*Energy Regulation
by the Federal Power
Commission*

Studies in the Regulation of Economic Activity
TITLES PUBLISHED

The Dilemma of Freight Transport Regulation
Ann F. Friedlaender

Technological Change in Regulated Industries
William M. Capron, Editor

Reforming Regulation: An Evaluation of the Ash Council Proposals
A staff paper by Roger G. Noll

International Diffusion of Technology: The Case of Semiconductors
John E. Tilton

Public Policy toward General Aviation
Jeremy J. Warford

The Local Service Airline Experiment
George C. Eads

Economic Aspects of Television Regulation
Roger G. Noll, Merton J. Peck, and John J. McGowan

Government and the Sports Business
Roger G. Noll, Editor

Energy Regulation by the Federal Power Commission
Stephen G. Breyer and Paul W. MacAvoy

Studies in the Regulation of Economic Activity

Energy Regulation by the Federal Power Commission

STEPHEN G. BREYER
PAUL W. MACAVOY

The Brookings Institution / Washington, D.C.

Copyright © 1974 by
THE BROOKINGS INSTITUTION
1775 Massachusetts Avenue, N.W., Washington, D.C. 20036

Library of Congress Cataloging in Publication Data:
Breyer, Stephen G   1938–
  Energy regulation by the Federal Power Commission.
  (Studies in the regulation of economic activity)
  Includes bibliographical references.
  1. Energy policy—United States.   2. United States.
Federal Power Commission.   I. MacAvoy, Paul W.,
joint author.   II. Title.   III. Series.
HD9502.U52B7   353.008'72   74-273
ISBN 0-8157-1076-3

9 8 7 6 5 4 3 2 1

THE BROOKINGS INSTITUTION is an independent organization devoted to nonpartisan research, education, and publication in economics, government, foreign policy, and the social sciences generally. Its principal purposes are to aid in the development of sound public policies and to promote public understanding of issues of national importance.

The Institution was founded on December 8, 1927, to merge the activities of the Institute for Government Research, founded in 1916, the Institute of Economics, founded in 1922, and the Robert Brookings Graduate School of Economics and Government, founded in 1924.

The Board of Trustees is responsible for the general administration of the Institution, while the immediate direction of the policies, program, and staff is vested in the President, assisted by an advisory committee of the officers and staff. The by-laws of the Institution state, "It is the function of the Trustees to make possible the conduct of scientific research, and publication, under the most favorable conditions, and to safeguard the independence of the research staff in the pursuit of their studies and in the publication of the results of such studies. It is not a part of their function to determine, control, or influence the conduct of particular investigations or the conclusions reached."

The President bears final responsibility for the decision to publish a manuscript as a Brookings book or staff paper. In reaching his judgment on the competence, accuracy, and objectivity of each study, the President is advised by the director of the appropriate research program and weighs the views of a panel of expert outside readers who report to him in confidence on the quality of the work. Publication of a work signifies that it is deemed to be a competent treatment worthy of public consideration; such publication does not imply endorsement of conclusions or recommendations contained in the study.

The Institution maintains its position of neutrality on issues of public policy in order to safeguard the intellectual freedom of the staff. Hence interpretations or conclusions in Brookings publications should be understood to be solely those of the author or authors and should not be attributed to the Institution, to its trustees, officers, or other staff members, or to the organizations that support its research.

Foreword

THE ENERGY CRISIS has occasioned debate over the policies needed to guarantee to industry and the consumer adequate fuel supplies at reasonable prices. Some have argued that the role of regulatory agencies should be expanded—that the Federal Power Commission, for example, should regulate oil as well as natural gas and electricity. It is thus both timely and helpful to examine the FPC's performance during a busy decade prior to public recognition of the gravity of the energy problem.

This book seeks to measure the effectiveness of FPC regulation in the 1960s. In the early part of that decade, hopes for success of the commission ran high. The regulators were high-minded and competent. Their major task—controlling the field price of natural gas—was regarded as difficult but important. And the commission embarked on such ambitious projects as the promotion of increased coordination in electricity production. How did the commission, over the course of the decade, actually change the performance of the industries that it regulated? Did those changes work to the benefit or to the detriment of the consumer?

The authors investigate the three major areas of the FPC's work—natural gas pipeline prices, natural gas field prices, and electricity production. They conclude that the commission helped neither the consumer nor industry. They contend that regulation had little effect upon pipeline prices and that it did not significantly promote a better coordinated electric power industry. Although the commission kept gas field prices low, in doing so it may have created a shortage that hurt consumers more than low prices helped them.

Since the commission's tasks—controlling monopoly power, transferring income from producer to consumer, planning for more efficient production—are typical forms of economic regulation, the study has a number of implications regarding the regulatory process in general. These are discussed in the final chapter.

vii

The authors gratefully acknowledge the help provided by a number of perceptive critics: M. A. Adelman, Alfred E. Kahn, Edmund W. Kitch, Stewart Myers, Roger G. Noll, Joseph A. Pechman, Merton J. Peck, Richard A. Posner, Haskell P. Wald, and the staff of the Federal Power Commission. The manuscript was edited by Robert Erwin; the index was prepared by Helen B. Eisenhart.

This book is the ninth in the Brookings series of Studies in the Regulation of Economic Activity. The series presents the findings of a program of research focused on public policies toward business. The program is supported by a grant from the Ford Foundation and has been directed by Joseph A. Pechman, director of the Brookings Economic Studies program, and Roger G. Noll, formerly a Brookings senior fellow and now professor of economics at the California Institute of Technology. Earlier versions of Chapters 2, 3, and 4 appeared in the *Bell Journal of Economics and Management Science,* the *Harvard Law Review,* and the *Southern California Law Review,* respectively. Stephen Breyer is professor of law at Harvard University, and Paul W. MacAvoy is professor of management science at the Massachusetts Institute of Technology. Both are members of the Brookings associated staff.

The views expressed in this book are solely those of the authors and should not be ascribed to the trustees, officers, or staff of the Brookings Institution or to the Ford Foundation.

KERMIT GORDON
President

April 1974
Washington, D.C.

Contents

1. Introducing the Federal Power Commission   1
   Goals 2
   Major Efforts 4
   Results 13

2. Regulating the Natural Gas Pipeline Companies   16
   The Public Utility Approach 16
   Regulatory Rules on Prices and Profits 22
   Effects of Regulation 38
   The Net Result 54

3. Regulating Natural Gas Producers   56
   Regulating Producer Sales 57
   The Objectives of Producer Price Regulation 59
   Regulating Prices through Individual Rate Cases 66
   Area Rate Proceedings 69
   The Shortage of Natural Gas 72
   Alternatives 87

4. Planning the Production of Electricity   89
   The Trend toward Interconnection 90
   The Potential Gains from Coordination 94
   The Coordination Problem 107
   FPC Planning 112
   The Need for Change 119

5. The Lessons of Regulation   122
   Theories of Regulatory Failure 124
   Steps toward Reform 132

Notes   135

Index   159

Tables

1-1. Estimated Expenses for FPC Regulation during a Typical Year in the 1960s   14

2-1. Allowed and Earned Returns on Investment for Florida Gas Transmission Company in Selected Years   29

2-2. Florida Gas Transmission Company's Return on Equity versus Cost of Capital for Alternative Investments   30

2-3. Decisions on Gas Pipeline Rates of Return and Estimated Cost of Capital for Alternative Investments, 1961 and 1962   31

2-4. Decisions on Gas Pipeline Rates of Return, 1968 and 1970   32

2-5. Zone Prices Set by the FPC for Gas in the New York Metropolitan Region, 1970   35

3-1. Curtailment of Gas Deliveries by Interstate Pipelines, April 1971 to March 1972   74

3-2. Estimated Demand by Companies for Natural Gas Reserves, before and after FPC Regulation, and Actual Additions to Reserves, 1964–68   77

3-3. Actual Prices and Simulated Unregulated Prices, Production, and Changes in Reserves of Natural Gas, East Coast and Midwest, 1961–68   82

3-4. Natural Gas Sales to Ultimate Consumers by Pipelines and Distributors, 1962 and 1968   84

3-5. Sources of Natural Gas Sales to Industrial Consumers, 1962 and 1968   85

3-6. Initial-Year Production of Natural Gas under New Interstate and Intrastate Contracts in the Permian Basin, 1966–70   85

4-1. Electric Power Pooling by Region and System, 1963 and 1970   100

4-2. Power Capacity, 1970, and Planned Additions to Capacity, 1971–80, by Study Area   102

5-1. Estimated Cost-Benefit Gap Accompanying FPC Regulation during a Typical Year in the 1960s   123

*Energy Regulation
by the Federal Power
Commission*

CHAPTER ONE

Introducing the Federal Power Commission

AT THE HEIGHT of the New Deal the Federal Power Commission was transformed into a regulatory agency required by statute to control the profits, prices, and services of certain firms "affected with a public interest." The Federal Power Act of 1935 assigned the task of "assuring an abundant supply of electric energy throughout the United States with the greatest possible economy and with regard to the proper utilization and conservation of natural resources." The Natural Gas Act of 1938 brought an additional energy source under regulation and implied a responsibility to instigate better service. In both cases the commission was also charged with securing "just and reasonable" prices.[1]

The firms regulated by the commission are those that produce natural gas for sale in interstate commerce, those that transport natural gas (primarily by pipeline) for resale in interstate commerce, and those that market electricity at wholesale across state lines.

For nearly forty years FPC decisions (and reviews of those decisions by the federal courts) have reflected a desire to protect consumer interests.[2] To achieve the aim of "reasonable" prices the commission has required that companies sell electric power and natural gas at rates approximately equal to the costs of providing the service. The commission has said that prices ought to be set close to average past costs of service, as found from the income accounts of the company, because this (accounting) "cost-of-service formula is the one best adapted in determining just and reasonable rates in this industry where costs are known."[3]

New facilities for producing and transporting natural gas and electricity under FPC jurisdiction must first be certified by the commission, which investigates the prospective builder's financial resources and fuel capacity to see that the installation could "meet those demands which it is reasonable to assume will be made upon them."[4] Moreover, in order to increase

1

production and reduce costs the commission has joined in the planning and forecasting activities of the industries it regulates.

During the 1960s, the Federal Power Commission substantially increased the scope of its jurisdiction. An effort was made in the late 1950s to meet the requirement, laid down in 1954 by the Supreme Court decision in the *Phillips* case, to regulate gas producing companies.[5] But at that time the commission's approach resembled orthodox public utility regulation: find the development and production costs of each of the thousands of natural gas producing facilities and then set individual price ceilings on the contracts for the gas sold by each of them. Given limits on staff, the FPC was able to complete its findings for only a few companies in the 1950s. In the early 1960s, the commission cleared out a backlog of cases by taking a new approach—that of setting common price ceilings on all gas sold in each major "field," or geographical area, where gas is produced. The Federal Power Commission thus had gained full control of gas contract prices by the middle 1960s. In the same period, the commission also made efforts to extend its jurisdiction over prices for sales of electricity by requiring the filing of all wholesale prices when any part of these transactions were in interstate commerce. In the aftermath of the 1965 blackout in the Northeast, the FPC became involved in establishing "safe" and "reliable" national transmission of electricity.

The broadening of the commission's power over pipeline companies and electricity producers in interstate commerce aroused little controversy, and initial objections to area price setting for gas producers soon subsided. By 1970, the so-called Ash Council, established by the President to review the activities of the regulatory agencies, could find little to complain about in the Federal Power Commission's performance.[6]

Goals

The duty of the FPC might be formulated as holding prices down and keeping service coverage up for the benefit of consumers of gas and electricity. This conception of an FPC "mission" is unsophisticated economically, but it does not *necessarily* conflict with more comprehensive economic aims. Keeping prices low is consistent with eliminating monopoly profits. Increasing the accessibility and reliability of power service improves product quality and may stimulate consumer demand. Planning in units larger than the single company might reduce the production costs of all the generating or transmitting companies and even reduce social costs (such as pollution or congestion) that are likely to be ignored in the companies' separate calculations. It is therefore permissible to assess the commission's performance in terms of economic efficiency. Such an assessment fits a framework of regulatory and antitrust law that seeks to achieve the benefits of competition if possible (although to prevent exploitation where industries cannot or do not support competition).

From the economist's point of view, then, the goals of the Federal Power Commission in the 1960s, within its mandate, were (1) to induce a more nearly equal distribution of income and (2) to increase economic efficiency. It is possible for these objectives to coexist peaceably. Limiting a monopolist's prices tends to bring about an increase of output and to redistribute income, probably toward equality. Sometimes, however, the redistributive goal conflicts with the efficiency goal. To hold prices below the competitive level may lead to a more nearly equal distribution of income (in the economic sense) but wastefully reduce supply (because the producers have no incentive to keep output high) and stimulate excess demand. Eventually the buyer faces a shortage that is created by lower prices. How is the Federal Power Commission to decide which consumers should, in effect, receive additional income through low prices at the expense of other consumers who, because of the shortage, must turn to a less desirable substitute? Giving primacy to the efficiency goal over the redistributive goal is in some instances a sensible way to resolve this dilemma, since it avoids the impossible task of evaluating transfers between groups of consumers.

At times, without quite acknowledging it, the commission has lapsed into pure "protectionism." At other times it has acted as though politically acceptable compromise ought to be the primary goal. The tacit assumption often seems to be that FPC is performing satisfactorily when its "clients" —gas producers, electric power companies, pipeline companies, and organized consumer interests—do not complain loudly. In some contexts, "neutral" political goals along these lines make sense. The inability to measure the value people set on clean air versus cheaper power, for example, may force reliance upon "fair procedures" to resolve pollution arguments by accommodating the interests of several groups. But, to jump from such a judgment about pollution to the conclusion that one cannot measure the value of, say, higher or lower gas prices except in terms of political reaction is unwarranted. Economic results (conceivably harmful ones) continue to flow from FPC activity whether or not the commission attains political tranquility. Once again, the economic efficiency goal appears superior for assessing the agency's performance—and indeed for *guiding* performance.

The pursuit of an efficiency goal consistent with an incomes goal is bound to be demanding, the more so because of inclinations to play the role of political mediator or the role of "protector of the innocent." Under the circumstances, what policies and procedures did the commission choose in the 1960s?

First, the FPC committed itself to setting prices equal to the costs of service. Elaborate procedures were established for determining investment costs—procedures for averaging past figures, collecting large amounts of accounting information, and listening to experts present their individual opinions about cost factors in great detail at numerous hearings. Somewhat simpler, more mechanical procedures were used by the commission to determine operating costs of the regulated companies, but all in all this style of regulation was (and is) laborious.

Second, the FPC sought "quality" service. It employed complex methods to calculate efficient scale and adequate reserves in given instances. In the case of electric power companies especially, numerous rulings about plant layout and interconnection were laid down.

Major Efforts

The commission's major efforts went into regulating the profits and prices of natural gas pipeline companies, setting the field price of natural gas, and promoting coordinated planning among firms engaged in interstate electric power transmission. On the average, 25 percent of the FPC's annual budget had to do with pipelines, and about 20 percent had to do with gas producers. The share of FPC budget allotted to electric power planning was relatively small. The activity, nevertheless, was important, for it was the commission's most serious and sustained effort to foster increased production efficiency.

To analyze the commission's performance in these three areas is to see all the important policies and procedures at work. Moreover, three functions which the typical regulatory agency must manage are represented here: (1) control of monopoly power; (2) control of economic rent; and (3) planning for increased efficiency in production. FPC effectiveness can be judged according to what was accomplished in these areas.

Natural Gas Pipeline Companies

The Federal Power Commission has broad authority to regulate the prices charged by companies transporting gas across state lines for sale to parties other than direct users. (Thus industrial and residential consumers are outside FPC jurisdiction, though of course affected by its decisions.) Any pipeline company whose operations fall into this category is regulated from the initial design of a project to the day of final disappearance of its equipment from a balance-sheet statement of capital assets. The regulatory process begins with an application for a certificate of public convenience and necessity by the company seeking to introduce service into some market. The certificate application is examined for "sufficiency" of the demand for the proposed service and of the capacity of the company to provide the service. After certification has been granted and service begun, the prices submitted by the firm are reviewed by the staff of the FPC pipeline division. If company and staff propose different and irreconcilable price schedules, a hearing examiner reaches a decision, which in turn may be brought for review before the Federal Power Commission proper. Finally the commission's decision may be appealed to the federal courts.

A fairly large number of companies come under this jurisdiction, and the combination of production conditions and regulatory requirements has made their business quite complex. In 1970, more than 80 pipeline companies were covered by commission regulation, with combined sales rising from $4.6 billion in 1961 to $7.8 billion in 1970. In the latter year operating costs were $5.6 billion, and for purposes of computing capital costs net plant was valued at $17.9 billion.[7]

The interstate pipelines have some of the characteristics of natural oligopolies—economies of scale in transmission would seem to justify no more than two or three pipeline sources of supply in any regional market with population less than 10 million.[8] In the typical instance, these pipelines have purchased gas from producers in the field for resale over a 10- to 20-year period to city distributing companies some miles removed from producing wells. Resale contracts signed between pipelines and distributing companies require delivery of the produced gas over the same period.

Regulation has been important in setting the terms in these contracts. The obligation to provide gas over lengthy periods has made the contracts inherently uncertain ventures for the pipeline firms. Certification procedures require the pipelines to present enough field purchase contracts to demonstrate a 10-year or 20-year supply of reserves and sufficient resale

contracts to show a 10-year or 20-year demand for these reserves. This requirement has secured volumes of gas to be delivered but, since the contracts often specify that the final price will be set (in accordance with regulation) at the time of delivery, it has not secured price. Rather, prices are
usually pegged to ceilings set and reset by the commission from time to
time. The demands for contract information, for the signed purchase and
resale contracts, and for geological studies and legal documents establishing the volume of the underground gas and its ownership have added to the
complexity of new undertakings to construct pipelines. Market conditions
necessitate keeping prices flexible even though quantities supplied remain
fixed. Consequently regulation centers on year-to-year control of prices.

The procedures in price control have been designed for reaching a finding on historical unit costs. Pipeline companies seeking to raise prices must
justify the proposed new prices as, on average, approximate to recent costs
of providing service under the relevant contracts. The commission's staff
has often disputed or denied a company's estimates of these costs. In such
instances, the dispute has usually revolved around (1) the proper allocation of fixed costs among different regulated services or between regulated
sales to retail public utilities and unregulated sales to direct industrial consumers and (2) the proper rate of return allowed on capital investment.
The desire to allocate costs and define rates of return with extreme preci-
sion has led to detailed yet inconclusive studies of historical expenditures
on plant, land, and interest as well as on accounting depreciation and the
"proper" rate of dividends to maintain stockholders' equity.

Controls over particular prices have been quite specific. For example,
the commission devised, although it does not always apply, the Atlantic
Seaboard Formula, requiring half of all capital costs to be allocated to
customers on the basis of relative annual purchases and half on the basis
of volumes bought during a designated peak-load period.[9] These allocations have seemed to set price differences between regulated and unregulated buyers. They have been controversial where applied, and rebuttal
arguments based on adverse demand conditions—on the inability to make
sales at the higher price implied by the "burden" of the allotted fixed costs
—have caused the FPC to abandon the formula entirely in some cases and
to apply it only partially in other cases. Generally, the companies and the
agency have negotiated cost figures upon which to base prices.

Estimates of the "proper" return on capital have been exceptionally
detailed, even in comparison with cost-allocation studies. Allowed rates of
return have depended on assumptions about possible alternative uses of

capital by the investor and about how much extra return should be awarded a company for "good service." Both assumptions have engendered dispute. In a typical proceeding, numerous financial and economic experts have made different assessments of required capital returns, leaving it to the examiner and the commission to sort out and evaluate the assessments and finally announce the "correct" rate of return.

The Federal Power Commission exercises its right of review over more than 1,500 price schedules each year. Customarily those calling for rate increases have been suspended until an investigation has been made. Then, after informal conferences, the suspended rates either have been withdrawn and revised to meet FPC price limits or have become the subject of formal rate proceedings. On a few occasions the FPC has initiated proceedings without waiting for a proposal for a rate increase—the aim being not merely to prevent increases but to lower rates already in effect. Cases in which a firm asked for formal proceedings rather than revise a proposal and cases initiated by the agency have together amounted to about 30 individual rate deliberations in process each year. After completing one of these cases, the staff carries out compliance reviews to make certain that price adjustments flow through to final consumers of gas.

Regulation of natural gas pipeline companies cost the Federal Power Commission about $3.5 million during the late 1960s.[10] The costs for defendants and intervenors must have been not far under that figure. In 1968, for example, private costs of regulation for the gas pipelines totaled $2.5 million.[11] Commission procedures may change from time to time, and increases in interest rates during periods of significant inflation increase the number of requests for rate increases. During the 1960s, the combined government-company charge to regulation of the pipelines was roughly $6 million per annum, for a group of firms whose sales totaled $4 billion to $6 billion. If the sales would have taken place at higher prices except for regulation and if regulation entailed no other costs, then clearly the commission performed well. The validity of these premises is investigated in Chapter 2.

✓ Gas Field Prices

Since the 1954 Supreme Court decision in *Phillips Petroleum Company v. Wisconsin,* the commission has exercised jurisdiction over prices charged by natural gas producers on sales to interstate pipelines. The first attempts to carry on price regulation copied the procedures for controlling pipeline resale prices, with cost-based standards for review of the prices of each individual company. These attempts failed because there were too many producers and too many elements of cost to be found on each sale of each producer. The determination of costs of service was exceptionally controversial and prolonged when gas came from wells jointly owned by a number of producers, each with different historical costs of exploration in that field, or when gas from different fields but in the same sales market was debited with different exploration and production expenses. Cost differentials produced a variety of prices within any one market, allowing windfall gains to those buyers getting the "low-cost" gas. Faced with having to approve arbitrary price differences on cases that waited years for decision, the commission moved away from prices based on company-by-company costs of service and turned to setting area price ceilings intended to reflect area-wide average costs of exploration and development. In 1960, the commission set provisional prices for "new" and "old" contracts in twenty-four gas producing areas and at the same time began proceedings to find out average historical costs in each of the various producing areas and thereby to determine formal area ceiling prices. In 1968, the Supreme Court affirmed the legality of the area pricing method and the particular prices set for the Permian Basin in southwestern Texas and southeastern New Mexico, the first producing region that the commission had reviewed.[12] Until the subsequent gas shortage caused the FPC to depart from this policy as a practical matter early in the 1970s (but without relinquishing the concept), reviews to set formal area ceilings were the central regulatory activity with regard to gas producers.

Consolidated area rate reviews have not turned out to be notable successes as simplifiers and time-savers. They are prolonged and complicated and consume far more administrative resources than might reasonably be expected. The first case began in December 1960 with hearings on prices charged by 351 companies for gas in the Permian Basin. The hearings were completed in September 1963, a commission decision followed in August 1965; and the Supreme Court affirmed the decision in May 1968.[13] The commission subsequently began to put these ceilings into effect in place of "provisional" or "interim" prices originally announced in 1960. Thus the first area-price proceeding took almost a decade to complete.

The commission began six more area proceedings in the late 1960s and early 1970s. Since they could in part build upon some of the evidence, findings, and experience arising from the Permian Basin case, these later proceedings have taken less time and legal resources. But application of regulatory rules has been just as complex. In all the area proceedings, the commission has tried to find historical average costs of exploring for, developing, and producing gas and then has used these costs to set maximum ceiling prices. The lack of analytical techniques for allocating joint costs incurred in exploring for and developing oil and gas has presented critical problems. Trying to estimate accurately the costs of capital for exploration and development poses a problem similar to finding the historical investment costs for research on one project in a multi-project laboratory. The difficulties of determining historical costs and relating them to future prices bring forth voluminous and conflicting testimony from expert witnesses and prolonged cross-examination and rebuttal hearings. The extended procedures have added to regulatory costs, both direct administrative costs and those resulting from regulatory delay.

Although area proceedings require prolonged deliberation, they have not by any means eliminated individual producer regulation. The commission throughout the 1960s continued to issue certificates of convenience and necessity to individual producers seeking to enter into new contracts with pipelines. The certificate reviews led to FPC judgments on the extent of each producer's gas reserves and on the "reasonableness" of the proposed sales prices. The reviews were designed to show to the FPC staff's satisfaction that the would-be producer's reserves were sufficient and also that the proposed prices were within the commission's provisional guidelines for area rates. This type of individual-producer certificate proceeding, to supplement the broader, multi-company area rate proceedings, caused the amount of administrative detail and complexity of regulation to creep upward again.

The number of certificate proceedings has been large. In the late 1960s approximately 2,000 applications for permanent certificates were filed with the commission per year. About 1,200 of these received attention within the year in which they were filed, and the remainder the following year. Since the large number of reviews produced delays ranging from 6 to 9 months, temporary certificates were instituted so as not to hold production facilities idle.

In sheer bulk, applications seeking exceptions to the field price set by the commission constitute a problem. Cases of this sort have not been dealt with rapidly; in fact, in fiscal year 1968, the commission completed review of only 500 applications for producer rate increases, although more than 7,500 had been filed up to that time (covering requests involving more than $130 million).[14] In that year a total of 84 producer "rate cases" were completed. Many of these pertain to prices on gas from areas where rates have not yet been set. In the others, a company attempts to prove through statistical and accounting data that its legitimate production costs (for drilling, say) have run sufficiently higher than area average to justify a price above ceiling.

Area proceedings have cost millions of dollars each year. The Federal Power Commission at the end of the sixties was spending more than $3 million annually to pay for staff preparation of area briefs, testimony, and drafts of decisions. The producers have undertaken extremely detailed and expensive investigations of drilling and production costs throughout the country, so as to prepare "findings" on historical costs for these proceedings. They have retained more than fifty law firms and more than a dozen economics and engineering consulting companies to provide testimony before the commission. Though their total costs have never been specifically calculated, the examiner in the Permian Basin proceedings allowed the producers to add 0.14 cent per thousand cubic feet of gas (Mcf) to their production costs to cover expenses on regulatory proceedings, and uncontested industry testimony in the Texas Gulf Coast area rate proceeding stated that these producer costs amounted to 0.15 cent per Mcf.[15] Since approximately 75 percent of the 16 trillion or so cubic feet sold annually to the interstate pipelines has been subject to area rate regulation, these figures indicate that total producer administrative expenditures under the "streamlined" area system could run as high at $18 million per annum.[16]

Total administrative costs of regulating natural gas producers can be estimated from these various sources, but only very imprecisely. The commission itself spends $3 million annually on area proceedings alone; the companies show expenditures of $18 million on the large area rate cases. There have been further costs for the individual rate reviews—the 1,200 certificate applications and 500 rate-increase applications processed each year—but no estimate of these costs to the producers is available. The cost of regulatory delay depends on the investment value of producing now rather than later. Possibly these opportunity costs have been greater than the accounting dollar costs.[17]

Even doubling the estimate, however, would not make the total costs large relative to the *potential* gains from price reductions. The gas pipeline companies bought more than $4.5 billion of gas from producers in 1970.[18] If regulation did hold prices down by even 1 percent, consumers presumably gained as much as was spent in the regulatory process. The question of whether this much has really been gained (and whether a dollar of rate reduction can be so assessed against expenses) is investigated in Chapter 3.

Interstate Electric Power

Like gas pipeline companies, electricity producers wholesale their product under conditions of natural oligopoly; for economies of scale in transmission are so extensive that only two or three sources of supply exist in a regional market. Also, the method for price setting in the electric power field has been quite similar to the method used with regard to pipelines. The Federal Power Commission has regulated both power and gas pipeline companies by finding cost of service from historical accounting expenses and allowing average revenue or price to go no higher than those costs of service.

Here similarity ends, primarily because of important differences in the extent to which the two industries have been subject to FPC regulation. While most natural gas is sold across state lines (and is therefore subject to FPC price jurisdiction), interstate electricity wholesale transactions made up no more than 7.3 percent of all power company dollar transactions in 1970.[19] With only a minor portion of the industry's capacity under FPC jurisdiction, attempts to estimate costs of this capital for price setting have been subject to a high probability of error and a high degree of regulatory effect. Small changes in the fraction of total cost attributed by FPC to the service under its jurisdiction could have the effect of doubling or halving officially recognized costs of service and hence regulated prices.

During the 1960s the FPC staff each year reviewed approximately 2,200 rate schedules proposed by the power companies. On the average, the commission approved all but about 50 proposed rate schedules annually but subjected those 50 to extensive "rate studies." Ultimately, the findings in about 30 of the studies conducted each year were contested in formal proceedings.[20] The commission usually disposed of these cases by affirming the prices set by its staff or by a compromise settlement.

Much of this activity was new in the 1960s, initiated by commission decisions that defined interstate sales to include almost all wholesale transactions between companies that were connected with out-of-state generating facilities. With this expanded scope of electricity regulation, the FPC in 1968 spent about half as much on administration in electric power as on pipeline regulation ($1.6 million).[21] The companies spent an almost equal amount. Approximately $100,000 was spent in total by the applicants in a typical year on preparation and defense of those rate filings not contested by the commission staff.[22] Those proceedings that became "formal cases" were more expensive; the 29 cases listed in the 1968 FPC annual report involved company costs ranging from $7,000 for proceedings on a single rate in Maryland to $305,000 for a full-scale rate review on service to a group of cooperatives in North Carolina.[23] A conservative estimate of company costs for the 29 cases in process that year would be $1.5 million, which would make the total public and private costs of regulation of wholesale electricity prices close to $3.2 million per year.[24] This estimate is conservative because it does not take into account the costs which protracted proceedings imposed in the sense of delaying electricity service; nor does it gauge the costs to any of the parties of uncertainty about future prices as a result of regulation.[25]

The Federal Power Commission has also undertaken a program to add to the quality of service in electricity generation. "Quality" has been defined very narrowly, at least in the context of formal case proceedings (a wider definition is used in Chapter 4). This program has centered on requiring the larger producers to provide power to small retailers with whom these producers would prefer not to do business. So far, the campaign has had little effect, though it has imposed costs on defendants in litigation before the commission.[26] Such "extension of service" cases have cost hundreds of thousands of dollars each to conduct.

There has been another major administrative program in electricity regulation. Once prices are set, the commission staff keeps track of whether a company in its day-to-day operations follows the commission rulings. More than 200 electric utilities filed documentation on capital assets in use, and more than 350 companies filed studies of classification of original capital expenditures, in a typical year in the late 1960s. If capital equipment is dedicated to interstate sales, it has to be used for production and distribution under these regulated-price transactions. The staff carries out "field surveys" to ascertain actual equipment usage.

Since these studies have sometimes been useful to the firms in their own operations—telling some firms, for example, where their capital equipment was being utilized at a given time—the costs cannot be entirely attributed to regulation. But regulated companies have not classified these surveys as purely "cost effective"; there were some regulatory costs involved here.

In sum, service-connection decisions and surveillance cost the Federal Power Commission approximately $1.3 million in 1968 with respect to "quality" furtherance, and the cost to private companies was approximately $1.9 million. Thus total costs of regulation were $3.2 million for price regulation and $3.2 million for dealing with the issue of "quality" in the production and distribution of electric power.

The foregoing estimates of the costs of regulating wholesale interstate electric power could well be in error. Variation in the cost of individual cases might make the total amount spent annually on price regulation as low as $1.8 million or as high as $4.7 million. The parties to proceedings concerned with quality of service may have spent $1.7 million annually, or they may have spent as much as $3.7 million.

What matters here is that the range be established. Probably the expenses of regulating electricity ran from $4 million to $8 million a year in the late 1960s, on industry sales under the commission's jurisdiction of $1.1 billion to $1.4 billion.[27] A related point that seems reasonably well established: about the same amount was spent on price control as on regulation having to do with quality of service.

Because federally regulated sales constitute only a minor portion of total electricity sales and because regulated and unregulated services are produced jointly, it is not easy to measure the benefits which regulation "buys." It may be most useful to appraise commission efforts to promote coordinated power planning. These efforts, designed to increase the efficiency with which electricity is produced, might have brought significant savings for consumers at comparatively small regulatory cost. Whether they did so is examined in Chapter 4.

Results

From the account given of the commission's work in each of the stipulated areas, it is possible to show approximately the total direct expense of regulation during a typical year in the late 1960s. Table 1-1 sets forth a single column for FPC expenditures, derived from budget information. Two columns are offered for company expenditures. One lists a "most probable" figure in each category of activity; the other shows the range within which the precise amount could fall. Some record-keeping and reporting expenses are routinely imposed on the companies by FPC regulations. Other administrative expenses are "initiated" by the companies on the supposition that the decisions obtained thereby may benefit them. Both forms of company expense count as costs of regulation in Table 1-1 and throughout this book.

Table 1-1. Estimated Expenses for FPC Regulation during a Typical Year in the 1960s

Millions of dollars

| | | Expenditures | | |
| | Federal Power Com- | Companies | | |
Activity	mission	Estimate	Range	Combined
Gas pipeline price and systems regulation	3.5	2.5	2.0 to 3.0	6.0
Gas field price regulation	3.1	18.0ᵃ	18.0 to 76.0	21.1
Electric power				
Price regulation	1.6	1.6	0.2 to 3.1	3.2
Systems evaluation	1.3	1.9	1.4 to 2.4	3.2
General FPC administration	1.1	...	...	1.1
Total	10.6	24.0	21.6 to 84.5	34.6

Sources: Col. 1 derived from data in *The Budget of the United States Government—Appendix*, various issues; cols. 2 and 3 estimated on the basis of information discussed in the text.

a. Area rate proceedings only; excludes certification expenses and individual price cases.

The combined agency and private expenditures set the minimum value of the benefits that regulatory activities must "buy" if the game is to be worth the price of admission. From the public's standpoint, regulation is not worthwhile unless it produces benefits greater than the total regulatory expense. Knowing generally what the commission regulates, the way it operates, and how much it costs, need the reader who is not involved with the industry or the agency read on after the results of FPC action are summarized to conclude this chapter? The Ash Council found no fault with the way the commission handles its workload as measured by the standards of the federal bureaucracy. Sales priced at billions are regulated for only about $35 million a year and seem to be controlled in the consumer's favor but without undue hardship for the producer. Surely all that remains is to indicate the percentage or rough dollar value of benefits "bought" by regulation?

Unfortunately the reader *cannot* take the utility of the Federal Power Commission for granted or assume that the remaining chapters merely cover technicalities and fine points. On the contrary, economic analysis reveals that in the late 1960s, with the commission operating at full steam, results were dismal: prices collected by the pipeline companies were not perceptibly lower than they would have been without regulation; setting field prices for natural gas did the residential consumer more harm than good by affecting the market so as inadvertently to bring on a gas shortage; and with federally regulated sales constituting only a minor portion of electricity sales, manifold opportunities to shift costs tended to render federal pricing ineffective. Commission planning efforts faltered.

These disappointing and unexpected results underscore the importance of the efficiency goal, which, as argued in the beginning, must be paramount in any workable mix with the commission's redistributive, protectionist, and mediator goals. A gap has opened between the *goal* of efficiency and a set of *procedures* more suitable for mediation.

The lesson to be learned from the poor results of FPC regulation in the 1960s does not stop with awareness of that gap. None of the currently accepted theories of regulatory failure adequately explains the unfortunate outcome. The commission's shortcomings cannot easily be blamed on its personnel, for able and energetic men led the commission in the 1960s and had the support of a competent staff. Nor was the agency "captured by industry." Rather, the causes of failure lie in the structure of regulation itself. The chapters that follow assess not only FPC performance but also the limits of the regulatory agency as an instrument of social policy.

CHAPTER TWO

Regulating the Natural Gas Pipeline Companies

AN IMPORTANT OBJECTIVE of the Federal Power Commission has been to hold down the prices that natural gas pipeline companies charge to retail gas utilities. Traditionally, to this end, the commission has determined appropriate limits on the profits that pipelines earn for transporting natural gas for resale in interstate commerce. But this has not been all: it has set wholesale prices directly by declaring what counts as cost, then allocating costs, including allowed profits, to various classes of buyers and requiring that prices be no greater than these specific costs.

Surprisingly, examination of the results in the late 1960s fails to show a pattern of prices held down by regulation. As mentioned before, only wholesale transactions are subject to FPC control. Sales to final users (industrial in the case of pipelines) go unregulated. Some price differences did exist between particular items in one category and items in the other category, but regulation does not seem to have constrained the pipeline companies to such an extent that measurable effects on the overall level of wholesale prices can be detected.

The Public Utility Approach

In explaining the negligible impact of regulation, the first aspect to consider is what the commission accomplished through the kind of controls traditionally imposed on public utilities. It may be that agencies act for half-conscious bureaucratic reasons, such as the desire to reduce case load or fear of controversy. Perhaps they do not really act for economic reasons at all.[1] Nevertheless, the justification given for FPC activities is that final consumers gain from this price-reducing effort.

The public test of regulation from this point of view is whether prices have been reduced under the jurisdiction of the commission. This test may be simplistic; and where the commission receives a good mark, the results may be disastrous for the consumer (if the lower price is accompanied by shortages). But, in any event, where the commission has attempted exclusively to regulate the prices charged by firms with monopoly or oligopoly power, we can take the test as our standard and ask whether regulation has in fact accomplished this goal.

There are two ways in which regulation might operate to lower the prices of a "public utility company." First, the mere *presence* of an agency could discourage unbridled monopoly or oligopoly behavior—even if the agency made little effort to investigate prices or to enforce general profit controls. The power of the FPC to set limits on prices and readiness to "make an example" of some firm charging "outrageously high prices" could act as a check on pricing even if large numbers of complaints were not actually brought against producers. Second, an agency could actually set prices company by company. The commission has done a good deal of this, and of course it has made its "presence" known. Either way, the "price savings" supposedly brought about by such activity would amount to the difference between the allowed price and the firm's "desired price" (which it would charge without regulation).

Ardent claims about price savings have come forth from the Federal Power Commission. Allegedly, companies consider it unrealistic to propose true "monopoly" prices to FPC, and those they do submit get pared down. The commission measures differences between regulated and desired prices in this manner to its satisfaction and equates the price savings with benefits.

The *1968 Annual Report of the Federal Power Commission* stated that, during the previous fiscal year, "of 10 major proposals to increase [pipeline] rates by a total of $63,380,200 annually . . . , one . . . proposal, involving $2,687,100 annually, was rejected, and two involving $95,400 annually were accepted without suspension" (p. 59). Other rate increases totaling $12 million, proposed in earlier years, were disallowed or withdrawn by the companies in commission proceedings completed in 1968, and reductions totaling $13.9 million were required of the pipelines after FPC surveillance reviews. According to the commission, its actions with respect to the gas pipeline industry that year resulted in price savings worth $29 million, and these savings accrued to the retail distributors of natural gas.

For two reasons, such savings might not be a useful measure of "tangible" benefits from regulation despite the commission's claim. First, the extent to which FPC was in fact responsible for them is not clear. Some price decreases could have taken place in the absence of regulation, as a result of cost reductions and interindustry competition. During the 1960s the gas transmission industry achieved economies of scale and faced competition from coal and oil in industrial markets. Some of the pipeline companies could well have held rates down for these reasons and yet credited the results to vigorous regulation by the commission. Second, whether gas retailing companies passed on price savings to consumers depended on competition or regulation in local markets, so that FPC actions may not have reduced final prices.

Even if the commission did hold prices down, not every dollar of regulation-induced price savings can be set down as a benefit for final consumers. Some dollar benefits might have been obtained more cheaply through the use of other government powers, such as taxation. Other dollar savings should not have been obtained at all, because the resulting price level turned out to be lower than was necessary to clear markets. What is needed is a set of operational indicators of *net consumers' gains* from the price savings engineered by a regulatory commission.

Ideally, in measuring benefits one would like to know what consumers would be willing to pay for alternative volumes of gas and to know the marginal cost of the various volumes, but the information is not available. Because of data constraints and the politics of regulation as it operates in the United States, we shall vastly simplify the measuring process by assuming that, within limits, the goal of price regulation is to see that consumers get more than they would otherwise for what they pay, with some dollars of consumer gains "worth more" than others. The simple measure is illustrated in the figure below: a two-dimensional price-quantity diagram for contract sales of gas to final consumers in a well-defined energy market. The gains to these consumers can be defined in terms of what they would be willing to pay rather than give up the regulation-induced price savings.[2]

Two categories of benefits are represented by showing two distinct areas in the illustrative figure on the facing page. Area A represents benefits that accrue to established consumers from a working year of commission price control. Without commission price surveillance, consumers would find price maintained at level P_1 rather than level P_2. The gains of established consumers are equal to $(P_1 - P_2)Q_1$, where Q_1 is the amount that would have been demanded at the higher price. Area B represents further benefits

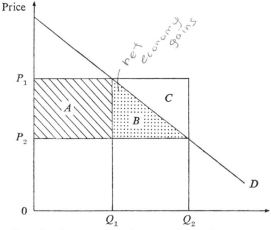

Quantity of gas purchased per year by final consumers

from expanding the amount of service. Given market demand D, the commission-induced price savings increase the quantity demanded from Q_1 to Q_2. The consumers' net additional gains from Q_2 are the dollar equivalent to what they would pay for $(Q_2 - Q_1)$ over and above their actual payment $P_2(Q_2 - Q_1)$ rather than go back to price P_1 and quantity Q_1; this dollar amount is Area B under the demand curve.[3] If regulation were to reduce price from P_1 to cost-of-service levels at P_2, and the reductions were completely passed on to final consumers, then the regulatory gains would be the sum of Areas A and B.

Two important limitations to using these measures make some of the gains "worth more" than others. The gains in A are strictly gains for final consumers of gas rather than net gains for the economy as a whole. Some consumers experience price savings, but others who are stockholders in gas and electricity companies lose potential income from their dividends as a result of the price savings. The first group's income gains are to some extent counterbalanced by the second group's losses. The dollar amount shown as Area A represents a net social gain only insofar as the new income distribution is more "socially acceptable" than the distribution at the higher price level. Only the quantity increases in benefits as shown by Area B can be considered net economy-wide gains. The extra consumption generated by the price savings can produce net gains, for direct consumers gain additional gas without causing dividend receivers to miss income.[4] Thus Area A is worth less than Area B if consumers of other goods besides gas are to be considered.

The second limitation is the ceiling on the amount of price savings which can be considered beneficial. If the measures which produced $A + B$ were carried to the ultimate, maximum benefits would follow from requiring a zero price. But if the commission were to require service to be provided for no compensation, then the result would be extensive sales for less than costs—costs which measure the value from using the resources elsewhere in the economy. Sooner or later, dissipation of the producing companies' assets would result in zero service, thus depriving consumers of gas. Even when not taken to the extreme of zero price, the principal result of below-cost pricing holds: some consumers must do without if prices are set below long-run marginal costs, and practical means do not exist for compensating them from the gains of those receiving price savings. Price reductions which result in service reductions cannot be unambiguously credited with benefits to final consumers.

The question is whether with the known data Area A and Area B can be measured precisely enough to evaluate FPC case and surveillance regulation. As an experiment toward answering this question, consider the FPC estimates of consumer benefits from regulation. Of the $29 million of 1968 price savings credited to regulation of pipelines, the sum of $14 million was confusingly classified at the same time as "in large part the flow-through of supplier refunds and rate reductions" (from natural gas field price regulation), so that about half has to be attributed to field price regulation.[5] Moreover, the remaining sum of $15 million must still be adjusted to take into account the fact that the putative savings flowed from disallowed price increases, not price reductions. The commission has an unconvincing way of calculating total dollars gained from preventing price increases. The quantity of gas Q_2 being distributed at the time is multiplied by the proposed increased price P_1. From the resulting figure, the same quantity Q_2 multiplied by the current lower price P_2 is then subtracted. Such a measurement overstates $A + B$, for it counts as gain the triangle of revenue C that would not in fact have been obtained at the higher price. That is, the triangle C lies beyond the demand curve and would not be realized as price increased.

After subtraction of the amount equivalent to C (estimated to be $1 million), the remaining amount should be further reduced to achieve an approximation to $A + B$. All "prevented" price increases that would not have been passed on to final consumers as price increases at that level should be excluded. For example, approximately 20 percent of the retailers' final demand has been attributable to industrial consumers, and these companies may or may not pass along their factor-cost increases as higher industrial prices, depending on market or regulatory conditions on final sales.[6] These sales in all probability cannot be shown to carry with them gains to final consumers from price controls on gas inputs. The same circumstances prevail with regard to pipeline sales to retail gas utilities— the utilities may not pass on price "savings" in whole or in part to final consumers.

The final calculations of regulatory benefits can thus be made to vary quite widely. Assuming that all of the savings are passed through, but that Area A savings are mere income transfers and not to be counted in economy-wide savings, benefits are $1 million. Assuming that industrial and gas utility buyers pass through only half of price savings to final consumers, the final consumer gains $A + B$ would have been only $6.5 million per year. Assuming that none of the savings to industry but all of the savings available to retail utilities were passed through to home consumers, benefits $A + B$ could be reckoned at more than $10 million (that is, 80 percent of $13 million, since sales by retailers to home consumers constitute this percentage of total sales).[7]

Exact calculations are unnecessary here if it can be determined roughly what benefits amounted to in comparison with the costs of regulation. The benefits could have been as low as $1 million or as much as $10 million for one year's denials of price increases that pipelines wished to charge gas utility retailers. Even the last figure does not seem large when compared with typical regulatory costs of $7 million annually to attain these benefits —given the substantial uncertainty about the extent to which price savings pass through to final consumers and about whether income-transfer benefits should be counted.

This exercise with benefits and costs demonstrates little more than that the FPC way of reporting benefits cannot survive close examination. But the analysis does raise some questions. Since most of the benefits consist of income transfers in Area A—approximately $9 million of $10 million— could not the tax system perform the same job more cheaply? Perhaps so. At least what the Internal Revenue Service spends on taxing profit income is only a small fraction of the amount of dollars thus collected, whereas FPC expenses roughly equal the amount actually transferred in a year by means of regulation. IRS does not of course redistribute the taxes to gas consumers, but it is by no means clear that such pinpointed redistribution is appropriate.

On the other hand, in making a case for regulating pipelines, FPC does not stop simply with comparing money benefits and administrative costs *in a year's surveillance*. The calculation includes benefits that the *mere presence of the commission* supposedly brings to the consumer. Regulated firms are said to ask for significantly lower prices than they would charge in the absence of any commission regulation. Such basic gains from the mere existence of pipeline regulation remain to be estimated. Since they depend on what the regulated firms believe the commission will do in the face of "transgressions," the first step is to describe the major, known rules that limit price requests. In essence, these rules are designed to ascertain the price that earns the company a return equal to its average costs, including a proper rate of return on capital investment in pipeline transmission. The next section discusses the commission's methods for deciding what rate of return is proper, what amount of investment is proper, and (sometimes) what prices will be allowed.

Regulatory Rules on Prices and Profits

The case regulation of the Federal Power Commission can be distinguished from the ongoing surveillance activities of the commission's staff. The case decisions in effect set upper bounds on prices requested by the companies, and they do so by making explicit a set of rules. These rules control the collection of information and the disposition of the issues that underlie most findings on the proper level of prices. The rules focus the activities of the commission and the companies; they simplify the administrative procedure for reviewing prices so that thousands of actual charges on individual transactions do not have to be considered one at a time.

Once the rules of procedure were set, a few case decisions on numerical limits on the rate of return might have been enough to achieve the goals of regulation. Say ten precedent-setting decisions in a decade could have effectively controlled prices even without surveillance by the commission staff. Companies perhaps automatically conformed to the numerical standards set in such decisions because of the obvious futility of trying to override the commission for higher profits and prices. For example, a limit of 8 percent on the average rate of return allowed Company A would apply to Company B without commission review if Company B had to request price increases to make more than 8 percent. A few FPC decisions on profits each year throughout the 1960s might, in principle, have held all residential gas prices down significantly. But that would depend on how and at what level prices were set; prices under the regulatory norms could have been as high as unregulated market prices, or they could have been considerably lower. The limits on profits set by the commission would be decisive.

This is to say that the case decisions could have been sufficient to achieve price savings, but only if they constrained profitability of the companies. The formal procedures for making case decisions, developed in great detail in the course of determining costs of service, had a bearing on that question. Problems of rate design related to setting particular prices that allow for seasonal and zonal price differences also should be considered.

The Cost-of-Service Approach to Profit Regulation

The Natural Gas Act of 1938 made it necessary for the pipeline companies to apply to the commission for price increases on sales to retail utilities, in accordance with the statutory standard that prices be "just and reasonable" and not "unduly discriminatory." These words have been interpreted by successive commissioners to require a particular procedure for finding "reasonableness": the cost-of-service method. According to this method, prices should yield from regulated sales pipeline revenues sufficient to cover the total costs of providing regulated service. The costs of service are defined as the total of gas purchase costs, operating and maintenance expenses on the pipeline, federal and state income taxes, depreciation of past capital investment, and an "acceptable" rate of return on the undepreciated portion of that investment. Finding the costs calls for the collection and use of accounting data on all these elements in a designated test period in the recent history of the company. The estimation of some costs, such as capital charges, relies heavily on the judgment of the commission because historical accounting data are not sufficient. The maximum price the commission allows—known as required earnings (R) per thousand cubic feet (Mcf) of gas—is arrived at through the following cost formula:

$$R = p_{gas} + c_o + \left\{ d_t + r(1 + T) \left[\sum_1^t (k_t - d_t) \right] \right\} / v,$$

where p_{gas} is the average field price of all gas purchased, c_o the unit costs of operation, d_t the costs of depreciation for year t, r the average rate of return on the rate base (or undepreciated original costs of equipment)

$$\left[\sum_1^t (k_t - d_t)\right],$$

k_t capital at purchase price for year t, T is rate of tax on income, and v is total volume of gas. The company's average price should not exceed R. Thus the "best estimate" of each of these elements of costs is the issue among pipelines, gas buyers, and the Federal Power Commission in cost-of-service proceedings on applications for price increases.

An early description of standards for finding costs of service was provided in *Natural Gas Pipeline Company of America* (2 FPC 218) in 1940; a more elaborate definition and specification was provided in the landmark case of *Hope Natural Gas Company* (3 FPC 150) in 1942. These cases established the pattern under which certain aspects of cost finding became quite routine while other aspects remained perennial sources of controversy.

The calculation of gas purchase and operation expenses was reduced to more or less routine submittals. The calculation of federal and state income taxes was a matter of minor controversy, and then only because the Internal Revenue Service and the courts allowed regulated firms to use one method of tax accounting for price-setting purposes and other methods for determining tax payments to the government. The commission defined depreciation as "the loss in service value not restored by current maintenance incurred in connection with the consumption of plant in the course of service."[8] In practice, the company defendants have accounted for depreciation by multiplying the original cost of capital equipment by a fixed percentage that would reduce these costs to salvage value at the end of a specified or negotiated "life of the plant." They have disagreed to a limited degree about the determination of original cost and the formula for "writing down" equipment.

The element of cost that led to the most controversy was the calculation of a fair rate of return; here, no standards based clearly on accounting or engineering data emerged from court or agency decisions, and so "judgment" became paramount. On the one hand, the courts and the commission have sometimes emphasized that rates of return must be high enough to prevent a firm's financial failure and to provide the management with an incentive for efficiency. By themselves, these objectives could justify a monopoly rate of return. On the other hand, the courts have made clear that returns should be limited to an amount comparable to that earned in more competitive industries. In *Bluefield Water Works,* for example, the court stated that the rate of return should equal "that generally being made at the same time, and in the same general part of the country, on investments in other business undertakings which are attended by corresponding risks and uncertainties."[9] This standard could have justified holding returns down to the marginal return on an alternative investment in a competitive industry. To some extent these objectives can be reconciled: profits that are equal to the economic cost of debt and equity capital should, in principle, equal profits earned by firms of comparable risk in more competitive industries while still providing an adequate cushion against financial failure. But such a standard still does not determine whether, or the extent to which, regulated firms should be allowed to earn more than this cost in order to provide an incentive for efficiency. Moreover, even if the commission were to adopt such a standard, there would be room for considerable disagreement about how to calculate these profits. Unfortunately, accurate determination of profit figures is as important as it is difficult. Slight variations in the cost of debt or equity can lead to substantial differences in final prices. If, for example, profits account for about 20 percent of total costs of service—a reasonable estimate—a single percentage point increase in the rate of return, say from 5 percent to 6 percent, can lead to a 4 percent increase in the final price of natural gas. Mistakes in the rate base are also unusually important, both because they show up in profits when the rate base is multiplied by the rate of return and because they also show up in the amount of depreciation allowed for the year.[10]

In the face of both the vagueness of statutory directives and the importance of finding the "correct" estimates, the commission has formulated rather elaborate and detailed standards for evidence. The commission's approach, and the formalism it involves, can be seen by reviewing an example. The 1958 Dockets G-3123 and G-12157, involving the determination of a rate of return and rate base for the Natural Gas Pipeline Company of America (19 FPC 1002), provide a good example; most aspects of FPC procedures were present, and the commission gave an unusually complete statement of reasons for its decision. The commission dealt first with the purpose of rate control, stating that "the primary aim of the Natural Gas Act [is] to guard the consumer against excessive rates" (at 1006); the agency then proposed to see whether an agreement by the pipeline company and its retail utility buyers over the pipeline's proposed rate increases was "fair, reasonable, and in the public interest." (An investigation was necessary, of course, since the agreement was very likely based on what the buyers and the seller thought the commission would approve. An FPC position of "no investigation at all" in such cases would permit monopoly prices to be charged wherever a pipeline company had the power to control supply in the market.) FPC quoted *Hope Natural Gas* to indicate its "legitimate concern with the financial integrity of the company" and then compared the terms agreed upon by buyers and sellers with the findings of an examiner. The examiner had offered a choice between (1) a rate of return suggested in testimony showing "comparable earnings" on investments in unregulated companies with "comparable risk" and (2) the previous level of earnings of Natural Gas Pipeline. The commission in the end preferred the buyer-seller agreement on the grounds that the examiner's figures were "too low": "under these circumstances it is of greater benefit to the consumers that Natural's financial integrity be assured, its credit maintained . . . , rather than the consumers be recipients of a temporary gain" (at 1007, 1008). Thus the commissioners weighed the financial history of this and supposedly comparable companies against their own impressions of rates of return required for "financial integrity"; an additional factor was the existence of an agreement between the buyers and the seller about what constituted a reasonable rate of return. All these factors were weighed somehow so as to allow the commission to make a judgmental decision.

Although the method just described sounds extremely vague, one simply cannot find any systematic use of more discriminating standards. Later case decisions mention other determinants, some of which are defined rather specifically. For example, in the *Northern Natural Gas* decision in 1961 (25 FPC 431), the commission said that "the most pertinent index is a comparison of recent earnings-price ratios of the major pipelines, considered in relation to return on book value of common stock and variations in the business risks and advantages of the individual companies" (at 441). But, despite this specificity in defining factors, nowhere is there any indication of the relative weights to be given to the many different factors involved in arriving at the allowed rate of return. Some official statements sound exact. In the *El Paso Natural Gas Company* case of 1962 (28 FPC 688), the agency characterized itself as "determining the cost of the company's debt and of its preferred stock, by making an allowance for its common equity based upon earnings-price ratios and other factors, and by applying these amounts to the company's capitalization so as to arrive at a rate of return" (at 691). Yet even here the weight given "other factors" was not indicated, and the commission went on to say that "to use this approach alone . . . places too great an emphasis on the exact percentage of the equity ratio . . . ; therefore we think it important and realistic also to consider the end result."

The method of judging profit rates is well illustrated by a 1969 case (42 FPC 74) in which the commission completed a full review of the rate of return of the Florida Gas Transmission Company and allowed 7.25 percent. Florida Gas in August 1968 had requested higher prices on its regulated sales, and FPC let these go into effect in 1969, subject to refund in the event of unfavorable review. The FPC staff investigated actual costs of debt interest in the designated test period from June 1968 to February 1969, looked at actual rates of return on equity of "comparable" companies in the same period as well, and recommended a rate of return accordingly. The returns on equity were supposed to indicate the opportunity costs of investors, the idea being that if equity holders did not receive comparable profit rates on shares in the Florida company in the future, they would be expected to sell out, reducing share prices and thus the amount received by the company from selling more shares. But the commissioners did not accept the method used for these staff calculations—"we have repeatedly stated that the relative weight to be given the varying factors (in rate of return) does not lend itself to precise mathematical determination" (at 83). The company offered alternative estimates of the proper rate, estimates based on testimony of experts familiar with both internal operations and "standing" in the capital markets. Given a choice of a 7.5 percent return advocated by the company's economics witness and a 7.0 return recommended by the staff, the commission found 7.25 percent to be "the fair and reasonable rate of return" (at 81).

What were the commissioners doing in this case? They started from the premise that actual historical costs would be a good measure of future costs for future pricing purposes, whether the historical costs were those of Florida Gas or of "comparable" companies. They raised the allowed rate of return in light of "the higher inbedded debt cost during the [latest] two docket periods" and "a slightly higher rate on equity which we believe is justified in the light of the shift in capital from 64.46 percent debt as of the time of RP66-4 to 71.73 percent debt in the [latest] docket" (at 89). The higher rate on equity was also said to be justified on grounds that the particular figure was lower than in "the three most recently contested cases determining rate of return before this Commission" (at 88). Somehow the commission drew comfort from the fact that the difference between the opposing estimates of rates of return was small and from its supposition that the company would continue to "do well" with a 7.0 to 7.5 percent rate. "Consideration of the evidence in this record and particularly the Company's own evaluation of its accomplishment over the nine-year period of its existence leaves little doubt that it has made tremendous strides in growth of physical plant and average daily throughput, made impressive increase in earnings, and secured adequate financing on the rates of return we have allowed" (at 88). Thus the agency seemed to rely on historical data but regarded the extra-historical fact that staff and company were not far apart in their statements as confirmation. As to the decision itself, placing emphasis on an "impressive increase in earnings" would suggest that the commissioners were striving for profits for Florida Gas, while emphasis on "growth of physical plant and average daily throughput" would, to the contrary, imply that they were seeking to increase sales to final consumers. The invocation of both more profits and more sales as desirable obscures whatever the *process* was through which the commission reached its decision.

Of course, the commissioners may very well have known what they were doing, despite espousal of conflicting goals; they may have decided on that exact rate of return which best achieved goals not stated in the decision. If so, we will be able to infer their reasons and their methods by examining the allowed rates of return themselves.

The Regulated Rates of Return

Allowed rates of return can be classified as "low" or "high" according to whether they were roughly equal to or greatly exceeded the company's costs of obtaining capital from investors. These classifications are crude, since they are drawn by comparing after-the-fact realized returns with approximations of the realized costs of equity capital. But the categorization might indicate the motives of the commission. If the commission deliberately set rates of return "low" compared with capital costs, then the FPC sought to keep consumer prices close to long-term production and transmission costs. If rates were "high," then the commission was ratifying monopoly profits.

The examination of actual rates might well begin with the return in the Florida Gas case. The Florida Gas Transmission Company in 1960 was allowed an overall return on capital of 6.0 percent, implying a 12.5 percent return on equity in view of the fact that equity accounted for 15 percent of capital. Adjustments in the overall return were made in 1962 (to 6.5 percent), in 1965 (to 7.0 percent), and in 1968–69 (to the aforementioned 7.25 percent). In keeping with these changes, the allowed equity rate of return was supposed to stay close to 12.5 percent until 1963, thereafter fall to 10 and then 9 percent as the equity-capital ratio increased to 35 percent. The last decision reversed this decline by allowing an equity return of 9.9 percent in 1968 and 1969, with an equity ratio of 28 percent.

Might these limits be termed generous in the sense of allowing this firm to make more than the competitive level of profits? Florida Gas in fact was given more opportunity for profit-making than it achieved: in the first seven years of operation, it earned only from one-half to two-thirds of its allowed return on equity. One possible explanation for this result is that the firm might have had to pay more for debt capital than originally forecast in 1960 so that, given the 6 percent to 7 percent limit on overall earnings, higher interest payments reduced the residual equity returns. As can be seen in Table 2-1, such an explanation is not sufficient. Not only did Florida Gas fail to earn the allowed equity rate, but the firm also failed to earn the overall allowed rate of return for five years. Competition from other fuels in relatively limited industrial markets kept Florida Gas from earning what the commissioners had allowed; in that sense, the commissioners set no limits on the profits of this regulated firm. But the Florida company probably still made "high" profits, even though below what the commissioners had allowed. Profits can be considered high when the rate of return on capital is substantially greater than the costs of capital—greater than the costs of drawing capital away from alternative investments. The costs are elusive, but not so much so that an order of mag-

Table 2-1. Allowed and Earned Returns on Investment for Florida Gas Transmission Company in Selected Years

Year	Rates of return (percentage of capital investment)			
	Allowed overall	Earned overall	Allowed equity	Earned equity
1962	6.5	6.4	14.7	8.5
1964	6.5	5.4	9.2	5.9
1966	7.0	6.4	9.4	8.3

Source: Compiled from the examiner's decision in 42 FPC 74 (1969) at 95–120.

nitude cannot be indicated. The costs of equity can be measured by the rate of return ρ_i that the investor had to give up by buying shares in the gas pipeline company rather than dividends and capital gains from the shares of other companies with comparable riskiness of enterprise, which can be expressed as $\rho_i = D_t/P_t + \Delta P_t/P_t$, where D_t equals dividends per share per year t, P_t the share price, and ΔP_t the change in share price. The dividends, when looked at on a per-share basis, are that portion of earnings Y_t not reinvested as I_t or not derived from the sale of additional shares ΔS_t. That is,

$$D_t = \frac{1}{S_t} (Y_t - I_t) + \frac{\Delta S_t P_t}{S_t}$$

for number of shares outstanding S_t. These two relationships, together with an explicit definition of the growth path of new investment, have been used to find the required rate of return ρ_i from data on alternative investments in the same risk class as the gas pipelines.

Three studies have been completed of these opportunity costs for the gas pipeline investor. Malkiel first, then Litzenberger and Rao, and finally McDonald have fitted regression equations—of rates of return on share prices, dividends, number of shares, income, and the growth in profitability of new investment—to samples of "alternative investments" in the 1960s. The samples were drawn from the retail gas and electricity industries, on the assumption that utility companies comprised an equivalent risk class.[11] The costs of capital derived from the statistical regression equations in the Litzenberger-Rao study are shown in the cost column of Table 2-2, as estimated from marginal rates of return on alternative investments with the same debt rate and variance in earnings as actually experienced by

Table 2-2. Florida Gas Transmission Company's Return on Equity versus Cost of Capital for Alternative Investments

Percentage of investment

Year	Return on equity earned by Florida Gas Transmission Company	Cost of equity capital for alternative investments
1962	8.5	6.0
1964	5.9	5.4
1966	8.3	6.0

Sources: On earnings, 42 FPC 74 at 104; on costs, R. H. Litzenberger and C. Rao, "Estimates of the Marginal Rate of Time Preference and Average Risk Aversion of Investors in Electric Utility Shares: 1960–66," *Bell Journal of Economics and Management Science*, Vol. 2 (Spring 1971), pp. 266–69. Cited hereafter as "Time Preference and Risk Aversion in Electric Utility Shares."

Florida Gas Transmission Company. The actual Florida Gas earnings rates are shown in column 1. The earned returns substantially exceed the estimated costs of capital for two of the selected years shown; for the entire 1962–66 period, actual rates of return were 1.5 percentage points greater than the estimated costs of capital.

Perhaps the Florida Gas experience with profits was exceptional. But there were a number of earlier decisions on rates of return in the 1960s in which the commissioners allowed high returns as well. The equity rates of return allowed in all of the formal proceedings completed in 1961 and 1962 were in the range of 9 to 12 percent (as shown in Table 2-3). Although FPC justified these allowances on a number of grounds, all duly recorded in the case decisions, the results were nearly the same.[12] In four out of five of the important pipeline rate cases decided in 1961, the commission fixed rates of return between 6.0 and 6.3 percent. The rate allowed in the fifth case was 6.5 percent, a figure used in two of the three cases decided in 1962. Whatever the payment of interest on bonds in all these companies (left to the market to decide), the rate of return allowed for equity was whatever was required to yield an "average" or "overall" rate of return below the 6.5 percent ceiling.

This ceiling continued to hold through 1967, in a period in which there were only two cases (Midwestern Gas Transmission in 1964 and East Tennessee Natural Gas once more in 1965). During 1968, 1969, and

Table 2-3. Decisions on Gas Pipeline Rates of Return and Estimated Cost of Capital for Alternative Investments, 1961 and 1962

Percentage of investment

Company (and year of decision)	Allowed rates of return		Estimated cost of equity capital (alternative investment)
	Equity	*Overall*	
United Gas Pipe Line (1961)	10.3	6.3	4.8–5.0
East Tennessee Natural Gas (1961)	12.0	6.0	4.8–5.0
Northern Natural Gas (1961)	10.5	6.3	4.8–5.0
Kansas-Nebraska Natural Gas (1961)	10.8	6.5	4.8–5.0
Panhandle Eastern Pipe Line (1961)	12.0	6.0	4.8–5.0
Alabama-Tennessee Natural Gas (1962)	9.3	6.5	5.0–5.2
Michigan Wisconsin Pipe Line (1962)	9.9	6.5	5.0–5.2
El Paso Natural Gas (1962)	12.0	6.1	5.0–5.2

Sources: The allowed rates of return are given in the case decisions for the companies named in the years indicated (respectively 25 FPC 26, 295, 431, 448, and 787; 27 FPC 1180; and 28 FPC 482, 952). The cost of equity capital for alternative investments is derived from Litzenberger and Rao, "Time Preference and Risk Aversion in Electric Utility Shares."

1970, many more applications for rate increases were made as companies sought to recover higher interest costs and rising equity costs. The overall rates were held below 7.0 percent in 1968 but were allowed to increase to the 7.3 to 8.5 percent range by the end of 1970 (as shown in Table 2-4). The accompanying rates of return on equity stayed within the 9 to 12 percent range (except for El Paso's 13.7 percent in 1970).

During the entire ten-year period, the allowed rates of return exceeded the estimated costs of capital for equity investors in the gas pipeline companies. In the early 1960s, allowed equity returns were more than twice estimated equity costs. During 1968 and 1970, costs rose to more than 9.0 percent but were still 1 to 3 points below the allowed limits on equity in eight of the nine cases decided during those two years. As costs of equity capital increased sharply and unexpectedly, the allowed rates of return on equity were increased even more sharply.

The results do not appear to have been adverse for the companies. They were advantageous for the commission by keeping down the number of cases. The companies had the privilege of initiating the cases and would do so whenever costs approached returns. In an economy with a strong upward trend in interest rates, the allowed returns had to exceed the costs of capital in the years immediately after case decisions if they were not to be reopened and additional cases brought every few months. Thus the com-

Table 2-4. Decisions on Gas Pipeline Rates of Return, 1968 and 1970

Percentage of investment

Company (and year of decision)	Allowed rates of return		Estimated cost of equity capital (alternative investment)
	Equity	Overall	
Natural Gas Pipeline of America (1968)	9.5	6.9	7.0–7.5
Panhandle Eastern Pipe Line (1968)	11.2	6.6	7.0–7.5
Cities Service Gas (1968)	11.2	6.6	7.0–7.5
Algonquin Gas Transmission (1970)	10.4	7.5	9.0–9.5
Pacific Gas Transmission (1970)	11.6	7.3	9.0–9.5
El Paso Natural Gas (1970)	13.7	7.7	9.0–9.5
Southern Natural Gas (1970)	11.0	8.5	9.0–9.5
Consolidated Gas Supply (1970)	9.4	7.8	9.0–9.5
United Gas Pipe Line (1970)	11.4	7.9	9.0–9.5

Sources: The allowed rates of return are given in the case decisions for the companies named in the years indicated (respectively 40 FPC 448, 98, 1033; 43 FPC 53, 837; and 44 FPC 753, 567, 997, 1556). The cost of equity capital for alternative investments is derived from Litzenberger and Rao, "Time Preference and Risk Aversion in Electric Utility Shares."

mission, by allowing substantial returns-cost margins in 1961 and again in 1968, kept abreast of its docket of untried cases.

To sum up, the commission may have limited extreme profit-taking, but allowed rates of return seem to have exceeded costs. Although this state of affairs reduced the commission's case load, it added more to pipeline profits than to consumer price savings.[13]

Fixed Costs and the Direct Regulation of Prices

The Federal Power Commission supplemented profit limits with direct intervention in setting prices. This intervention involved the agency in rate design with respect to *season* of the year, *location,* and regulatory *jurisdiction.* The commission had established principles under which prices varied as a function of these dimensions of service. Over the course of the 1960s, these principles were greatly eroded by individual case exceptions. The resulting pattern of prices reflected the conflict between rules and company efforts to discriminate in price.

The rules for pricing dimensions of service were initially developed as a result of controversy over how to determine the rate base. Capital expenditures in the rate base had to be attributed to particular consumers to determine relative prices. When the commission first became concerned with the allocation of overhead early in the 1940s, examiners held that capital expenses should be levied on customers by "demand charges," or monthly charges based on the relative amount of gas taken by the individual during "peak demand," while operating expenses should be levied in "commodity charges" of cents per thousand cubic feet (Mcf) of gas actually delivered.[14] Both demand and commodity prices were based on system-wide average costs, but demand prices included all fixed expenses such as depreciation and capital returns, to the extent the traffic would bear them; commodity prices were for actual deliveries and were set by variable costs.

These propositions established the theory of the "tariff and service" contract rules in FPC Order 144.[15] However, they were not adequate for apportioning fixed costs among customers who purchase at different locations but all buy gas at the time of peak demand. It could be argued that rate schedules calling for the same demand charges per Mcf for all customers were discriminatory; for the capital costs of providing service to customers closer to the producing fields were arguably less than the costs of serving others farther away. The FPC dealt with these complaints from closer buyers by establishing zone prices to take account of distance. In a case against Northern Natural Gas Company, the commission required the establishment of three zones and calculated the demand prices for each on the "Mcf-mile" method (calculating the proportion of capital charges for each zone as the proportion of Mcf-miles in that zone to total Mcf-miles). This was in agreement with the argument made by zoning's supporters that one price for a system 600 miles long "requires communities situated nearer the source of gas supply to subsidize those communities located more distant . . . ;" and FPC rejected the contrary argument that "the large volume of gas distributed on Northern's system, increasing through the years, has benefited all of Northern's customers through lowered transmission costs . . . [with] the large volume sales made in the upper reaches of Northern's system."[16] The commission reasoned that, although there indeed was evidence that costs per Mcf were less the greater the gas volume in a pipeline, the predominant factor in costs was distance: "It is a simple economic fact that the delivery cost of natural gas increases in close proportion to the length of the transmission line. . . . The distance factor is the prime determinant of the cost of rendering service."[17]

Although the rule was straightforward enough, application turned out to be far from systematic. In the Northern Natural case itself, there was as much reason to set distance-related differential commodity prices as demand prices; yet the commission—accepting the argument that "an increase in [commodity] rates will result in the loss of industrial sales to competitive fuels by some of Northern's customers"—did not apply zone differentials to commodity charges.[18] Although the Mcf-mile method was reaffirmed in reviewing Tennessee Gas Transmission's price differentials in 1962, the qualification was added that, "as between two allocation procedures both economically defensible, that one should be preferred which minimizes the differentials in zone rates." Moreover, in cases decided between 1955 and 1962, the practice had developed of giving some weight to other cost-related matters such as the line's load factor and the total volume delivered to particular points on the line; and the "relative weight to be given in each case to one or more of these factors is a matter of judgment."[19] These other factors resulted in prices at farther locations below those that would have been set with the Mcf-mile method.[20] By occasionally tolerating submissions of price schedules without any zone differentials (such as those of the Michigan Wisconsin Pipe Line), the commission further diluted the distance rule. By the end of the 1960s, the case and administrative exceptions, rather than the Mcf-mile method, set the pattern of regional price differentials. The pricing pattern in some of the important markets reveals the imprint of regulatory compromise.

Consider first the New York regional market. The gas delivered into New York comes from three pipelines—Transcontinental, Texas Eastern, and Tenneco. These companies developed over the same time period in the late 1950s and early 1960s, with Tenneco the largest of the three in capital outlay because of substantially greater pipeline mileage in its storage and delivery system. Tenneco had the lowest accounting costs of operation per Mcf in 1970, through lower gas purchase prices in the field and greater economies of scale from its larger volume of gas in transmission (as shown in Table 2-5); with commodity price set on the basis of operating costs, Tenneco's prices should have been the lowest in the group. But this company also had the highest rate base, because of more extensive looping of the main line and more recent extensions, which should have resulted in Tenneco listing the highest demand price.[21]

In fact, Tenneco's commodity price was the highest, and its demand price was relatively low (Table 2-5). Most important, the differences among charges of the separate pipelines were quite small. The commodity prices were approximately the same for the three companies, as one might expect on deliveries of a homogeneous product by three suppliers to the same market. The demand prices, though varying from $3.30 to $3.97 per Mcf, were set so that even at 50 percent of the capacity delivery rate the

Table 2-5. Zone Prices Set by the FPC for Gas in the New York Metropolitan Region, 1970

Pipeline company	Total system mileage	Accounting costs (cents per Mcf)		Demand price (dollars per Mcf)	Commodity price (cents per Mcf)
		Operation	Maintenance, regulation, and taxes		
Transcontinental Gas Pipe Line	8,507	24.3	7.3	3.30	27.7
Texas Eastern Transmission	8,727	25.9	8.6	3.97	28.0
Tenneco	12,729	22.8	8.0	3.64	30.2

Sources: H. Zinder and Associates, *Summary of Rate Schedules of Natural Gas Pipeline Companies as Filed with Federal Power Commission, April 30, 1970* (Zinder, 1970); Federal Power Commission, *Statistics of Interstate Natural Gas Pipeline Companies, 1970* (1971).

differences were less than 5 cents per Mcf when averaged over actual deliveries. The two-part pricing schedules for each pipeline turned out to be more similar to each other than to the Mcf-mile rules in the *Northern Natural Gas* and *Tennessee Gas* decisions.

The pricing pattern for deliveries into the populated areas of southern Michigan, to offer another example, showed no adherence to Mcf-mile rules. The three pipelines into the region had entirely distinct zone differentials—Trunkline Gas Company with one differential across two zones, Panhandle Eastern with two differentials among three zones, and Michigan Wisconsin with none. The Trunkline and Panhandle companies showed operating costs of 5 cents per Mcf less than Michigan Wisconsin, and maintenance-depreciation costs at least 8 cents less; but all the lines had commodity prices from 26 to 28 cents per Mcf for lower Michigan in 1970, and their demand charges averaged to within 4 cents of each other at scheduled rates of delivery. The Mcf-mile zone rates in Michigan would have been much higher for Michigan-Wisconsin, both because costs were greater and because deliveries in that region were relatively greater. The older FPC principle governing zone prices simply was not followed. The actual price schedules seem to have been designed so that they would work out the same for the three companies.

Most prices on pipeline sales where there were two or three sources of supply showed this accommodation in the late 1960s. Rather than strict adherence to higher charges at farther distances, the agency allowed lower commodity prices at farther locations if "in line" with those of another pipeline. Prices on sales where there was only one pipeline source of supply showed more conformity with the rules—Transcontinental Pipe Line's sales in the Carolinas, where it was the only large supplier, were priced in keeping with Mcf-mile rules even if this company's New York sales were not. Similarly, El Paso Natural Gas Company's sales across Texas and New Mexico followed the rules on mileage differences. On Northern Natural Gas Company sales in Minnesota, both commodity prices and demand prices followed Mcf-mile principles after revisions in the early 1960s. In brief, Mcf-mile rules applied where markets were securely held by a single pipeline; where there were more pipelines, the rules were bent to allow matching prices.

Other rules governed prices for gas delivered during different seasons of the year and for deliveries to regulated, as opposed to unregulated, customers. The Atlantic Seaboard Formula allocated a substantial part of capital and other elements of costs normally classed as overhead to commodity charges and thus reduced demand charges.[22] Since peak consumption and thus demand charges were usually greater in the case of regulated sales to retail utilities than in the case of sales to industrial consumers, the formula had the effect of reducing prices on regulated sales.[23] But the formula was habitually "tilted" in case decisions, so that by 1968 it no longer applied even to the Atlantic Seaboard Corporation itself. In a review of Atlantic's price schedule, a circuit court noted that, whereas in the early 1960s "roughly half of fixed costs were recovered by the commodity rate . . . , after the revision only 6 percent was recovered through that rate."[24] As the court said, "the Commission may modify its doctrine or even change its policy," and FPC had already explicitly altered the formula for subsidiaries of the Columbia Gas System. The reason for granting Columbia's modification was that entry of competing pipelines had caused the subsidiaries to lose off-peak customers who had been served at the relatively high commodity prices endemic under the Atlantic Seaboard Formula. The court was convinced by its review of FPC variations from the formula for Atlantic Seaboard, Columbia Gas, and other systems that "the purpose of the [exceptional] rates is to restrain the customer from shifting its purchase from the historic supplier to a certified second supplier."[25] As in zone differentials, the seasonal and jurisdictional differentials embodied in simple regulatory rules were significantly distorted in cases justifying varying price-cost margins to meet competitive entry or competitive pricing conditions.[26] The erosion of regulatory principles through case-by-case decisions in the end produced a pattern of actual prices not very different from what the companies would have charged without regulation.

Although simple guidelines for pricing patterns, as laid down in *Northern Natural* and *Atlantic Seaboard,* were not observed, there was some consistency in regulation. The tariff and service contract rules called for the imposition of demand prices and commodity prices on regulated sales to retail utilities. Since this two-part method of figuring charges applied to sales by the major pipelines to retail utilities but was rarely used on unregulated sales to industrial buyers, the commission clearly did mold one sector's prices. What resulted from insisting upon demand and commodity price calculations for sales to retail utility companies? Most likely, if we judge by the results in New York and Michigan, the regulated sales at locations farthest from the gas fields took place at lower prices (given the additional costs of transmission) than did unregulated sales at comparable locations.

The two-part charges, based roughly on prescribed limits to the rate of return on capital, were paid by retail utilities and may or may not have brought price savings to the final consumer. To assess this possibility—potentially the most important result of all—requires an investigation of the relative prices of regulated transactions.

For that purpose a model has been derived and is set forth in the next section. The reader who does not wish to follow the technical analysis may proceed directly to the summary of results, which begins on page 54.

Effects of Regulation

The rates of return allowed by the FPC apparently did not constrain the profits of pipeline companies. Also, the commission's rulings in zone and peak pricing cases seemingly had little effect on price patterns where more than one pipeline sold in a wholesale market. Although this suggests that regulation in the 1960s achieved almost nothing in the way of price savings, the evidence adduced so far is impressionistic. A more thorough economic analysis of the structure and level of regulated prices is needed before this conclusion can be fully justified.

Whether prices have been affected by the regulatory process can be confirmed or disproved by comparing prices subject to FPC regulation with prices on unregulated sales. It is well to begin the comparison by outlining some relevant economic models of the effects of regulation, the best source for these being the "A-J-W models" which were developed from analyses of regulated pipeline activity.[27] Setting forth models is a way of finding testable propositions on regulated as compared with unregulated prices. Subsequently, statistical equations can be fitted to data on pipeline prices for testing.

Hypotheses on Price Determination

For analytical purposes, the market for gas can be divided into two categories: fuel for households and fuel for industrial furnaces. The Natural Gas Act limits the commission's price-setting power to sales for resale in interstate commerce. Most sales to the retailers who serve the household market fall into this category and so are regulated by the commission, but most industrial sales are not for resale and so are not regulated. Models of prices can be based on residential-industrial separation of markets, with demands independent and pipeline costs jointly determined (in the sense that the commercial and residential users share the same transportation capacity K at the same time).

The pipeline enterprise faces demands for gas by retail public utility companies, seeking an annual amount q_1, and by direct industrial consumers, seeking q_2 during the same period. Both sets of customers expect continuous rather than interrupted service. The amount demanded by each class of customers depends on the price of service. In the gas industry, a customer faces a two-part price: a "demand" charge (α_1 and α_2, respectively, for the two groups) that is independent of the amount of service purchased and a "commodity" charge (P_1 and P_2, respectively) per unit of service. The amount of service demanded depends on prices for gas from other sources and for gas substitutes. As with other commodities, these prices are determined by the interaction of costs and demand.

On the supply side, gas prices depend on production and transmission conditions that fix costs. The pipeline enterprise incurs total costs $C(q_1, q_2, K)$, composed of the operating expenses to provide output $q_1 + q_2$ and the amortized capital costs of existing capacity K. The amounts of these costs vary, in large part, with the volume of gas and the distance it is transported.

Gas prices are also significantly affected by the extent to which a pipeline firm controls its market. A pipeline company could control prices if there were few sources of supply or if suppliers made themselves "few" by forming a cartel to allocate market demand among themselves. A cartel can be effective in raising prices only if the members agree upon an acceptable and enforceable allocation scheme, a price-setting mechanism, and an effective means for enforcing the set prices. Enforcement is likely to be especially difficult if the number of firms in the cartel is large. Even a cartel with a sound allocation scheme and enforcement procedure could be ineffective, particularly on industrial sales, because of extensive interfuel price competition.

On the demand side, the important determinants of prices include the number of fuel users, the extent to which users cooperate in establishing their own price-setting mechanism, and the closeness of substitute forms of energy.

The effects of supply and demand conditions, including the presence or absence of regulation, can be analyzed within the framework of the following model. Each pipeline firm is assumed to maximize its profits, given the cost and demand conditions it faces. In each instance, prices are assumed to be "discriminatory." That is, if buyers differ in intensity of demand for service and if low-price buyers never resell gas to high-price buyers (which will be the case so long as the means of transport belong exclusively to the pipeline firm), then prices will differ among groups of buyers. Using the notation defined above, a pipeline firm seeks to maximize profits R as follows:

(2-1) $$R = \alpha_1 + \alpha_2 + P_1 q_1 + P_2 q_2 - C(q_1, q_2, K),$$

subject to the capacity constraint, $q_1 + q_2 \leqq K$.

Prices without Regulation

If markets are not regulated, the price-setting mechanism can be either an enforced cartel agreement or the independent profit-maximizing price decisions of individual firms. In the former case, each firm must accept as predetermined the prices for each class of user and is free to vary only the amounts sold to each group, q_1 and q_2.[28] Assuming demand is great enough for the firm to sell to each group at the given prices, to maximize profits, outputs are set so that:

(2-2) $$P_1 = P_2 + [MC(q_1) - MC(q_2)]$$

where $MC(q_1)$ and $MC(q_2)$ are the marginal costs of each type of service.[29] In practice, since the gas being supplied to each class of customers is identical, these marginal costs are transportation costs—that is, the costs of transporting one more unit of gas to each of the two groups of customers when the quantities provided to each are q_1 and q_2. Equation 2-2 has two equivalent verbal interpretations. (1) Prices for the two classes of customers should differ only by the difference in marginal transport costs. (2) The divergence between price and marginal transport cost must be the same for both services.[30]

If the industry does not have an enforceable collusive agreement, firms are free to vary prices as well as outputs. The prices that maximize profits will then be related as follows:

$$P_1(1 + 1/e_1) = P_2(1 + 1/e_2) + [MC(q_1) - MC(q_2)],$$

where e_1, e_2 denote the price elasticities of demand in the two markets.[31] In that case, the relative prices can be expressed as:

(2-3) $$P_1 = \frac{(1 + 1/e_2)}{(1 + 1/e_1)} P_2 + \frac{1}{(1 + 1/e_1)} [MC(q_1) - MC(q_2)].$$

The ability of the sellers to classify buyers as "retail utility" and "industrial" results in price differences that depend on differences in the marginal costs of transportation and on relative elasticities of demand.[32]

Prices When Retail Utility Sales Are Regulated

The FPC method of control is to set limits on profits through the artifice of finding fair rates of return on investment. It will simplify the analysis to assume that the commission directly limits total profits on regulated sales q_1 to M, so that $P_1 q_1 - \gamma C \leqq M$, where γ is the proportion of total costs attributed to regulated sales.[33] Since the profits on industrial sales are not regulated at all, total revenues only partly reflect regulatory constraint. The conditions for maximum profits, subject to this partial regulation and the capacity constraint, specify the two prices as:

$$(2\text{-}4) \qquad P_1 = \delta \frac{(1 + 1/e_2)}{(1 + 1/e_1)} P_2$$
$$+ (\delta - \gamma\delta + \gamma) \frac{1}{(1 + 1/e_1)} [MC(q_1) - MC(q_2)],$$

with respect to which the coefficients on P_2 and $[MC(q_1) - MC(q_2)]$ must be non-negative.[34] With $\delta > 1$, relative regulated price is greater.

The effect of imposing regulation can easily be to *raise* the relative price for the regulated service.[35] Suppose that before regulation the profit-maximizing strategy for the firm was to produce output $q_1 + q_2$ and thereby fully utilize capacity K. Then, when regulation is imposed, the firm is required to reduce the profits from its regulated service. Since the old prices, α_1, P_1, α_2, and P_2, and outputs, q_1 and q_2, were optimal, profits on the regulated service can be reduced through either increases or decreases in sales.

If, when regulation is imposed, sales in the regulated market are increased, then, because of the capacity constraint, sales must be reduced and prices increased in the unregulated market. But, since profits were maximal before regulation was imposed, such a change causes profits to fall in the unregulated market as well. Consequently the firm will have greater total profits if it leaves the service in the unregulated market unchanged while raising prices and lowering output in the regulated market. Only if the profit limit cannot be obtained by price increases will the firm choose to lower prices for the regulated service.

If capacity was optimal before regulation, and if the firm can reach the regulatory profit limit with a price increase, then the imposition of regulation will cause excess capacity. If capacity was less than optimal before regulation, the regulated firm will, if it increases prices and reduces output for regulated service when regulation is imposed, also lower prices and increase sales in the unregulated market. This is because, in the pre-regulation solution, if capacity is less than the amount that would yield highest profits, marginal revenues will exceed marginal costs in both markets (see n. 33, p. 140). If new capacity becomes available in either market, as it would for unregulated service if the regulated service were cut back, firms find it profitable to expand sales through a reduction in price.

In the long run, there would be a number of impelling reasons to increase capacity. Urgings of a regulatory agency and opportunities to increase total profits M by getting the agency to allow higher capital costs as the base for rates would encourage firms to build greater capacity than they would without any regulation.[36] Most of the additional capacity would go into unregulated sales because marginal output in the unregulated sector would now be relatively more profitable. Both regulated and unregulated prices could be reduced as a result of capacity expansion, but the regulated price would stand relatively higher in that regulated sales would increase relatively less. In other words, the regulated sector with reduced profits in all probability would experience a long-run relative decline in sales and a relative rise in prices.

Pricing Summary

At this point, the array of theoretical price variations might well be summarized.[37] The price hypotheses considered here differ from each other because they reflect possible differences in the degree of market control and in the extent of regulation. If for each category of service pipelines enforced collusive prices, and if there were no regulation, the coefficients a, b in the equation $P_1 = aP_2 + b[MC(q_1) - MC(q_2)]$ would take on values of 1.0. If for reasons of rivalry between pipelines in the same market prices for all amounts of gas turned out to be uniform to all industrial or all retail utility buyers but still could be set separately for the two classes, the elasticities of demand e_1 and e_2 would enter coefficients a and b such that

$$a = (1 + 1/e_2)/(1 + 1/e_1) \quad \text{and} \quad b = 1/(1 + 1/e_1).$$

Effective regulation will cause still different coefficients—the "regulatory constraint" terms δ and γ are found in a and b. The δ and γ terms normally can be expected to increase the regulated price relative to the unregulated price.

Collecting Data

The information on prices charged by the interstate pipelines, though voluminous and complicated, is not altogether useful for testing the effects of regulation. The companies file annual reports on sales revenues, as well as price schedules or "tariffs," for each contract over which the agency has jurisdiction (often referred to as Form 2 Reports). The companies also file reports on sales revenues (but not tariffs) on unregulated transactions involving delivery under contracts previously certified in the pipeline construction process. Information on physical volumes is also copious and also treats regulated transactions differently from unregulated transactions. With regard to gas delivered under regulated contracts, measured in units of 1,000 cubic feet, the commission requires annual accounts by tariff, by buyer, and by location of delivery. Information on the unregulated sales is limited to the amount of gas and the identity of the buyer.

The figures collected by the commission do not show demand charges, commodity charges, and volume by contract and therefore are incomplete for purposes of gauging price effects. The appropriate prices can be roughly estimated for regulated sales by correlating annual quantities of gas delivered with the tariff sheets. This has been done for the contracts of seven pipelines as shown in their 1969 annual reports: Arkansas-Louisiana, Cities Service, Panhandle Eastern, Southern Natural, Transcontinental, Tenneco, and United Gas. The prices for unregulated sales are taken to be the total revenues from each industrial sale divided by physical volume of deliveries on that sale.[38]

The price information so computed is used to estimate a, b in ($P_1 = aP_2 + b[MC(q_1) - MC(q_2)]$) for the effects of pipeline and interfuel competition and for the effects of regulation. Since the equations are derived with reference to marginal prices, the commodity charge on regulated sales is designated to serve as P_1, and the unit price on unregulated sales is designated as P_2.[39]

Marginal Costs of Transport

The marginal costs of transport, $MC(q_1)$ and $MC(q_2)$, can take on many different values, and finding the proper value depends on choosing the relevant time period, on allowing for the location of the pipeline, and on allowing for differences in factor prices of capital and fuel. For purposes of examining the results of price regulation, the time period of a single year, averaged from activity in the interval 1952–67, has been chosen, and the costs counted are those recognized by the commission: expenditures on operations, maintenance, administration, transmission, storage, and depreciation. Eight large interstate pipeline companies are included in the analysis. They were chosen because they were built over similar terrain with similar technology in their main lines and because they had much the same system length and capacity, with more than 1,000 miles of total mainline pipeline, 75 percent of which had diameter equal to or greater than 15 inches.[40]

The most general equation suitable for expressing costs on these systems is $C = \alpha + \beta\, m \cdot q$ with m equal to mileage and q the annual throughput volume of gas. The length of the main line of each transporter has been estimated by inspection of maps and engineering drawings, to provide data for the variable m, and throughput of gas has been extracted from sales figures in the annual volumes of *Statistics of Interstate Natural Gas Pipeline Companies* issued by the commission. When fitted to the sample, the equation (with $R^2 = 0.958$) proved to be $C = 44.7(10^3) + 0.57\, m \cdot q$ in cents per 1,000 cubic feet of gas transported for 100 miles. Attempts were made to account for differences in input factor prices among the transporters, and for the mix of volume and mileage as well, but they did not improve the fit as measured by R^2. The introduction of variables to account for the year of the observation and/or to account for the particular pipeline did not change the values of α or β or increase the value of R^2. The measure of marginal costs is 0.57 cent per hundred miles, so that values of transport cost differences $MC(q_1) - MC(q_2)$ are taken to be 0.57 $(m_1 - m_2)$, where m_1 and m_2 are 100 mainline miles of distance from a common gas field origin point to the points of resale of regulated gas q_1 and unregulated gas q_2.

Elasticities of Market Demand

The price sensitivity of gas demands has been estimated in a number of recent studies but analyzed only with regard to sales to consumers or else with regard to sales at the well head (to discover the effects of regulation of field producer prices).[41] There have been no studies of the specific elasticities of demand of those buying gas at wholesale from the interstate pipelines. In order to make first estimates of e_1 and e_2, a sample of contract prices and quantities has been constructed and a regression analysis of the sample completed with equation forms suggested by the more detailed studies.[42]

In most cases, markets for gas supplied by the pipelines encompass whole metropolitan regions. The purchasing retail distributors can go to alternative sources of gas that deliver within their metropolitan regions, whether pipeline company or liquid natural gas company; the industrial consumer can go to the same sources or to suppliers able to provide large volumes of coal and fuel oil. Data have been collected on transactions in seventeen such market regions: specifically, the 1969 home fuel prices, gas tariffs, and industrial prices reported to the FPC have been assembled, as well as figures on natural gas delivered under contract to both regulated and unregulated buyers.[43] From these data, demand functions have been estimated of the form:

$$\log q_1 = \alpha + \beta \log P_1 + \gamma \log P_F + \partial \log Y + \epsilon \log N + \phi \log TDD,$$

where q_1 is annual gas receipts of retail utilities, P_1 is the commodity price to these utilities, P_F is the price index of alternative home heating fuels, and Y, N, and TDD are, respectively, the "market size" variables per capita income, population, and temperature-degree days. The residential demand function proved to be:

$$\log q_1 = 8.106 - 1.907 \log P_1 + 0.390 \log P_F + 0.545 \log Y$$
$$(1.342) \qquad (0.816) \qquad (2.792)$$
$$+ 0.564 \log N - 0.445 \log TDD$$
$$(0.337) \qquad (0.711)$$
$$R^2 = 0.374,$$

a relationship in general agreement with empirical regularities found elsewhere in energy-demand studies. Gas price increases had the effect of decreasing quantity demanded; and increases in income, population, and the prices of other fuels had the effect of increasing demand.[44] But the regularities are not extremely marked—the coefficients are not statistically significant, and we observe that the equation explains only 37 percent of the variation in the quantity variable (as shown by $R^2 = 0.374$). Although at first glance the price elasticity seems quite high—the coefficient equal to the e_1 estimate is -1.907, clearly in the elastic range—it is not statistically different from zero. The estimate also seems to be subject to wide variations. After 1968 data on q_1 and N were collected for the same seventeen locations, the same equation was estimated except that output in the previous year, $q(t-1)$ was included as an explanatory variable. In this regression, the coefficient for $\log P_1$ equaled -0.950 and for $\log q(t-1)$ equaled $+0.970$; both were statistically significant, and $R^2 = 0.998$. Thus the conclusions from this demand analysis must be limited. All that can be suggested is that the elasticity coefficient of residential distributor demand may be as low as zero but that it is most likely to be between -1.0 and -1.9, where demand is elastic.

The 1969 figures on industrial demand, including price and quantity information on forty-nine direct pipeline sales, have been used to fit a least-squares regression equation. With corporate employees EES taken as a measure of size of market, the industrial demand regression was found to be:

$$\log q_2 = 11.372 - 1.785 \log P_2 - 0.249 \log dP32 - 0.144 \log dP33$$
$$\quad\quad\quad\quad (0.980)\quad\quad\quad (0.114)\quad\quad\quad\quad (0.125)$$
$$\quad - 0.205 \log dP29 + 0.681 \log EES$$
$$\quad\;\; (0.168)\quad\quad\quad\quad (0.192)$$
$$R^2 = 0.306,$$

where $dP32$, $dP33$, and $dP29$ are dummy variables for price additives on sales to three industries. The coefficients for price P_2 and for number of employees EES are statistically significant, and the first of the price additives (for the stone-clay-glass industry) is also different from zero. The remaining coefficients do not differ from zero, and R^2 indicates that only 30 percent of the variance in q_2 is explained by the regression. But industrial demand would appear to be quite elastic as compared with the retail distributors' demand: the elasticity for the chemicals industry is -1.785; for the stone-clay-glass industry it is -2.034; for primary metals -1.929; and for petroleum refining -1.990. Each of these seems to be close to -2.0, or at the lower end of the range from -1.0 to -1.9 estimated for the elasticity of retail distributors' demand.

Further regression analysis suggests that industrial demand is even more elastic than these estimates indicate—particularly where there are close gas substitutes. Data were available for a more limited sample of thirty-nine sales contracts with buying companies in the chemicals, glass, and primary metals industries, including price P_2, quantity q_2, and industrial coal prices P_c as well at the locations of gas delivery. The regression from this sample was:

$$\log q_2 = 10.954 - 3.471 \log P_2 - 0.962 \log dP32 - 1.070 \log dP33$$
$$\quad\quad\quad\quad (0.918)\quad\quad\quad (0.542)\quad\quad\quad\quad (0.673)$$
$$\quad + 1.578 \log P_c$$
$$\quad\;\; (1.346)$$
$$R^2 = 0.378.$$

Here the estimated elasticities varied from -3.47 (on sales to firms in the chemicals industry) to -4.54 (on sales to companies in the primary metals industry). Demand apparently was less elastic when the gas was used as a process raw material for which no close substitutes existed (as in chemicals) and was more elastic in the case of gas used as boiler fuel with very close substitutes (as in metals).

Equations have also been fitted for two of the industries separately where there were sufficient data. These show substantial price elasticities and indicate substantial differences in particular industries' reactions to gas price changes. (Perhaps industry differences produced the low R^2 values in the combined-industries equations.) The equation for demand for gas in the chemicals industry P_2 (28) is:

$$\log q_2 = -2.021 - 3.486 \log P_2 + 0.839 \log EES + 4.049 \log P_c$$
$$(2.118) \qquad (0.315) \qquad (1.938)$$
$$R^2 = 0.567$$

for twelve observations; and demand in the stone-clay-glass industry is:

$$\log q_2 = 11.641 - 2.778 \log P_2 + 0.819 \log EES + 1.163 \log P_c$$
$$(1.371) \qquad (0.239) \qquad (0.998)$$
$$R^2 = 0.232$$

for nineteen observations. These equations indicate values of price elasticity $= -3.49$ and -2.78, respectively, and as such add to the impression that industrial demand elasticity e_2 lies in the range from -2.0 to -3.5. Since the industrial sales observations encompass individual transactions rather than whole markets—so that they understate quantity responsiveness to price—the market elasticities have probably been greater. But this range, from -2.0 to -3.5, along with retail demand elasticity between -1.0 and -1.9, will be used in the calculations for the δ effects from regulation.

Elasticities of Demand for the Individual Pipeline

So far we have measured the market elasticity of demand—the demand schedule faced by a monopoly. Such a schedule measures the effect of competition from other fuels on the gas seller's price, but it does not measure the effect of competition from other pipelines. In fact, we are interested in the demand schedule that faces the individual pipeline. Such a schedule will reflect *any* competition that tends to cause a pipeline to lose sales as it raises prices or to gain them as it lowers prices. Competition among gas pipelines, in other words, might lead the individual pipeline to set prices that are lower than the profit-maximizing level that our measure of market elasticity implies.

Rivalry among pipelines serving the same industrial buyers, or even the same retail utility, could by itself have lowered prices more than did the actions of the commission. The additional element of separate pipeline price initiatives can be taken account of by modifying the elasticity calculations to include so-called Cournot elements. The Cournot argument is that each firm, assuming the sales of other firms are given by contract, sets its own sales and prices to increase its market share. Thus e_1 is replaced by ne_1 for n equivalent-sized firms subject to e_1 market-wide elasticity.[45] It is important to assess the extent of such individual price-reducing initiatives, in terms of finding ne_1 rather than e_1, ne_2 rather than e_2, in the relative price equation $P_1 = aP_2 + b[MC(q_1) - MC(q_2)]$.

Consider the relative price equation $P_2(x) = aP_2(y) + b[MC(q_{2x}) - MC(q_{2y})]$, where $P_2(x)$ and $P_2(y)$ are both industrial prices, one for sales to industry x and the other for sales to industry y, and $MC(q_{2x})$, $MC(q_{2y})$ are the marginal costs of transporting to each of the points in the sample. This equation can be fitted by least-squares regression to the data from seven pipelines' industrial sales in 1969. According to the analysis in the last section, the estimate for a is $(1 + 1/e_{2y})/(1 + 1/e_{2x})$, and for b is $1/(1 + 1/e_{2x})$, since both sets of industrial sales prices were unregulated. If systematic Cournot rivalry occurred in the 1960s, the a and b would be too low to be "explained" by the values of e_{2x} and e_{2y} found above, and these values of e_{2x} and e_{2y} should be replaced by ne_x and ne_y with n as "observed" in this regression—that is, with $b = 1/(1 + 1/ne_{2x})$, then $n = 1/[e_{2x}(1/b - 1)]$.

This equation has been fitted by least squares to forty observations of 1969 annual sales of four pipelines to companies in the petroleum industry and the primary metals industry. The prices are P_2 (29) for petroleum and P_2 (33) for primary metals; the marginal costs are $MC[q_2$ (29)] and $MC[q_2$ (33)] for transporting along any one of the four pipelines. The relationship to be estimated is:

$$P_2(29) - P_2(33) = \Delta P_2 = (a - 1)P_2(33)$$
$$+ b\{MC[q_2(29)] - MC[q_2(33)]\} + d,$$

where the constant term, d, measures pipeline-to-pipeline differences in transport costs, which would be excluded otherwise because $MC(q_2)$ is estimated as 0.57 cent per hundred miles for all services. The first comparative equation for price is:

$$\Delta P_2 = -0.936 \, P_2 \, (33) + 1.301 \, \{MC[q_2 \, (29)] - MC[q_2 \, (33)]\} + 26.64$$
$$\quad\quad\quad (0.048) \quad\quad\quad (0.182)$$
$$R^2 = 0.947,$$

with all prices in cents per Mcf of gas and the implied elasticity of demand of buyers in petroleum $b = 1/(1 + 1/ne)$ or $ne = -4.32$. The second comparative price equation is for eighty-seven observations on P_2 (33) primary metals against P_2 (49) electricity:

$$\Delta P_2 = -0.572 \, P_2 \, (49) + 2.581 \, \{MC[q_2 \, (33)] - MC[q_2 \, (49)]\} + 19.86$$
$$\quad\quad\quad (0.603) \quad\quad\quad (0.572)$$
$$R^2 = 0.245,$$

with the implied elasticity of demand in primary metals $ne = -1.63$. The third comparative price equation is based on two hundred forty-two observations of contracts with stone-clay-glass manufacturers (32) and the electricity generating companies (49):

$$\Delta P_2 = -0.407 \, P_2 \, (49) + 1.061 \, \{MC[q_2 \, (32)] - MC[q_2 \, (49)]\} + 13.59$$
$$\quad\quad\quad (0.064) \quad\quad\quad (0.298)$$
$$R^2 = 0.161,$$

with the elasticity of demand of stone-clay-glass manufacturers $ne = -17.66$. The fourth comparative price equation, from forty-four observations of P_2 (28) chemicals against P_2 (33) primary metals, is:

$$\Delta P_2 = -0.927 \, P_2 \, (33) + 1.504 \, \{[q_2 \, (28)] - [q_2 \, (33)]\} + 34.99$$
$$\quad\quad\quad (0.120) \quad\quad\quad (0.426)$$
$$R^2 = 0.735,$$

and the implied elasticity of demand ne for chemicals is -2.98. Two of the four equations (petroleum and glass) show estimates of ne that are somewhat larger than those for market demand e given above; and the other two show the same values for ne as for e.

In general, it has to be concluded that the elasticity of demand for the purposes of individual pipeline price setting was greater than the industry-wide demand elasticity. The difference in regression coefficients suggests that n would stand between 1 and 2. Apparently price-reducing effects resulted from the presence of more than one pipeline on the supply side of most industrial gas purchase markets.

The price-setting practices in markets for pipeline sales to retail gas utilities seemingly differed from those in industrial markets. The pipelines set two-part prices on contracts with retail utility companies. The marginal or commodity prices were not set at a level in keeping with the residential market elasticities of demand. Instead, they were calculated as if they were being used to add to marginal consumption while the initial or demand prices accumulated the bulk of the net revenues from providing service. This can be seen from using a sample of twenty-six paired residential sales which occurred in 1969, half at location x and half at location y, to estimate $\Delta P = b[MC(q_{1x}) - MC(q_{1y})]$.[46] The equation is:

$$\Delta P = 0.869[MC(q_{1x}) - MC(q_{1y})]$$
$$R^2 = 0.312$$

with the estimated value of b less than 1.0. The commodity prices at farther locations did not compensate for marginal transport costs to those locations.

A second regression was fitted as follows:

$$\Delta AR = 2.451[MC(q_{1x}) - MC(q_{1y})]$$
$$R^2 = 0.317$$

for AR equal to the average revenue from demand plus commodity charges; here the elasticity ne implied by the fitted value of b is -1.70. The ΔP regression indicated that commodity prices have not been set with respect to demand elasticity. In fact, the *commodity* prices are more similar to the model for perfectly discriminatory prices (when all pipelines operate together to control the market for maximum joint profits) than to any other model used here. But the price differences are too small to have been perfectly discriminatory—they were less than the calculated differences in costs of transport. This behavior, rational when marginal buyers are large relative to the intramarginal (closer) buyers, indicates that the primary rationing mechanism for these companies has been the commodity price. If regulation were effective, then, in reducing profits, it would increase the commodity price and release capacity for industrial use (rather than increase the *demand* price, forcing out marginal users entirely).[47] On the other hand, the ΔAR regression indicates that the average of demand and commodity prices has been set close to the equivalent "best profit" single charge if market demand elasticity were close to -1.70. Since the value of -1.70 is within the range of elasticities observed for retail gas utility markets in 1969, it has to be concluded that *ne* equals the market elasticity *e*.

On the whole, prices for gas to industries seem to have been set with regard to individual seller demand elasticities ne_2 higher than market elasticities e_2, in keeping with some pipeline rivalry. The number of pipelines at any industrial consumption location has made a difference for the level of prices there—for price setting, the number of independent suppliers *n* is between 1 and 2, and price differences have been reduced by as much as one-half of the monopoly level because of this number.

In contrast, prices have been set for retail utilities in two parts. The initial or demand price, making up one part of the tariff, has been in line with market demand elasticity. The commodity price, making up the other part, has been designed to induce sales at or even below marginal cost, without regard for individual seller demand elasticity. It is profitable to go below marginal costs on the commodity price if the demand price can be set for that class and for other buyers so as to make up more than the marginal loss. Thus the regulated tariffs in effect amounted to monopoly and discriminatory pricing.[48]

Testing Regulated against Unregulated Prices

Finding the extent to which profit regulation affected prices in the 1960s now requires calculation of the coefficients a, b in $\{P_1 = aP_2 + b[MC(q_1) - MC(q_2)]\}$. Here the sample of 1969 contracts for seven pipelines with industrial and retail utility buyers is used to fit a regression of regulated marginal price P_1 to unregulated unit price P_2, the difference in costs of transport $[MC(q_1) - MC(q_2)]$, and a constant. In this least-squares equation:

$$P_1 = aP_2 + b[MC(q_1) - MC(q_2)] + d_1L_1 + d_2L_2 + \ldots + d_6L_6.$$

The constant term is a series of dummy variables, $L_1, \ldots, L_6$, taking on values of 1 for six of the seven pipelines (to account for the effects of differing gas field purchase prices on the absolute levels of resale regulated prices). The observations consist of nine hundred eighty-six paired residential-industrial transactions, and the least-squares regression from this sample is:

$$P_1 = 0.906P_2 + 0.501[MC(q_1) - MC(q_2)] - 2.532L_1 - 4.617L_2$$
$$- 13.625L_3 - 8.300L_4 - 8.500L_5 + 8.783L_6.$$

The relationship indicates that prices were lower on regulated sales, and less-than-compensatory price markups were taken on increased transport costs to regulated sales at farther locations.[49] Once account is taken of differences in demand elasticities, however, it appears the regulated prices were not greatly different from unregulated prices under the same demand conditions.

With the estimated value of $a = 0.906$, and with $a = \delta[(1 + 1/e_2)/(1 + 1/e_1)]$, we can insert various probable values of the coefficients of elasticity e_1 and e_2 and thereby derive δ. The elasticity of industrial demands takes on values from -2.5 to -5.5; and so as to obtain all "reasonable" values of δ, it is assumed that for e_2 the probability of values -3.0, -4.0, and -5.0 occurring is 0.3 and that the probability of values -2.5 and -5.5 occurring is 0.05. The elasticity of retail utility demand e_1 is eliminated from this calculation because of the structure and nature of two-part prices on sales to utility buyers. There is variation in the estimate of a as well. Taking five values of e_1 and twenty values of a (as determined by a normal distribution with standard deviation of 0.008), the values of δ range from 1.475 to 1.109 (with probability 0.05). Therefore the average value of δ equals 1.206. Since without regulation δ would equal 1.0, the Federal Power Commission profit controls appear to have had some effect. But stringent regulation would have produced much larger values of δ. (With $\delta = 1/(1 - \lambda)$ and $\lambda \to 1.0$ as regulation increases in stringency, $\delta \to \infty$.) And these results do not account for the effects of uncertainty, which add to the size of δ as well. Within the range of "reasonable market demand conditions," as shown by the chosen values of e_1 and e_2, and the calculated range of a, regulation had only a very modest effect.

The other parts of the regression equation are also revealing of the price-setting process. The coefficient b for $[MC(q_1) - MC(q_2)]$ has low values in the estimated equation—prices increase much less with greater distance than is called for by transport cost differences. With monopoly application of two-part prices on the regulated utility sales (and regulated sales were in the majority at farther locations), the calculated value of b should be "too low" for price differences to equal cost differences. In fact, it is too low, so that the results of discriminatory two-part prices on regulated sales appear in this second coefficient.[50]

The process of regulatory control might be viewed here as having taken place in two steps. First, price setting under regulation involved the use of two-part prices, with substantial initial charges on annual service but with relatively low marginal charges per Mcf of delivered gas. The marginal charges were substantially lower than *average* prices on unregulated sales even though they may have actually been more profitable (as only one part of two-part prices). Second, regulation raised the relative commodity price above that which would have been charged without regulation, although the magnitude of this effect was modest.

Although regulation by two-part pricing might be credited with price savings at farther locations, did such discrimination bring about a lower price level for all consumers? This depends on the extent of the second effect of profit regulation. Accurate estimation of this effect alone is impossible, because the two-part prices were the only prices available—there was no set of single-price regulated sales with which to compare single-price unregulated sales. Only the crudest indication can be found of the effects of regulation alone—from comparing average revenue AR_1, the average of demand and commodity prices on regulated sales, with the unregulated price P_2. The "price" AR_1 can be considered the "equivalent" one-part tariff, given that the commission had set rates of return on capital such that the same overall profits were made as were collected under the two-part tariffs. The equation $\{AR_1 = aP_2 + b[MC(q_1) - MC(q_2)] + d\}$ then shows the relative price effects from regulation in the a, b coefficients.

The equation has been fitted to the sample of nine hundred eighty-six paired industrial-retail utility sales in 1969. The resulting least-squares regression is as follows:

$$AR_1 = 1.086P_2 + 0.750[MC(q_1) - MC(q_2)] - 2.931L_1 - 14.049L_2$$
$$- 3.362L_3 - 5.937L_4 - 2.094L_5 - 0.739L_6.$$

This indicates that higher relative prices prevailed for regulated sales than shown in the marginal price comparisons.[51] But this is deceiving, because the implied values of δ have to be much closer to 1 in this case, inasmuch as the assumed value of e_1—without a two-part tariff—lies in the range from -1.0 to -2.0. In fact, the estimated values of δ are less than 1, ranging from 0.15 to 0.80, so that measurable effects from rate regulation alone were nonexistent (if one accepts AR as the regulated unit price). Of course, this appraisal does not take account of uncertainty, which should increase δ. All that can be concluded, given these findings on the relationship of regulated to unregulated average prices, is that the effects from profit regulation alone were probably negligible.

This conclusion must be brought together with what we learned from the comparisons of marginal prices and from the earlier price equations on industrial sales free of the effects of regulation. The assessment of average price is quite tentative, since it is not possible to define precisely what is being measured by "price" in terms of the average revenue from a two-part tariff. But if buyers were to give equal weight to the demand price and the commodity price, the effects of regulation would be shown by the value of δ. The two all-sample regressions carried out above yielded values of 1.2 (using P_1 and P_2) and 0.8 at the most (using AR_1 and P_2). The first value implies some effect from regulation, and the second suggests that there was no effect. The higher value of δ implies that a $1.00 increase in the allowed returns would actually increase profits by $0.17; the lower value of δ implies that a $1.00 increase in allowed returns would have *no effect* on actual returns, because actual returns were already at the market maximum.

The Net Result

The Federal Power Commission's treatment of the natural gas pipeline industry has now been measured along several dimensions. First, a year's activity in price surveillance has been reviewed. The chief discovery: price savings brought about through surveillance were not much greater than the costs of litigation. Even then, the "reductions" were measured from levels sought by the companies, and there may have been many reasons for artificially high proposals. Second, the standards set by the commission in the profit-control cases were reviewed. These standards cannot be called stringent, for the realized profits were much greater than estimated costs of capital for the pipeline companies. Third, the standards for specific prices varied from case to case, but the difference between prices at near and far locations of sale was smaller than the difference in the cost of transportation. Fourth, prices were compared as between regulated and unregulated sales. The actual transactions prices on regulated sales apparently did not differ consistently from those on unregulated sales, if account is taken of variations in costs of transmission and in demands for natural gas.

Unhappily, these assessments lead to one inescapable conclusion. Namely, the value of Federal Power Commission price-setting activities has been either very low or zero.

Given the combination of elaborate procedures and negligible results, it is difficult to believe that holding prices down for final gas consumers was really the goal. The "public rationale" does not explain the expansive rulings on rates of return in the 1960s, or the variations allowed in pricing structure, or the lack of effect on the relative prices of regulated transactions.

In the final analysis, the commission took on the role of arbitrator, seeking to reduce controversy between pipelines and wholesale buyers. This is evident from the voluminous proceedings in consideration of each point of view. It is clear that the critical issues in a case are resolved by the interested parties. This is to be expected, for these parties can appeal unfavorable decisions and can introduce further cases. The commission keeps itself and the pipeline companies busy assembling information about expenses which can be documented by accountants. When it absolutely must act in the more controversial matter of setting profit limits, the FPC proceeds as "inoffensively" as possible, choosing rates of return by reference to estimates outside the regulatory process (such as "comparable earnings"). Taking this means to reduce controversy closes off the possibility of achieving significant economic results through regulation.

In fact, the rate of return allowed by the commission turned out to be nonrestrictive in the 1960s for two reasons. First, lower estimates would have brought about case "stacking" by the pipeline companies, whereby they initiate new proceedings before the old ones are completed. Second, the reference indicators of "reasonable" rates of return on which the buyers could mount their own initiatives generally took on high values in this period. The agency paid attention to proposals based upon "how well" other companies had done historically—and other companies had done well in the 1960s.[52]

Much the same pattern of response emerged from the individual pricing cases. The commission offered simple rules—the "Mcf-mile" and "Atlantic Seaboard" rules. And where they produced price variations not in keeping with the competitive conditions in pipeline sales markets, even these uncontroversial rules were breached with selective reductions on the initiative of the pipeline companies.

The commission evidently became absorbed in the notion that it was making the gas pipeline industry run smoothly. Whether the agency made all that much difference and whether smoothness was of primary importance are doubtful. Caught up in "cases," the FPC acted without having any significant impact on prices.

CHAPTER THREE

Regulating Natural Gas Producers

IN RECENT YEARS the Federal Power Commission has devoted considerable effort and about 30 percent of its budget to regulating the prices at which producers sell natural gas. Most producers search for gas by drilling wells on leased land; they bring gas to the surface, gather it in central locations, and sometimes refine it in the sense of removing liquids that they can sell separately. They sell most of their gas to interstate pipeline companies which transport it from the field and resell it as described in the previous chapter, either to industrial users or to distributing companies that in turn resell to industry or to home consumers. Thus regulation of producers has in practice consisted of putting an FPC ceiling on prices in this first sale, given existing ceilings on second sales.

Before World War II, natural gas was mainly a by-product of the search for oil, and as such it was sold at prices that merely covered production costs. However, the growth of pipelines capable of bringing gas from fields in Texas, Oklahoma, and Louisiana to distant markets increased demand to the point where higher prices stimulated greatly extended supplies. By 1970, one-third of national energy consumption was from natural gas. Less than 25 percent of the gas comes from oil wells; most comes from wells that produce only gas, found in the search for gas itself. Naturally the pipeline industry has also expanded. Before 1955 many fields were worked by hundreds of producers but served by only one pipeline; at the beginning of the 1970s at least two or three pipelines were competing to buy gas in nearly every producing area.

Since the early 1960s, commission regulation has been remarkably effective in holding down producer selling prices. Whether this regulation benefited the nation or even the consumers it was designed to help is another matter. Low prices have led to heavy buying and consequently to a substantial shortage of natural gas; they have also led producers to sell to

56

unregulated industrial or intrastate customers instead of regulated interstate pipelines. To explain how this state of affairs arose and what should be done about it, the present chapter explores the objectives of producer price regulation and the methods used by the commission to achieve them.

Regulating Producer Sales

In 1954, somewhat to the Federal Power Commission's surprise, the Supreme Court held in *Phillips Petroleum Company* v. *Wisconsin* that the commission was responsible for regulating sales by the gas field producers to the interstate pipelines.[1] Since that time, arguments about the validity and implications of the Supreme Court decision have made producer regulation an important political as well as economic issue. Debates about whether producers should be regulated have raged before the commission, in the courts in further cases, and before Congress. Despite the sometimes extreme criticism of the decision, the Supreme Court's logic in that case is not wholly unreasonable, though neither is it totally satisfying.

The court held that, although certain language in the Natural Gas Act appears to grant producers an exemption, the act does in reality provide for regulation of producers. Somewhat ambiguously, the act states that "the provisions of this chapter shall apply . . . to the sale in interstate commerce of natural gas for resale . . . but shall not apply . . . to the production or gathering of natural gas."[2] If a field producer's sale to an interstate pipeline is "a sale in interstate commerce for resale," how is it possible to exempt "production or gathering" of natural gas from regulation? Possibly the physical production and gathering operations themselves can be held distinct from sales and other operations, but no guidelines are offered.

Although the legislative history of the Natural Gas Act has little to say about producer regulation, what is said seems to support the Supreme Court's decision. A House of Representatives committee report states that the words "production or gathering" are "not actually necessary, as the matters specified therein could not be said fairly to be covered by the language affirmatively stating the jurisdiction of the Commission."[3] This statement, if it accurately indicates intention, suggests that Congress did not mean to exempt from regulation sales by producers to pipelines at the wellhead, for such sales surely could be said "to be covered by the language affirmatively stating the jurisdiction of the Commission" over sales for resale in interstate commerce. The producers perhaps anticipated this reading of the law. Although the Federal Power Commission consistently refused to regulate producers, at the urging of the gas companies Congress passed a bill in 1949 granting a clear producer exemption—a bill that President Truman vetoed. The producers, the Congress, and the President all acted as if without a new law the producers might be regulated.[4]

Despite the logic of the court's position, it can still be criticized. The court did not examine, more than superficially, the economic purposes that producer regulation might serve. Without such an examination, the court could not tell whether producer regulation was a consistent application of economic policy, in the sense of being consistent with regulation of "monopoly" distribution companies in the gas industry. If producer regulation did not further economic policy, then to assume a congressional intent to regulate in the face of ambiguous language and an uncertain legislative history was not warranted.

After the decision in *Phillips Petroleum Company* v. *Wisconsin,* Congress passed a bill exempting field sales of natural gas from regulation. President Eisenhower vetoed the bill, not because he favored regulation but because he disapproved of the fact that lobbyists had overtly offered campaign contributions from the industry in return for congressional votes for the bill.[5] At that point, once it became clear that Congress was not going to force through exemption for producers, the Federal Power Commission began to struggle with the problem of how to regulate. The first approach was to treat producers as individual public utilities and set prices on the basis of individual costs of service. After this approach proved unwieldy, the commission set regional ceiling prices, allowing all individual producers within each gas production region to charge less than, but no more than, the regional ceiling. To accomplish this, FPC in 1960 divided the Southwest into five geographical areas, set interim ceiling prices at the 1959–60 levels for new contracts, and began hearings to determine the final, legally binding ceiling prices for each area.[6] Over the 1960s, hearings, agency decisions, and court reviews took place in formal array for prices in the Permian Basin of West Texas and New Mexico and in Southern Louisiana. At the close of the decade the process had not yet been completed for the other areas.

Because of statutory limitations on commission authority, the area rate proceedings could set limits on prices only *prospectively,* that is, from the time an area rate proceeding was completed. To control producer prices during the many years that the proceedings were in progress, the commission worked out a legally complex, though operationally simple, procedure.

Price increases for existing contracts presented little problem, for any such increases took effect subject to an obligation to refund any excess above the "reasonable rate" which the area rate proceeding was to find. Prices for new supply contracts were controlled by the certificate-issuing procedure. The commission, with the help of the courts, developed the practice of withholding certificates allowing producers to sell newly produced gas in interstate commerce if the producer intended to sell the gas at more than the interim ceiling prices.[7] Although some certificates were issued to producers proposing higher prices, the commission adopted the practice frequently enough so that new gas prices generally were priced roughly at the interim ceilings.

Because the area rate proceedings lasted through the decade, the provisional prices held all new contract agreements to near the 1960 unregulated average. The first complete area rate proceeding in 1968 set prices for the Permian Basin only slightly higher than the provisional (or 1960) prices. The second proceeding set ceiling prices for Southern Louisiana at about the 1960 level, but the reopening of the case raised the ceiling by about 25 percent.[8] Since the remaining area rate cases were not complete and thus the 1959–60 interim ceilings remained in effect, contracts for new reserves throughout the decade were written as if economic conditions had not changed since the late 1950s.

The Objectives of Producer Price Regulation

The area rate proceedings have moved very slowly and have been expensive. Whether this is "good regulation" depends on the reasons for wanting to regulate gas producers and on the results achieved in pursuit of this rationale. Upon close inspection, two conceptually distinct purposes for this regulation emerge. That neither the agency nor the courts took pains to distinguish between them makes the task of evaluating regulation more difficult.

Control of Market Power

Restraint of market power is a traditional economic rationale for regulation. Stated in highly simplified and direct terms, where one firm or a very small number of firms produces the entire output for a market, it is usually expected that output is going to be less than the amount that would be provided by competitive suppliers. Monopoly or oligopoly firms restrict market output in order to increase the market price, assuming the higher price is more profitable to them. In many cases prices would presumably be quite high. Monopolistic tendencies can in theory be controverted by public agencies, such as antitrust and regulatory commissions. If it is costly to introduce competition into an industry via antitrust policies—because economies of scale make production by a greater number of firms less efficient—the government is moved toward trying to restrain prices directly.

It is often claimed that state regulation of gas distributors and federal regulation of interstate pipelines have been needed to curtail market power and to eliminate arbitrary price behavior. Supporters of producer regulation have advanced similar reasons for field price controls. Some of them have asserted that gas production has been concentrated in a few petroleum companies—so few that the largest have controlled the supply of gas to the interstate pipelines.[9] Unless market power at the wellhead is checked, so the argument runs, pipeline regulation will not be effective. Monopoly prices paid for gas at the wellhead by pipelines and retail distributors will be passed through as costs to final consumers. In the words of the Supreme Court, "the rates charged [by producers] may have a direct and substantial effect upon the price paid by the ultimate consumers. Protection of consumers against exploitation at the hands of natural gas companies was the primary aim of the Natural Gas Act."[10] According to this rationale, the Federal Power Commission should determine the price at which gas would be sold under competitive conditions and should then forbid sales at higher prices.

The question of producer market power played an important role in the debate in the 1950s over the need for regulation of producers, but this concern has diminished during the more recent controversy on *how* to regulate the producers. The "market structure" evidence accumulated in the 1960s —on number of sources of new production and reserves of gas—has not supported the assertion that gas producers possess unbridled market power. Rather, decentralization of ownership is as prevalent in gas production as it is in many workably competitive American industries. As the Fifth Circuit Court of Appeals pointed out, "There seems to be general agreement that the market is at least structurally competitive."[11]

The principal indicator of market structure is the degree of ownership concentration in the production of gas or in reserve holdings for future production. Federal Power Commission statistics show that in the early 1960s the four largest gas producers accounted for less than 10 percent, and the fifteen largest for less than 50 percent, of national production.[12] Shares in particular geographical markets were not highly concentrated either, even when the market definition was narrow. For example, in the Permian Basin of western Texas and eastern New Mexico, the five largest producers accounted for somewhat less than 50 percent of production.[13] Commenting on similar dispersion for county-sized production districts, M. A. Adelman has characterized even this degree of production concentration as "low," in fact "lower than 75–85 percent of [industries in] manufactured products"; and James McKie has shown that entry into the industry is so unimpeded that, even if concentration were higher here than elsewhere, the largest producers would not be able systematically to charge higher than competitive prices.[14]

The rejoinder to indicators of wide ownership of *production* is that the relevant market is in sales of rights to produce from new *reserves* and that no doubt ownership of uncommitted reserves must be highly concentrated. Petroleum companies sell gas by committing new reserves for production in 10- to 20-year contracts. The contracts specify initial-year prices and procedures for making price changes. Once the contract has been signed, production has been "locked in," so that the critical price effects on supply have accrued at the dedication of new reserves. Proponents of regulation have argued that this new reserves market is so concentrated that a few producers have been able to raise prices and that the higher prices have been passed through by the device of "favored nations" clauses calling for the same prices in old as in new contracts.[15]

This argument, however, has little basis in fact. The four largest petroleum companies provided at most from 37 to 44 percent of new reserve sales in West Texas and New Mexico and a maximum of 26 to 28 percent in the Texas Gulf region—all in the 1950–54 period just before the *Phillips* decision. These levels of concentration in supply of new reserves were all less than half the concentration in the demand for these reserves by the four largest pipeline buyers in each of these regions. Power to control new contract prices probably did not exist on either side of the market, but if there were "a balance," then it lay with the pipelines rather than the producers.[16]

Of course, one can still argue that, despite its apparently competitive structure, the producing segment of the industry has behaved noncompetitively. Certain proponents of regulation, such as some of the gas distributing companies in the early 1960s, asserted that the rapid rise in the field price of natural gas between 1950 and 1958 was evidence of noncompetitive performance (prices rose from 9 cents per Mcf to a peak of 24 cents per Mcf in the Gulf Coast region). Economic studies of the markets for new contracts suggest, however, that anticompetitive producer behavior did not cause the price increase. Rather, during the early 1950s the presence of only one pipeline in many gas fields resulted in a monopoly buyer's (monopsony) price for new gas contracts. Thus the field price for natural gas was often depressed below the competitive level because of the lack of effective competition among buyers. During the next few years, several pipelines sought new reserves in old field regions where previously there had been a single buyer, and this new entry raised the field prices to a competitive level from the previously depressed monopsonistic level. New competition among entering pipelines, not concentrated market power, accounted for much of the price spiral that was later said to prove "the need" for regulation.[17]

Proponents of regulation also argued that competition among producers was bound to be negligible because their customers (the pipelines) had no incentive to bargain for low prices. Since the final sales made by the pipeline companies were regulated on the basis of costs plus a fixed profit on capital, the pipelines, instead of resisting price increases, would simply pass any purchase-price increase on as costs to be paid by the consumer. This argument is theoretically suspicious, for strict regulatory supervision would force the pipelines to worry about whether they would be able to pass along a price increase, whereas weak regulatory supervision would allow them to keep any extra profits they earned through hard bargaining with producers—at least until "regulatory lag" caught up. More important, the "passing on" argument applies to capital costs too. Given limits on price increases set by some combination of consumer demand and regulatory awareness, the regulated firm would prefer to hold down fuel prices (on which no "gain" was earned) in favor of enhancement of capital prices (on which a rate of return was allowed).[18] Moreover, the slim empirical evidence available suggests that pipelines did in fact bargain for minimum prices. In the 1950s, pipelines pushed field prices below competitive levels wherever possible, and, when the low price threatened to drive producers out of exploration and development, rather than raise prices for all producers the pipeline firms themselves went into the exploration business. They selectively produced higher-cost gas themselves, paying monopsony prices for the low-cost gas from petroleum companies, so as to reduce payments of producers' "windfall" rents to the minimum.[19]

In addition to conjectures about "ineffective competition," supporters of regulation point to producer profits as possible evidence that field price controls were necessary. And, in fact, profits did appear high in comparison with some other industries. Economic experts appearing for the distributing companies in the Permian Basin area proceedings reported average returns on capital between 12 and 18 percent for oil and gas companies at a time when the average return in manufacturing was less than 8 percent. This profit comparison, however, is not enough to establish the presence of monopoly pricing, for three special features of returns in the gas producing industry must be recognized. First, lucky discoveries in a world of uncertainty might earn unusually efficient or fortunate producers a high economic rent in natural gas because of the importance of the discovery process. Second, the Permian Basin figures reflect profits only of firms still in business, not of those that failed. The uncertainty in exploring and developing gas—seven out of eight exploratory wells have been dry in most years—suggests that risks of failure are unusually high; measuring the industry returns on the basis of companies that survive results in an upward bias. Third, the profit figures in the Permian Basin proceedings overstate the true return to capital because of the accounting procedures used. The rate-of-return estimates were calculated simply by dividing total profits that producers reported they had received by the total capital that they reported they had invested. This does not account for the extensive time lag in this industry before an investment begins to earn a return. The accounting return on a dollar invested here must be far lower in real terms than elsewhere if payment begins five years, rather than one year, after the investment is made; the simple bookkeeping profit rate must be adjusted to take the long lag between exploration and production into account. Producer witnesses in the Permian Basin case estimated that an "apparent yield" of 16 to 18 percent was equivalent, because of the lag in production, to a "true yield" of about 10 percent.

In brief, arguments to the effect that competition does not exist in the gas production industry are unconvincing. If the firms involved do not have the market power imputed to them, regulating them as though they have can cause nothing but trouble. The following chain of events becomes possible. The Federal Power Commission, believing in the monopoly rationale, pushes prices below the competitive level. Since lower than competitive price stimulates demand, some of the buyers able to get gas use this fuel even though the economy could provide for their needs with other fuels at lower real costs. Simultaneously the lower price reduces incentives to supply new reserves and production, for it cannot provide sufficient returns to the producers now at the margin. By increasing the quantity demanded and decreasing the quantity supplied, regulation causes a shortage.

Regulation To Reduce Rents and Windfalls

Even in a competitive market, the distribution of gains from production might be so unacceptable as to justify the regulation of prices. Price in a competitive market is equal to the cost of producing the marginal units that can be sold. Some producers can sell—at that market price—intramarginal units that are far less costly to produce, perhaps because they have special skill or expertise or because they control a resource that cannot easily be duplicated. Such producers realize economic rents, or returns in excess of those required to bring forth production. It has been claimed that these rents are exceptionally high in the oil and gas industries and therefore that price control systems should be devised that would deprive producers of such incomes and give them to consumers in the form of lower prices.

Although no one has measured the amount of rent that gas producers would have earned without regulation during the 1960s, there are reasons to believe that rents would be large compared to those earned in other industries. For one thing, gas is a wasting resource, and knowledge of its presence in the ground in commercial quantities is uncertain until exploration and development are complete. At that point, the price of the gas is set by the cost of marginal additional exploration and development (when demand is increasing sharply). The difference between this price and the production costs of fully explored reserves could constitute an appreciable windfall divided between producers and landowners. Meanwhile, the cost of finding and developing gas reserves has increased since 1950. Thus gas found and sold to pipelines fifteen years previously in reserve commitments, but still not tapped, would entail lower costs than new reserves. If this "old gas" were to be priced at new long-term marginal exploration and development costs, the windfalls or rents might constitute as much as one-half the payment.

Proponents of regulation wish to eliminate such windfalls and rents without interfering with the market-clearing mechanism. To do so, regulation would have to hold down the price of intramarginal volumes of gas while allowing marginal units to be sold at a price that equaled long-term exploration and development costs. In effect, regulation would have to set separate prices for each source of supply. Of course, such regulation would result in excess demands for the lower-priced intramarginal units. To "clear" the excess demand created by the lower intramarginal prices by auctioning off these volumes would be to give the windfall rents to the pipelines taking the highest bids; to "clear" through rationing would provide the windfall to the retail distributor.

This type of regulation would be somewhat unusual but not unheard of. Differential regulated prices are most commonly found in housing, where rent control laws may hold the price of existing housing at previous levels, while allowing the price of new housing units to rise so as to clear the market of demands for new rental units. But this policy requires extraordinary sensitivity to changes in supply so as to react with marginal price changes, and, even in the best of conditions, it requires also a complicated rationing procedure.

Where the primary aim is to bring about the redistribution of income away from windfall gains to producers toward higher real income for consumers, the problem is to do so *without* affecting output. This requires knowledge of the location and shape of the supply curve for both established and additional supply. Moreover, when reduced intramarginal prices bring about the increase in quantity demanded, the excess demand has to be limited by recourse to such rationing devices as classifying users and designating one or more classes as "low priority" so that they experience shortage. Finding the low-priority consumer—on some grounds other than willingness to pay—turns out to be a never-ending search.

Neither the Federal Power Commission nor the Supreme Court has clearly distinguished the two separate regulatory objectives of controlling market power and transferring rents to consumers. The commission often issues statements as though it were trying to achieve both of them at once. In recent years, there has been some shift toward the second objective. For one thing, the commission has expressed the belief or fear that efforts to limit prices have reduced the supply of new reserves and the actual level of gas production. Lowering prices from "monopoly" to "competitive" levels should have had the exact opposite effect of increasing both reserves and production by moving along the demand function, at least down to the point of equality of average price with long-run average costs. The commission's continued efforts to regulate, in the face of this result, suggest that it no longer sees itself as basically trying to control monopoly power. For another thing, the commission set two price levels in the area rate proceedings—higher prices on "new" gas and lower prices on "old" gas.[20]

The development of this procedure, along with expressions of concern as to whether the "new" gas price would be high enough to cover the costs of producing marginal supplies, suggests that limiting producer rents and windfalls has been the more important concern underlying more recent regulation.

This shift notwithstanding, the agency and the courts have not completely abandoned the notion that producers hold price-raising power. Still, in view of the lack of empirical support for the notion that producers are "monopolists," we shall assume that regulating producers' market power is not a sensible regulatory goal. It seems more reasonable—because it corresponds more closely to the facts in the gas industry—to try to limit producer rents and windfalls. It is almost necessary to hypothesize that this is what the commission has been trying to do.

Regulating Prices through Individual Rate Cases

The Federal Power Commission first tried to regulate gas producers as if they were public utilities allowed to earn "fair return on fair value." The procedure was the same as for setting gas pipeline prices, with the agency judging the "costs of service" and allowing prices sufficient for a company to recover these costs but no more. This way of regulating prices seemed to promise that no producing company would earn more than a reasonable return on its capital—or at least that companies with unusually low costs would instead of receiving windfalls have to pass them on as lower prices. This method also seemed to avoid the risk of serious shortages. If production costs were to increase and there was demand for higher-cost reserves, then under this regulation the supply would be available at higher (cost-justified) prices.

Although this method allowed producers with different costs to sell at different prices, it did not provide ways to determine who should get the cheaper gas. Also, this method took for granted that substantive information was available on elements of cost in great detail. The agency expected that costs for new additions to reserves could be determined in the same way as the historical costs from the accounting records of gas transporters and electricity generating companies. But, as the examiners found out, determining the cost of gas production is an especially difficult undertaking.

Since gas is often produced in conjunction with oil, finding the separate costs of natural gas posed several extraordinary difficulties. Joint expenditures on *exploration* may yield joint production of petroleum and natural gas, separate production, or no production—some gas from oil wells, some from gas wells, in addition to many dry holes. Expenditures on *separate development* of gas fields yield gas with liquids of a number of types, and expenditures on *gas refining* yield both "dry" gas and salable liquid. Outlays to produce jointly two products complicate the regulatory process because there is no direct way to decide whether or to what extent a specific dollar should be considered to be the "cost of gas production" or the "cost of liquid production."

The problem is distinctly a regulatory problem. Without price controls, under competitive conditions, producers would recover marginal joint costs from the sale of gas and oil, but the relative amounts recouped from each would vary from firm to firm.[21] With price controls over both oil and gas, the regulator might try to reproduce competitive market results simply by requiring that the combined revenues from the sale of the two equal the combined costs. The company could propose any combination of prices that would cover total costs. (In fact, this procedure has been followed generally in regulation of jointly produced industrial and residential electricity as well as peak versus off-peak long-distance telephone services.)[22] The distinct regulatory problem for gas has been that oil prices are not regulated by the Federal Power Commission. Therefore the commission had to find the exact costs of one of the joint products or else had to try for indirect regulation of the earnings on the unregulated sales of liquids.

The commission's efforts at exactitude were not successful. Attempts were made to apply various accounting techniques for allocating joint costs so as to find precise gas costs. One method allocated joint costs according to the ratio of separable costs of oil production to separable costs of gas production. A second method allocated joint costs in accordance with the number of thermal units (BTUs) contained respectively in the oil and gas produced. A third method, recognizing that BTUs of oil and gas might not be of equal value, multiplied the BTUs by a factor representing relative value (a circular procedure, since value determined cost, cost determined price, and price determined value). None of these procedures had much to do with the price that gas would command under competitive conditions. An economic analyst could not find long-term marginal costs of a single product by using them; nor could he produce with them an estimate of the historical average costs for that product. On the contrary, these accounting methods created the illusion of separable costs when in truth the costs were intermingled and could not be separated.[23] To let rate base figures compiled on any of the conventional theories of rate-making govern a rate for natural gas is little better than to draw figures out of a hat.[24]

The commission struggled with a number of further, extremely serious difficulties in finding costs for each company. Judging whether historical returns were comparable to those earned by firms in other industries where "risks are comparable" was especially difficult since the "comparable" industries were not readily identifiable. Though it could be acknowledged that gas production was more risky than providing telephone service, it could not be agreed that gas extraction was more subject to cost-and-demand changes than copper mining or steel production.

Even if a method had been found for choosing comparable industries, it was not then possible to compare costs of capital. Gas producers had insignificant debt holdings. Equity returns were not directly comparable: few of the smaller gas companies sold shares in organized trading markets providing price information, and the larger companies—though providing information on returns—produced both gas and petroleum.

The very numbers of producers of natural gas created overwhelming difficulties in rate-of-return regulation. In 1954 there were more than 5,000 producers, and by 1960 more than 2,900 applications for increased rates were awaiting FPC action. The individual case approach to regulation required findings on costs, including joint costs attributable to gas, and on the allowable rate of return and rate base for the hundreds of companies involved in the 2,900 suspended applications. This would have taken an intolerable amount of time. The decision in the first producer case —the *Phillips* case—took 82 hearing days, and 235 exhibits and 10,626 pages of testimony went into the record. Although further cases might have been handled in shorter time with less legal material, differences from case to case in joint costs and degrees of riskiness, and therefore in allowable rates of return, were obviously going to require numerous individual decisions. By 1960 the Federal Power Commission had completed only 10 of these cases. The remaining backlog led the Landis Commission, appointed by President Kennedy to study the regulatory agencies, to conclude that "without question," the Federal Power Commission represents the outstanding example of "breakdown of the administrative process."[25] Sheer glut caused the abandonment of the procedure of finding individual costs of service.

As the previous discussion suggests, however, glut and short-sighted management alone did not cause the commission's difficulties. Even if the commission had commanded ten times the staff, it would have encountered the substantive problems posed in trying to separate joint costs and in setting a proper rate of return. These problems continued to plague the commission as it turned to administratively simpler regulatory methods. The commission was further plagued by the task of rationing low-priced gas—for rationing becomes a burden for any agency that tries to regulate competitive markets by setting different producer prices for sales of the same product at the same place and time.

Area Rate Proceedings

In the early 1960s the Federal Power Commission embarked on a policy of setting producer prices in batches, dividing the country into five producing areas and determining price ceilings separately for "new" gas and for "old" gas in each area. This tier pricing system was designed to provide a fairly simple way of transferring rents from producers to consumers without seriously discouraging gas production. It was assumed that gas found in conjunction with oil and gas found several years before a hearing cost less to produce than new gas. More pragmatically, the agency assumed that low prices for such gas would not discourage production, given that its supply was relatively fixed. Both of these assumptions are plausible. Low prices presumably deprive the producer of possible rents, to the benefit of the consumer, while higher prices for new gas ought to encourage enough additional gas production to satisfy total consumer demands.[26]

Despite its apparent simplicity, however, the tier pricing system also exhibited a number of serious flaws. For one, it provided no way to ration the low-price gas. For another, there was no assurance that the two prices (for old and new gas) were equal to the long-term marginal costs of production. Any gas shortage resulting from these two flaws was bound to be compounded by the fact that the commission could regulate producers' interstate sales but could not regulate the price at which they sold gas intrastate in Texas, Oklahoma, and Louisiana. Thus, in times of shortage, producers were able to sell gas intrastate, where prices were allowed to rise, particularly to industrial purchasers on the margin of choice between petroleum, natural gas, and other sources of hydrocarbons. The gas that these industries purchased was likely to be diverted from retail distributors willing to pay a much higher price but unable under regulation to do so.

How likely is it that the commission in fact induced a significant shortage by setting new gas prices below the long-term costs of exploration and development? An examination of the methods used by the agency to set area prices suggests that the answer must be "highly likely." The first method used by the commission was to set the new gas price equal to the *average historical costs* of developing recent reserves. Thus, in the Permian Basin case, the commission staff surveyed both major and minor producers in order to find the annual total costs for the base year of 1960. Experts employed by the producers, and some employed by retail distributors, made similar surveys, and the results from the three sources produced a range of estimates of historical average exploration and development costs. In the Southern Louisiana case, such surveys were undertaken once again, this time for the base year 1963. After considerable dispute over the validity of the estimates, the commission used certain of them to support price ceilings roughly equal to the interim prices set in the early 1960s. For the Permian Basin, the FPC set a new gas ceiling at approximately 16.5 cents per Mcf; in Southern Louisiana it set new gas at 21 cents per Mcf. The interim ceilings had been 16 cents and 21 cents, respectively.

The similarity of the final ceiling prices to the provisional prices is not at all surprising, given the method. This is because the provisional price ceilings themselves probably biased the effort to ascertain the cost of new production. If producers surmised that they were unlikely to be able to sell gas at more than these 1960 prices, they would have developed only those reserves having marginal costs lower than such prices. This would have resulted in the average costs of new reserves being slightly below the interim ceilings. Thus using the historical average costs to set future prices was to use historical prices to set future prices. In principle, if the Federal Power Commission had set provisional prices at 1 cent per Mcf, it would have discovered in retrospect that the historical average costs of gas production were slightly less than 1 cent, for no gas that had higher marginal development costs would have been offered for new reserve contracts. If the commission had then used historical average costs in its standard way, they would have "confirmed" that the interim price was the correct future price.

The commission further increased the bias by using average costs rather than marginal costs. If the aim was to encourage new production, the ceiling prices should have been set as high as prospective marginal development and extraction costs. Given a wasting resource from a fixed stock of uncertain size, it is probable that the marginal costs were greater than the average costs of finding and developing new reserves.[27] The category of higher-cost producers included not only the unlucky or less skillful operators but also those forced to search farther afield or deeper underground after having exhausted their more promising leaseholds. Averaging their costs in with the new gas costs of fortunate or unusually skillful producers concealed the costs of some further new gas production. Setting ceiling prices on the basis of average costs would guarantee that the exploration and development of the marginal reserves would not take place.

The examiners tried to take account of "the margin" by adding an "allowance for growth" to the average historical costs of finding new gas. In the Permian Basin proceedings, for example, the commission added 1.11 cents per Mcf to the ceiling price in recognition that producing enough new gas in the future to meet growing demands would probably require the exploitation of more expensive reserve sources. But it did not determine the size of this premium by analyzing producers' probable marginal costs. Rather, an expert appearing for the distributing companies stated that in his judgment this was the proper amount, and experts for the producing companies in turn testified that in their judgment the proper figure was 2.15 cents per Mcf. The commission chose between the two without stating any guidelines of its own on (1) reduced probability of finding gas, (2) higher drilling costs, (3) the rate of return required to attract speculative capital into gas production, or (4) the long-term output of this industry. Thus the commission's use of historical average costs, along with its acceptance of the distributors' estimate of the premium required to encourage exploitation of marginal reserves, made it likely that the new gas prices would bring about a gas shortage.

Negotiated Prices

Facing continued difficulties, in the late 1960s the commission turned to a process of direct negotiation to set prices. In the Southern Louisiana case, representatives of the producers, distributors, and other customers bargained out a settlement which most of them then presented to the commission for approval. The agency and the courts took the negotiation under advisement, along with a great deal of information on historical costs, and decided to set price ceilings slightly below the settlement figures. When a deepening gas shortage led the commission to reopen the Southern Louisiana proceedings, once again the parties negotiated a settlement. This time the FPC adopted the settlement figures on its own, holding that they constituted reasonable ceiling prices.[28]

To set ceiling prices by negotiation comes close to abandoning both goals of regulation. Negotiation among interested parties to "settle" a Federal Power Commission proceeding does not constitute much of an effort to control monopoly power, since the process bears no resemblance to haggling among buyers and sellers in a competitive market. Rather than competing for purchases or sales, the parties bargain in blocs—the buyers together in one bloc, dealing with producers in the other bloc. The price may end up higher than, lower than, or equal to that set in a competitive market; it depends on the skill and power of particular blocs. Nor is this form of regulation likely to provide two-tier prices that will eliminate producer rents. The new gas price is unlikely to induce enough new reserves to clear excess demand—for the reason just given and for the additional reason that the parties are constrained in their bargaining by their knowledge that the agency and the courts have the power to approve or disapprove the result. In the Southern Louisiana case, for example, they knew that the commission was unlikely to approve any price out of line with past prices or any price that departed too radically from average historical costs, and so the first negotiation in this case produced a settlement very close to the interim ceiling price. Yet, once the commission reopened the proceeding, indicating that it expected to raise the ceiling to alleviate the gas shortage, renegotiation produced a price 20 to 25 percent higher. The negotiation process may produce little more than what the commission has implied it wants by past decisions.

The one undeniable advantage of setting prices through negotiation is administrative simplicity. The commission need not spend as much time gathering evidence, the number of warring parties is reduced, and a successful appeal to the courts to overturn an agency decision is less likely. Whether the prices set by this method could possibly alleviate the gas shortage that developed in the late 1960s, and at the same time reduce producers' rents, is the subject we want to investigate next.

The Shortage of Natural Gas

The economic problem with field price regulation was the lack of a way to set ceiling prices without causing excess demand. We have addressed reasons why FPC policy might bring about a shortage. We have hinted that a shortage did occur. Now is the time to address two questions in detail. How serious was the shortage? Could the commission reasonably justify the shortage as "worth it," in terms of the gains for the consumer in income transfer?

Initially, the shortage of natural gas took the form of a deficiency of reserves in the 1960s. The lack of large new *reserves* early in the decade curtailed *production* at the end of the decade. This was not generally recognized at the time. Whereas the current production shortage was widely noted and decried by 1971, only a few industry spokesmen had noted the diminishing reserve findings in the middle 1960s. Even buyers of gas at the wellhead eventually agreed that regulation created excess demand for production and that ceiling prices under new contracts were too low.

In 1971 and 1972, retail distributors had to announce restrictions on deliveries of gas to new customers in Illinois, New Jersey, and Pennsylvania. One of the pipelines serving the New York metropolitan region had to *reduce* winter deliveries by 8 percent—just when demands were increasing not only because of the season and increased population but also because of local pollution regulations that called for substitution of gas for dirtier fuels. There were frequent further instances of inability of pipelines and their buyers to obtain as much gas production as they wanted at regulated prices. In fact, pipeline firms reported to the commission substantial shortfalls on the quantities they were under contract to deliver. These are shown in Table 3-1 for the period from the spring of 1971 to the spring of 1972 as volumes of gas sought by buyers but not delivered. In this period, the reported shortfall was 3 percent of total pipeline deliveries and 2 percent of total national sales. A subsequent FPC study estimated that shortfalls as a percent of total sales were even greater: 3.6 percent in 1971, 5.1 percent in 1972, and an expected 12.1 percent by 1975.[29]

Those experiencing the shortage tended to blame regulation for this state of affairs. The chairman of the Columbia Gas System (a pipeline) announced that his company would limit its new sales commitments because "customers have recently made requests for next winter far exceeding [previous] requirements. . . . We cannot obtain the additional gas to meet these demands." This executive attributed the shortage to "unrealistic area pricing policies on gas production," combined with unforeseen increases in demand.[30] The chief executive officer of Consolidated Natural Gas Company in Pittsburgh (a retail utility) described that company's unsuccessful attempts as early as 1967 to secure more gas. "We were unable to contract with [pipeline] suppliers for any additional long-term supplies. . . . We were routinely met with the response that there was a shortage of

Table 3-1. Curtailment of Gas Deliveries by Interstate Pipelines, April 1971 to March 1972

Pipeline company	Reduction of deliveries contracted for (billions cu. ft.)
Algonquin Gas Transmission	3.6
Arkansas-Louisiana Gas	152.5
Cities Service Gas	18.6
El Paso Natural Gas	3.4
Natural Gas Pipeline of America	77.0
Northern Natural Gas	2.4
Texas Eastern Transmission	29.2
Transcontinental Gas Pipe Line	28.5
Trunkline Gas	49.6
United Gas Pipe Line	132.0
Total	496.8

Source: Compiled by the authors from curtailment proceedings before the Federal Power Commission as of December 1971.

gas for purchase in the gas fields in Texas, Louisiana, and the midcontinent areas of the United States." His investigations led to the conclusion "that the volumes of undedicated reserves which may be available for purchase by the pipelines are insufficient to meet current increases in utility demand . . . in large part because of the cumulative effects of regulation under the Natural Gas Act during the period since the *Phillips* decision in 1954. In my opinion, price reductions and price rollbacks and instability have stopped exploration operations while the resulting low rates have created an artificially high demand for natural gas."[31] Some distributors and some state regulatory commissions disagreed with these reasons given for the gas shortage, but the conclusions of these buying company executives were not untypical of the trend of views.

The commission itself not only acknowledged the existence of a substantial shortage but also suspected that regulated prices might be at fault. Staff reports showed that additions to gas reserves had been insufficient to meet the "unceasing market requirement for extended periods of time," that "the emergence of a natural gas shortage during the past two years [1971–72] marks a historic turning point—the end of natural gas industry growth uninhibited by supply considerations. . . ."[32] The staff's view was shared by the commissioners, who in their concern over the shortage decided that "the vital importance of future additional gas supply . . . warrants further proceedings looking toward possible revision of the area price ceilings for such gas."[33]

Neither these expressions of opinion nor measurements of production shortfalls reveal the full extent of the gas shortage. What is more, the sources of excess demand are as important as the magnitude, because consumers doing without might be subject to very high costs resulting from the technical disadvantages of using substitute fuels. The nature, extent, and incidence of excess demand are estimated here by recourse to an inventory analysis, in which attention is paid to both production and reserve *backing* that ensures more production.

The concept of production shortfalls is not altogether satisfactory for analyzing the extent of the gas shortage, inasmuch as gas is not purchased at the time of production. Both industrial gas customers and retail distributors enter into long-term gas contracts because they wish to buy not only gas for immediate consumption but also security of supply. In present-day markets, producers commit or dedicate reserves for future production only if buyers are willing to pay a premium for a long-term commitment. In other words, by refraining from selling all their gas for immediate use producers satisfy the pipelines and distributors—they insist on dedication— and in return receive a somewhat higher gas price from these customers. The FPC insisted upon certain reserve commitments but at the same time undercut the market mechanism that promoted reserves. Perhaps the agency acted on the theory that it was protecting residential buyers who were unable to bargain for the "desirable" reserve backup, but all parties to gas production sought reserve security anyway.[34] The extent of the shortage in the 1960s lay in the gap between the reserves needed to secure existing demand and the actual reserve requirements established by the commission.

An Inventory Approach to Reserves

As previously mentioned, the field markets for natural gas are not similar to those for other fuels. There are no large-volume spot transactions for the purchase and delivery of gas at any one location in one day. Rather, reserves of gas are dedicated to pipeline buyers, and these reserves are depleted by production into pipelines over an extended period of time. The dedications are made by contracts which specify initial prices, delivery period, and the rights to draw upon certain in-ground reserves of gas. The contract markets can be said to "clear" if newly dedicated reserves meet the inventory requirements for keeping new production going by pipeline to final industrial and home consumers.

These inventory needs obviously exceed a few years' production. Pipeline companies would not make connections for only 2 or 3 years of deliveries; in fact, they traditionally have sought 10 to 20 years of reserve backing for contracts to retailers. Optimal backing is a question of balance between the greater security that reserves provide a pipeline against default on its promised deliveries and the greater initial pipeline outlay necessary to have such reserves on tap.[35]

The FPC has considered the proper amount of reserves to be 20 times initial production, so that (regulated) demands for new reserves have been based on "the assumption that each new market commitment is backed by a 20-year supply."[36] Long before the commission had much influence on demand for reserves, however, both pipeline and nonpipeline buyers manifested a preference for reserve backing. In 1947 new reserves secured by both pipeline and nonpipeline buyers provided backing equal to 14.5 times new production, and in subsequent years additional reserves to support additional production rose until by 1957 new reserves equaled 24.5 times new production.[37]

A simple, rough estimate of demands for reserve inventory under ceiling prices in the late 1960s might be obtained by multiplying total new production—for all new contracts plus any renewals of expiring contracts—by either the FPC ratio for reserve backing or the "market" ratio that prevailed from 1947 to 1957. To do this, it is necessary to reckon, for each year of the "study" period, the extent of additional demand and the extent of replacement demand for production to be delivered to final home and industrial consumers.

To estimate total new production, we have assumed that in a given year gas was supplied from reserves that had been committed evenly over time to buyers who wanted roughly 14 years' backup (the national rate of depletion of new reserves in 1947).[38] Thus 1/14 of the production was for contracts that would expire in any one year. The total new production demanded, then, would equal the increase in production over the previous year, plus 1/14 of that year's production.[39] (The latter amount is for renewal or replacement of expiring contracts.) To estimate new reserve demands in each year, the total new production figure can be multiplied either by 20 (the FPC's recommended backup figure) or, to be very con-

servative, by 14.5 (the smallest backup demanded by buyers before regulation, in 1947).

The total demands for reserves for 1964–68 under these conditions are
set forth in Table 3-2. Total new production each year ranged from 0.9
trillion cubic feet to more than 1.6 trillion cubic feet. If companies wanted
to back that new production with 14.5 years of reserves, they would have
demanded each year amounts that ranged from 13.2 to 23.6 trillion cubic
feet of reserves, depending on the year. If they had wanted 20 years of
backing, they would have demanded each year amounts that ranged, depending on the year, between 18.4 and 32.8 trillion cubic feet of reserves.
The real supply of new reserves, as shown by the total commitments
actually made to the pipelines under new contracts, was far less, ranging
from 9.4 to 15.7 trillion cubic feet per year. For the 5-year period as a
whole, if pipelines' would-be "demand" for reserves is measured by 14.5
times new production, then that would-be demand amounted to 156 percent of the new reserves actually committed under contract. If measured
by the commission's standards (20 times new production), would-be demand amounted to 219 percent of the new reserves actually committed. In
other words, in the late 1960s, demand for new reserves ranged somewhere
between $1\frac{1}{2}$ and $2\frac{1}{5}$ times the reserves supplied.

Of course, this inventory analysis depends upon restrictive assumptions.
The increased demand for reserves is calculated on the assumption that the

**Table 3-2. Estimated Demand by Companies for Natural Gas Reserves,
before and after FPC Regulation, and Actual Additions to Reserves,
1964–68**

Trillions of cubic feet

	Reserves demanded to back new production		
Year	*14.5-year backing*	*20-year backing*	*Actual additions to reserves*
1964	19.8	27.4	10.7
1965	13.2	18.4	12.8
1966	22.1	30.7	14.9
1967	21.4	29.8	15.7
1968	23.6	32.8	9.4

Source: From or derived from Federal Power Commission, *The Gas Supplies of Interstate Natural Gas Pipeline Companies, 1968* (1970), p. 92.

preference of pipelines for security in reserve backings is constant—that no change occurs in the conditions that translate security needs into reserve demands. If this assumption holds up, it is fair to conclude that a "shortage" of reserves developed that injured buyers by reducing their security. One cannot really determine the extent to which higher prices would have ended this shortage (perhaps by eliciting more supply or by drying up demand for more reserves) without trying to determine how market-clearing prices would have affected supply and demand for reserves.

A Supply and Demand Analysis

In the absence of area price ceilings, higher prices would have been specified in new gas contracts, and significantly greater new reserve commitments might have been made. General increases in demands for energy, during a period in which the supply responses in coal and oil markets were a little sluggish, should have led to short-term price increases for new gas reserves. The gas supply response might have been substantial—enough to fill in part of the excess demand shown in the inventory analysis of reserve commitments. Without price ceilings, the demand response should also have been substantial; by rationing the new volumes available, the price increases would eliminate the rest of the excess demand.

To test these hypotheses, the first steps are to construct supply and demand schedules pertaining to the 1950s and to use these schedules to find the market-clearing prices in that period. Here supply and demand relations are fitted to data for the 1950s and used to find ΔR_{tj} (new reserves added in year t in producing district j) and P_{tj} (the average of the initial base prices on new contracts signed in year t in producing district j). Southwestern fields where gas was produced for resale along the East Coast are the ones scrutinized.[10] The values for ΔR_{tj} and P_{tj} that clear the supply and demand system in the 1950s appear to be close to the actual values of new reserves and prices for those years. As a result, it can be concluded that markets operated in the 1950s so as to satisfy demands as they arose. The model is then applied to the 1960s by inserting 1961–67 data into the supply and demand equations and then solving the system for market-clearing values ΔR_{tj}, P_{tj}^* characteristic of the 1960s. Differences between model values and actual reserves and prices are attributable to the rigidity imposed through regulatory ceiling prices.

The amount of new reserves found ("supplied") in a year depends on geological, technical, and economic factors. Over time, the density of deposits in a given region will become more or less evident. Drilling inputs further affect the amount of available reserves. (The only data on such inputs show number of gas development wells in the 1950s and 1960s by drilling district. These are not indicative of all inputs, because of great differences in depth and strata conditions, and wells themselves are joint factor inputs both of capital and of knowledge of surrounding geological conditions.) Finally, the supply of newly discovered reserves also depends in part upon the prices producers can expect to get for new gas.

On the demand side of gas field markets, prices are affected by the pipelines' costs of transport from each district. The volume of discoveries is important in setting these costs—large discoveries provide the opportunity to put in large-scale gathering lines which reduce the costs of transporting each additional Mcf of gas. Distance also is important—the greater the distance of the reserves from the final industrial and home gas users, the greater the costs to the pipelines.

As for the final consumer, in years in which prices of substitutes are rising and incomes or other determinants of personal consumption are increasing, demand is increasing, and so bid prices should be higher. An indicator of final consumer demand increase is an increase in the price of substitutes, as shown by the index of all fuel prices at retail.

Having listed the principal components, we are now in a position to prepare a model of the supply and demand relationships. Gas markets without price ceiling regulation are expected to clear gas reserves ΔR_{tj}, gas production ΔQ_{tj}, and the number of development wells W_{tj}, at initial contract prices P_{tj}. The market-clearing solutions depend on the outside or "exogenous" variables: district characteristics j; reserves demanded $\Sigma \Delta R_{tj}$; capital stock of gas-burning furnaces in the country K_t; index of all fuel prices at retail fp_t; distance M_j; rate of interest i_t; and oil price op_t (more gas drilling occurs where there are prospects of profitable oil discoveries).

Data series for each of these variables have been constructed for the pre-regulatory period 1955–60 in eleven drilling regions that provided gas on contracts to pipelines serving the East Coast and the Midwest.[41] These data are used to fit the supply and demand relations by two-stage least squares, with the four endogenous variables, ΔR_{tj}, ΔQ_{tj}, W_{tj}, P_{tj}, simultaneously determined. The procedure is to find "reduced form" equations for ΔR_{tj}, ΔQ_{tj}, W_{tj}, and P_{tj} separately, given the exogenous variables, and then use the fitted values $\Delta \hat{R}_{tj}$, $\Delta \hat{Q}_{tj}$, $\hat{W}_{tj}$, and $\hat{P}_{tj}$ to find the supply and demand equations.[42]

The fitted supply and demand equations are thus four least-squares regressions: one for the supply of new reserves, the second for the supply of wells, the third for new production, the last for the demand for new reserves. The number of wells and the supply of reserves for the 1955–60 period are given by the following equations:

$$W_{tj} = -648.60 + 11.46 \hat{P}_{tj} + 175.52 \, op_t + \sum_{1}^{10} a_i J_i$$
$$\phantom{W_{tj} = -648.60 +} (1.73) (1.73)$$
$$R^2 = 0.734$$

$$\Delta R_{tj} = -5.41 + 2.45 \hat{W}_{tj} + \sum_{1}^{10} b_i J_i$$
$$\phantom{\Delta R_{tj} = -5.41} (0.98)$$
$$R^2 = 0.831.$$

Note the positive cumulative effects from well drilling, new gas contract prices, and the all-fuels price index.[43] The elasticity of reserve supply with respect to new contract gas price is estimated to be equal to 0.51 at average 1956 price and 1956 new reserves, so that a 10 percent price increase theoretically leads to a 5.1 percent increase in discovery of new reserves.

The production equation is as follows:

$$\Delta Q_{tj} = -34.33 + 0.015 \, \Delta R_{tj} - 27.49 \, i_t + 11.37 \, fp_t$$
$$\phantom{\Delta Q_{tj} = -34.33 +} (2.89) (-2.27) (2.75)$$
$$R^2 = 0.693,$$

which shows a positive production–reserve relation, a negative production–interest rate relation, and a positive production–fuel price relation. The elasticity of production with respect to reserves was approximately 0.40 and was "statistically quasi-significant."[44] The elasticity with respect to interest rates was negative and with respect to the fuel price index was positive. Both coefficients were quasi-significant and had the expected effect on production: the higher the capital cost (i_t), the lower the production rate; the higher the price of alternative fuels, the higher the gas production rate.

The demand equation has also been estimated in the second stage of two-stage least squares as follows:

$$P_{tj} = 12.22 + 0.0012 \, \Delta \hat{R}_{tj} - 0.000094 \, \Sigma \Delta R_{tj} - 0.0013 \, M_j$$
$$\phantom{P_{tj} = 12.22 +} (8.93) (-1.12) (-1.95)$$
$$+ 0.088 \, fp_t + 0.00083 \, K_t$$
$$ (0.99) (5.02)$$
$$R^2 = 0.616.$$

The elasticity of gas prices with respect to total reserves $\Delta\Sigma R_{tj}$ at 1956 average values (the reciprocal of the usual elasticity of demand) was -0.06, while the elasticity of gas prices with respect to the fuels price index was $+0.02$ and with respect to the stock of gas-burning furnaces (an index of the size of the resale market) was $+0.05$. These values are low, indicating small responsiveness of bid prices to changes in the values of these variables. The elasticity of demand is substantial—a small change in prices P_{tj} brings forth large changes in total new reserves demanded $\Sigma\Delta R_{tj}$. This elasticity equals $(-1/0.00009)(P_{tj}/\Delta R_{tj})$. The other elasticities—for variables ΔR_{tj} and M_j, differentiating the drilling regions—are as expected from the economics of pipeline costs and demand.

This four-equation formulation indicates that the supply of newly discovered reserves and of new production depends upon new contract prices. These prices in turn depend on the size of total discoveries, on pipeline costs, and on conditions of demand in final gas resale markets. The four equations together make up an equilibrium system that describes well the actual prices and discoveries in the late 1950s. An indication of the closeness of description is the accuracy with which equilibrium in the four-equation system reproduces the actual values of new reserves, prices, and production in the 1955–60 period. The simulated prices and the actual annual average prices from the eleven-region sample (in cents per Mcf) compare rather closely, as can be seen when they are listed side by side.

Year	Average actual price	Simulated price
1956	17.0	17.9
1957	18.1	18.4
1958	19.3	18.8
1959	19.1	19.7
1960	18.4	20.0

The two sets of prices are quite similar, and the difference between average actual reserves and simulated reserves comes to less than a trillion cubic feet of gas for the five-year period analyzed here. These similarities make it likely that market clearing was accomplished by price changes within the year, in the years 1955–60, before price controls.

The question is whether markets cleared in the 1960s or whether the ceilings on prices in the early 1960s had such a substantial effect on gas reserve discovery and disposition that the shortage developed from the price controls alone. In order to formulate a judgment on these possibilities, the four equations have been used, along with 1961–68 values of the exogenous variables, to find the values ΔR_{tj}^*, ΔQ_{tj}^*, W_{tj}^*, and P_{tj}^* which solve the equations or, in other words, "clear" the gas market as if there were no price ceilings. These "unregulated" values are compared with actual values in Table 3-3.

The simulated or unregulated prices that would have cleared the reserve market were on the average 6 cents per Mcf higher than ceiling prices for the entire period and over 7 cents higher for the period following 1962. On the supply side, the higher prices—if they had been allowed—would have provided considerable incentive to add to the volume of new reserves. The simulated reserves are more than twice as high as the actual reserves over this period. On the demand side, the market-clearing price would have significantly reduced the amounts of reserves sought. The amounts demanded are not known, since all that have been registered are those reserves both demanded *and* supplied. That excess reserve demands would have been reduced is indicated by the rate of change in the total reserve demand function with respect to field price (the reciprocal of the coefficient -0.00009): demand would have decreased approximately 10 trillion cubic feet for each cent of price increase.

Another indication of the potential impact of clearing prices appears in the difference between the actual and simulated production series. Actual

Table 3-3. Actual Prices and Simulated Unregulated Prices, Production, and Changes in Reserves of Natural Gas, East Coast and Midwest, 1961–68

Year	Price P_{tj} (cents per Mcf)		Production ΔQ_{tj} (billions cu. ft.)		Changes in reserves ΔR_{tj} (billions cu. ft.)	
	Actual average price	Simulated[a]	Actual	Simulated[a]	Actual	Simulated[a]
1961	17.7	20.0	292	817	5,567	12,480
1962	19.0	21.1	230	755	5,805	12,858
1963	16.5	22.4	447	688	4,884	13,077
1964	16.7	22.9	200	814	5,512	13,221
1965	17.4	24.1	348	750	6,015	13,621
1966	17.2	25.5	347	627	4,204	14,147
1967	17.4	26.7	575	520	3,693	15,026
1968	18.0	27.8	434	548	951	15,572

Sources: American Gas Association (AGA), *Reserves of Crude Oil* (1969), pp. 175–219, Tables XVII-1 to XVII-45; AGA, American Petroleum Institute, and Canadian Petroleum Association, *Summary of Estimated Annual Discoveries of Natural Gas Reserves*, various issues.

a. The simulations are estimates of what the values would have been without FPC regulation.

production falls short of simulated production by approximately 52 percent over the eight-year period. It appears that unregulated prices would have brought forth much greater output.

The overall impression is that new reserve supplies might have been three times greater, and immediate production twice as great, if there had been no field price regulation.[45] The higher market-clearing prices would have brought forth additional discovered reserves more than twice the entire amount of additions to the interstate inventory over the 1961–68 period. The buyers' response to higher prices observed in our sample suggests that higher prices would have eliminated the remaining supply-demand gap observed in the inventory analysis. The shortage of natural gas can be attributed to Federal Power Commission field price regulation, in the sense that continuation of 1955–60 market processes rather than regulatory ceiling prices would have prevented excess demands for reserves.

As it was, a serious reserve shortage developed in the 1960s, invisible on the surface. It revealed itself in the pipelines' reduction of their reserve-to-production ratio, a change that reduced the security of service that many old customers with 20-year contracts desired and that many new customers sought. This "security loss," shared by all those connected to interstate pipelines, was soon translated into a more tangible actual production shortage. In 1971 and 1972, many pipelines had to curtail deliveries because they could not take gas from their reserves fast enough to fulfill their contracts. The reserve base was too thin to support full demand for production during the winter heating season. Thus the shortage became plainly visible, following directly from the reserve shortage which in turn was a creature of FPC regulatory policy.

The Impact of the Shortage

Before attempting to assess the results of gas field price regulation, we should try to determine who felt the shortage. Although the gains and losses are hard to pin down, and any conclusion is highly speculative, those who felt the shortage most were probably the interstate residential buyers —exactly the group regulation was designed to benefit.

Evidence supporting this view shows that, during the 1960s, home consumer reserves were reduced in the course of meeting the demands of unregulated customers. Three observed changes constitute especially strong evidence.

(1) The regulated pipelines—those selling gas interstate for resale—

obtained somewhat less than their proportionate share of new reserves in the late 1960s as compared with earlier years. In 1965 these pipelines held contracts for 68 percent of the nation's 284.5 trillion cubic feet of reserves. Between 1965 and 1971, additional gas totaling 92.9 trillion cubic feet was found, of which the interstate pipelines obtained 62 percent (only 57.9 trillion cubic feet), and their share of all reserves, to be used primarily to supply home consumers, fell to 67 percent.[46]

(2) As distinct from reserves, in the division of total annual gas production between residential and industrial users proportionately more went to industrial users over the decade. Table 3-4 shows that the percentage of gas sold to residential users declined about 2 percent between 1962 and 1968.[47] The decline was caused by a large increase in unregulated industrial sales.

(3) Sales to industrial users by intrastate pipelines and by producers themselves expanded far more rapidly than sales by regulated interstate pipelines. As shown in Table 3-5, between 1962 and 1968 the regulated pipelines increased their direct industrial sales by 24 percent; intrastate pipelines and distributors did so by 62 percent; producers themselves expanded their direct sales to industry by 39 percent.

That the reserve shortage hit the residential buyer—supplied by a regulated pipeline—most seriously is still more evident when certain particular

Table 3-4. Natural Gas Sales to Ultimate Consumers by Pipelines and Distributors, 1962 and 1968

	1962		1968	
Class of service	Quantity (millions Mcf)	Percent of total	Quantity (millions Mcf)	Percent of total
Residential and commercial	4,320	44.5	5,966	42.9
Industrial and other				
Sold by distributors and intrastate pipelines	3,267	33.6	5,284	38.0
Direct sales by interstate pipelines[a]	2,129	21.9	2,641	19.1
Total	5,396	55.5	7,925	57.1
Grand total	9,716	100.0	13,891	100.0

Sources: Industrial sales by interstate pipelines—FPC, *Statistics of Natural Gas Companies, 1962* (1963), Table 7, and FPC, *Statistics of Interstate Natural Gas Pipeline Companies, 1968* (1969), Table 3; other data—American Gas Association, *Gas Facts 1971* (1972), Table 64. Line 3 is derived by subtracting line 2 from line 4. The data from *Gas Facts* are converted from trillions of BTUs on the basis of 1,031 BTUs per cubic foot of natural gas, a figure derived from the general range of 1,000 to 1,100 BTUs per cubic foot.
  a. Classes A and B companies.

Table 3-5. Sources of Natural Gas Sales to Industrial Consumers, 1962 and 1968

Class of seller	1962 (millions Mcf)	1968 (millions Mcf)	Percent increase
All pipelines and distributors	5,396	7,925	46.9
Intrastate pipelines and distributors	3,267	5,284	61.7
Interstate pipelines	2,129	2,641	24.0
Producers	3,809	5,284	38.7
Total[a]	9,205	13,209	43.5

Sources: Lines 1, 2, and 3—Table 3-4; line 5—American Gas Association, *Gas Facts 1971*, Table 77; line 4—line 5 minus line 1.

a. Includes sales by utilities, non-utility producers, and others for field use, carbon black plants, petroleum refineries, Portland cement plants, pipeline fuel use, electric public utility power plants, and other industrial uses.

gas supply regions are examined. The Permian Basin, for example, held about 2.5 percent of total U.S. gas reserves in the early 1960s. In the late 1960s, additional discoveries raised this figure to about 10.5 percent. Six large interstate pipelines, two intrastate pipelines, and many direct industrial buyers bid for the new reserves. From 1966 onward, the intrastate lines and the direct industrial buyers obtained almost all of them. In fact, interstate pipelines, which absorbed 84 percent of production from new reserves in 1966, absorbed only 9 percent in the first half of 1970. (See Table 3-6.) Prices for new gas offered by intrastate buyers rose from 17.0 cents per Mcf in 1966 to 20.3 cents per Mcf in 1970. Toward the end of 1970, the intrastate pipelines bought more than 200 billion cubic feet of reserves at initial delivery prices of 26.5 cents per Mcf.[48] During the same

Table 3-6. Initial-Year Production of Natural Gas under New Interstate and Intrastate Contracts in the Permian Basin, 1966–70

Billions of cubic feet

Year	Production		
	Interstate	Intrastate	Total
1966	149.0	29.0	178.0
1967	60.4	16.8	77.2
1968	20.0	136.1	156.1
1969	29.4	146.4	175.8
1970[a]	10.3	103.1	113.4

Source: *Natural Gas Policy Issues*, Hearings before the Senate Committee on Interior and Insular Affairs, 92 Cong. 2 sess. (1972), Pt. 1, p. 298.

a. First six months of 1970.

period, interstate prices remained between 16 and 17 cents per Mcf—near the regulatory ceiling.[49] The interstate pipelines were simply outbid.

The gains of the consumers who, because of the regulation-induced shortage, received gas production at 6 cents less than market-clearing prices did not offset the losses of those consumers who had to go without. The losses from excess demands for new reserves are not observable, since they took place in the form of reduced backing on continued production; but gas pipelines were willing to pay an "insurance premium" of 6 cents to obtain *more than twice as much* reserve backing. If this willingness to pay indicates the value of guaranteed deliveries to the final consumer, then the losses exceeded the gains.[50] Those persons "deprived" of reserves were, for the most part, residential gas consumers who wished to buy them. On very conservative assumptions, these buyers wanted 14.5 years of reserves—an "insurance" that they bought before regulation in the 1950s. They would have been willing to pay 6 cents per Mcf, or $500 million per year, more for that reserve backup.

The losses from excess demands for production are observable; buyers willing to pay the 6-cent "premium" to obtain production curtailed by regulated prices lost more than was gained by others getting their deliveries at the lower prices, because they lost deliveries as large as the total production.[51] That is, the shortage was larger than the actual deliveries going to retail distributors, as shown in Table 3-3.[52]

These losses are not the end of the matter, of course. The economic costs of litigation and delay from the area price proceedings have been substantial. A further cost resulted from displacement of industry by price ceilings—even if this loss is not directly measurable. Industrial firms for whom energy costs were a large part of total costs moved to the producing states solely to obtain natural gas that in effect was kept off the interstate market through the interstate price ceiling. The extra costs from such a move are appropriately part of the cost of regulation. (There are no statistical estimates suggesting the amount of such costs at the present time, but it should be possible to trace relative industrial development in Texas, Oklahoma, and Louisiana over ten years to assess these costs.)

In total, the roughly measurable costs of producer price regulation seem high. Regulation induced a gas shortage of considerable dimensions, forced lengthy and expensive administrative proceedings on a highly complex, decentralized, and previously unregulated sector of the industry. And its major objective—benefiting the home consumer—was not achieved. The lower prices produced benefits with one hand that were taken away with the other. Excess demand generated from the reduced prices took away the benefits—regulation denied consumers gas reserves for which they would have been willing to pay.

Alternatives

The arguments against continued efforts to control the exact price of natural gas are strong. Regulation is not necessary to check the market power of producers. Moreover, there is no practical way to calculate and capture rents in competitive gas markets: setting the prices for producers individually is not feasible; setting area rates is administratively complex and of necessity produces a gas shortage.

Some consumer groups have argued that the Federal Power Commission should deal with the problems that arise from its regulatory efforts by introducing still more regulation. The FPC might, for example, seek to expand its jurisdiction over intrastate sales to end the "leakage of supply." It might then establish end-use controls, specifically allocating gas to particular individuals or classes of customers.[53] Such an approach, however, would not solve the problems raised here. More intense regulation would reduce even further the incentives to increase reserves or improve gas production technology. It would simply impose the additional burden upon the commission of determining which end uses were "superior" and which "inferior." Such a task is difficult, to say the least. In the 1960s, for example, to burn gas under an industrial boiler or in a power plant was considered an "inferior" use. Today, the "pollution-free" quality of natural gas makes such a judgment less certain. Once prices are abandoned as a measure of value, the number of claimants, citing a variety of economic and social imperatives, becomes impossibly large. There is no reason to believe that the commission—which was unable to determine the marginal cost of gas production—would find a proper solution to this still more complex problem. In all probability, it would simply arrange for a series of compromises among such claimants, as in the case of gas prices. Such compromises would lead to continued excess demand for gas and shortages in which, as likely as not, those who were supposed to benefit from gas regulation would still be left without.

The alternative is de-regulation. Our analysis strongly indicates that less, not more, regulation is required. The commission could obtain, through economic analysis, a rough idea of whether competitive conditions exist in each producing region. Unless the evidence strongly suggests that producers possess monopoly power, the commission should allow new gas prices to approach market-clearing levels. At the same time, by using prices in the competitive areas as benchmarks, the commission could set prices in those few producer regions where monopoly power existed.

A gradual return to market-clearing prices after an investigation and finding of competitive market conditions would be consistent with the commission's legal obligations as determined in the *Phillips* case. Nothing in that decision *requires* the commission to set prices; the decision simply gives the commission jurisdiction to do so. Moreover, if the commission maintains continuous supervision over market conditions, accepting as "just and reasonable" only prices set by workably competitive regional markets, it will carry out the statute's mandate (as interpreted in *Phillips*) that it regulate producers. *Permian Basin, Hope Natural Gas,* and many other cases provide an agency with very broad discretion over the methods used to achieve a statute's regulatory objectives. And, in this instance, there is no other way to carry out the statute's twofold purpose: gas sales "at the lowest possible reasonable rate consistent with the maintenance of adequate service in the public interest." (See *Atlantic Refining* v. *Public Service Commission,* 360 U.S. 378, 388.) In a workably competitive context, the market-set price will satisfy both objectives; any other price will be either too high, unreasonably taxing consumers, or too low, preventing adequate service. The legal attitude that best harmonizes the statute, legal principles of administrative discretion, and the economics of gas production is that reflected in a recent observation by the Fifth Circuit Court of Appeals. "The Commission," reasoned the court, "does not have to employ the area rate method, or for that matter regulate price directly at all, but it has chosen to fulfill its duty in that manner here."[54]

CHAPTER FOUR

Planning the Production of Electricity

BEFORE 1960, FPC regulation of the electric power industry had limited impact. The commission issued licenses to build certain hydroelectric facilities. It carried out orthodox rate-of-return review of wholesale prices for that small portion of the industry where one company produced electricity and another distributed it.[1] It collected information from companies within its jurisdiction but made no effort to plan for the industry as a whole. In fact, even these activities were difficult to carry out, for the commission followed a legal theory that made it virtually impossible to know, at any single point in time, over which companies it had jurisdiction (a point to be discussed later).

In the early 1960s—perhaps stung by the Landis report's criticisms—the commission with a new chairman and rejuvenated staff made a notable effort to plan a more efficient power industry.[2] In 1964 it published an extensive study of the industry, the *National Power Survey*, which reached the conclusion that by closely coordinating plant construction and operations the nation's electric companies could produce power far more cheaply.[3] The survey was followed in 1967 by a further extensive report suggesting ways to increase the reliability of the nation's transmission system.[4] More recently, the commission has encouraged formation of regional electric reliability councils with representatives from the companies and the government and has brought environmental considerations into the scope of its planning.

This chapter assesses these activities and the commission's ability to plan. The ability to plan is critical to the development of the FPC—indeed, the one promising strategy for improved regulation, given the poor results of the agency's price controls, would be to shift the emphasis from price control to planning.[5] The assessment focuses upon the first and most ambitious of the commission's planning activities: its efforts to attack the

89

electric power "coordination" problem. In the course of the chapter, some general conclusions about the relationship of a federal agency to the planning activities of private power companies emerge.

The Trend toward Interconnection

Electricity service is customarily viewed as consisting of (a) production of power by water or steam turbines, (b) transmission over high-voltage lines of the energy produced, and (c) local distribution for short distances over low-voltage lines to final consumers. By the accounting methods of the industry, more than half the costs are charged to production of electricity, one-eighth to transmission, and the rest to distribution. Several hundred firms owned by private investors provide approximately three-quarters of the nation's electricity supply. The remainder is produced by local, state, or federal installations. Nearly all private firms are vertically integrated, providing generating, transmitting, and distributing services as a single entity or through separate firms controlled by the same holding company.[6]

Since the opening of the first commercial steam generating plant in the early 1880s, the electricity industry has grown rapidly. In 1902, approximately 3,600 separate systems produced about 6 billion kilowatt hours of electricity; 70 years later, several hundred firms were producing more than 300 times as much.[7] The technology has grown apace. In 1900, the largest generating unit had a capacity of 1,500 kilowatts. The capacity of the largest unit was 208,000 kilowatts in 1930, 260,000 kilowatts in 1956, and more than a million kilowatts in 1970. Similarly, maximum transmission line capacity rose from 60 kilovolts in 1901 to 287 kilovolts in 1934, 345 kilovolts in 1954, and over 750 kilovolts by 1970.[8]

At first, changing technology provoked similar change in the pattern of regulation. As technology made large-scale operation more efficient, competition between companies within a single city began to disappear, and municipalities sought to regulate prices and service quantity through their prerogatives in issuing franchises. Then, between 1905 and 1920, local franchising gave way to comprehensive control by state regulatory boards.[9]

More recently, regulatory control has ceased to mirror the scale of operation that technology makes possible. To be sure, the federal government now exerts considerable regulatory authority. In 1920, the Federal Power Commission was created to administer the Water Power Act, which gave it licensing authority over hydroelectric facilities.[10] In 1935, the

Securities and Exchange Commission, under the authority of the Public Utility Holding Company Act, began to break up the corporate empires that typically controlled a myriad of utility assets located in widely separated states.[11] In the same act, the FPC was given statutory authority over electricity companies to regulate the price of wholesale sales across state lines (which might otherwise have escaped all regulation).[12] Nonetheless, today as in the 1930s electricity regulation takes place primarily at the state level; state commissions control the prices of retail sales and review all construction plans. Restraints imposed by the commission or other federal agencies are typically viewed as supplementary forms of regulation.

With the growth of scale in capacity, power companies recognized the importance of coordinating generation and transmission by combining them across regions larger than the single retail distribution area.[13] Recent technological change—increasing the size of efficient generating units— has in all probability increased the need for coordination. Operation of a group of generating units and a network of interconnecting transmission lines for service to multiple population centers as if the parts were one system can, in principle, produce cost savings in six categories.

Operating costs can be held to a minimum through a program to select for dispatch the power from those generators capable of producing it most cheaply. The program is formulated by tabulating the power stations in ascending order of marginal operating costs—the "first" station being the one with lowest marginal costs—and then by loading the plants on the system in that order as demand increases. Each plant is "started up" for power production when total demand exceeds full capacity of the operating plants already on line with lower marginal costs.[14]

The PJM system, for example, comprised of a dozen separately owned companies, can dispatch power to Pennsylvania, New Jersey, and Maryland from whichever generator within that area can produce and transmit it to a given point at the lowest incremental cost. When additional load is needed, the PJM central computer locates that generating unit with the lowest incremental cost of generating the incremental load; it will automatically signal the dispatch office belonging to that unit's owner to start that unit, and unless the owner takes steps to block that signal, the dispatch office computer will automatically increase the unit's load. The central dispatch system of American Electric Power Company, a large holding company, goes a step further, for its central computer automatically adjusts the load of each generator within its multistate system directly. New England

and New York consortia have installed similar computer systems. Costs can thus be reduced by coordination alone whenever the parts of different companies have different incremental costs and whenever central dispatching of power from all of them together allows fuller utilization of those with lowest marginal costs.

Costs for meeting peak demands for electricity can be reduced by taking advantage of the fact that demand varies according to the time of day and the season of the year. Two regions in which peak demands occur at different times can save generating capacity by using the peaking capacity in one to supply some part of the peak demand in the other. If in winter demand peaks sharply at about 5:00 P.M., two adjacent systems in different time zones may be able to share the equipment needed to supply their respective peaks. The same principle suggests the possibility of exchanges between areas which have summer peaks because of air conditioning and those where peaks occur in winter because of heating demand. Coordination across companies with different peaks results in what is sometimes referred to as demand-diversity cost savings.

Reserve costs are also reduced by coordination. Reserve generating capacity is kept in case peak demand has been underestimated or in case operating units break down and for use during periods of maintenance. Interconnection can save on the capacity needed to allow maintenance work if firms in a coordination group can stagger their maintenance schedules to allow each to use the same spare generator to substitute for the generator being overhauled. Coordination can also reduce the risk of underforecasting demand. The larger the interconnected system, the more likely that the effect of unusual weather and changes in industrial demand in one place can be absorbed by reserve capacity from another place.

Coordinating the operations of several systems also reduces the need for breakdown reserves. Pooling reserve capacity allows each firm to call upon the reserves of other firms if a generator outage occurs. And the reserves of the others will be available unless several outages occur simultaneously— a contingency that becomes more remote the larger the number of generators in the system.[15] Sharing such capacity can reduce investment in reserve capacity by an amount sufficient to compensate for the increased costs of interconnecting transmission lines.

Generating costs can be reduced by coordination if it allows firms to take advantage of economies of scale in generator size. Since capacity depends on boiler and turbine volume while costs very roughly depend on metal surface areas, costs per unit of capacity decline with total outlay. The larger the generator, the more cheaply it can produce electricity at the margin.[16] In fact, in estimating the elasticity of costs with respect to capacity, the consensus seems to be that costs increase by only 8 or 9 percent when capacity increases 10 percent.[17] Thus the most efficient way to make electricity usually is to install the largest generator that technology permits —a size that increased from roughly 400 megawatts (400,000 kilowatts) in the early 1960s to approximately 1,000 megawatts in the early 1970s. A large generating unit, however, requires a large backup unit in case it breaks down, and recently larger units have tended to break down more frequently.[18] Whereas a smaller firm may not face sufficient demand for its electricity to justify replacing a small generator with a large one, several small firms combined into a single system may be able to do so.

Transmission reliability costs can also be reduced through coordinated planning across a wide geographical area. When a generator breaks down, reserve generators must make up the deficit; but, during the first few seconds after a major breakdown (before the reserve generators can start up), more is needed. Power will rush into the deficit area, and the interconnecting transmission lines must be sufficiently strong to withstand the surge. Similarly, when a major line breaks down, power recoils and spreads itself out through the remaining interconnected lines of the system; those remaining lines must not break down, or they will aggravate the problem. Thus, once firms are interconnected at all, the generating or transmission plans of one will affect the need for lines elsewhere. Company X's installation of a large generator in State A may require the strengthening of Company Y's lines in State B, an area well outside Company X's service area. Unless Companies X and Y and others affected coordinate their plans, there is a risk of power failure, on the one hand, or waste, on the other.

Social costs, such as the adverse environmental effects from power generation, can also be reduced through coordination. Nearly every method of making electricity affects the environment in some way. Fossil-fuel plants pollute the air; nuclear plants heat nearby rivers and lakes; hydroelectric plants and their accompanying transmission lines disturb the biotic equilibrium and scenic attraction of wild areas. Coordinated planning over a wide geographic area can reduce total construction and help to locate the area's plants so as to produce the desired level of power at a lower cost to the environment.

At this point, one might wonder whether a single, nation-wide electricity system is called for. After all, most of the factors mentioned above seem to suggest that the bigger the system the better. But such is not the case. For one thing, as a system gets bigger, the marginal or additional benefits from further increases in scale become smaller beyond a certain point. Combining two 20,000-megawatt systems may save little, if any, reserve capacity. At the same time, as previously unconnected systems are combined to extend over a progressively larger geographic area, the outlay on transmission to connect them becomes progressively greater. Management costs may also grow when the complexity of a vast, single system makes administration increasingly unwieldy. The largest central dispatch system thus far developed has a capacity of 30,000 megawatts spread over a 50,000 square mile area.[19]

Degrees of coordination vary. Interconnected firms might lower costs to some extent by: buying and selling power to each other at intervals; making power available to each other in times of emergency; reviewing each other's future plans and adjusting their own accordingly; planning future capacity jointly.

The FPC has actively encouraged coordination since the 1964 survey. The remainder of this chapter examines the effectiveness of the agency in carrying out this policy. By examining the unrealized potential gains from coordination in 1964, when the policy was first adopted, and in the early 1970s, an estimate can be made of the speed with which the electricity industry, prompted by the FPC, is rationalizing power production and distribution.

The Potential Gains from Coordination

The FPC in its *National Power Survey* of 1964 made an extensive effort to estimate the need for increased coordination and, by doing so, to widen the scope of power planning. The survey report was written by commission staff members on the basis of studies undertaken jointly with 120 representatives of the industry. The industry trade association described these men and women as representing "the best talent available in the industry." They contributed 20,000 man hours of work and "received many thousands of man hours of help from the technicians in their respective organizations."[20] While disagreeing with many of the survey's conclusions, most industry leaders praised its method of analysis and accepted its general conclusion that greater coordination was necessary.

In particular, the 1964 survey divided, and progressively subdivided, the nation into 2 zones, 4 sectors, 8 statistical regions, 16 study areas, and

48 power supply areas. It surmised that, as of 1964, coordination was reaching effectiveness within the 16 study areas, although interconnection and organization up to that level were not complete. The authors of the survey then estimated the savings that would result if by 1980 coordination among the nation's electric power producers reached the 4-sector level.

By taking advantage of demand diversity, the survey claimed, 4-sector coordination could reduce by 12,000 megawatts the total peak demands which a less coordinated group of producers would need to be prepared for; 2-zone coordination could reduce the collective peak needs by 21,000 megawatts; and nation-wide coordination could reduce them by 28,000 megawatts. Assuming that one megawatt less of "demand contingency" implied one megawatt less of capacity, and assuming construction costs of $130,000 per megawatt, potential demand-diversity savings were estimated as $1.5 billion to $4.0 billion for generating capacity. In terms of annual expenditures (applying an annual fixed charge of 12 percent), these savings would range from $180 million to $480 million per year.[21]

By pooling safety margin reserves, the survey estimated that 4-sector coordination would reduce the need for capacity by 36,000 megawatts, 2-zone by 46,000 megawatts, and a nation-wide single system by 50,000 megawatts by 1980. With costs calculated as before, construction savings would run between $4.7 billion and $6.5 billion, with annual savings between $564 million and $780 million.

Finally, the survey estimated the saving that would flow from increased ability to install generating units of efficient size. Here the survey assumed that if firms were coordinated at the 16-area level, the grid would be large enough to absorb the largest generating units and would make feasible the gradual replacement of smaller units with larger ones. This regimen would save $3.5 billion in construction costs by 1980, or $420 million annually. In sum, the survey found that through greater coordination savings of $1,164 million to $1,680 million annually could be achieved by 1980.

The survey's conclusions are open to a certain amount of criticism. For one, the industry claimed that the demand diversity found in recent years was unstable and over time would tend to disappear. As air conditioning became more popular, progressively more of the country would experience summer peak demands, limiting the possibility of seasonal interchange. Moreover, since summer peaks tend to last for several hours, the possibility of interchange between time zones is also limited. The remaining amount of diversity would occur too erratically to become the basis for planning capacity interchange. Figures published in 1971 suggest that the industry view was correct, for the most part, since seasonal peaking has been less significant than the survey suggested, and consequently regional coordination would have been a less significant source of demand-diversity savings.[22]

In estimating the benefits of moving from coordination at the 16-area or 8-region level to full coordination at the nation-wide level, the survey did not subtract the full social costs of the required additional interconnection. These costs would be extensive, since major east/west and north/south high-voltage tie lines would have to be built. Finally, the survey was wrong—in the opposite direction—in assuming that 16-area coordination was far advanced in 1964.[23] Thus the survey probably underestimated the need to encourage coordination at the 16-area level and overestimated the benefits attainable from coordination beyond that point.

On the other hand, the survey's general conclusions receive considerable support from the cautious, detailed study by William R. Hughes.[24] Hughes measured the difference between the actual cost of producing power and the presumed cost that would arise with an "optimal" level of coordination as of the early 1960s (which he assumed to be the 4-sector level). He estimated savings from taking advantage of demand diversity at between 0.7 percent and 1.4 percent of total bulk power costs, and he estimated savings through reserve sharing at 2 to 4 percent of bulk power costs. He also measured the extent to which firms installed units of less than optimal size during the 1950s and early 1960s, from which he concluded that this tendency raised bulk power costs in 1963–64 by 3.1 percent. If, for purposes of comparison, bulk power costs for 1980 were to be the $30 billion projected in the survey, the annual cost savings (from not having to build) would come to between $210 million and $420 million for demand-diversity savings, to between $600 million and $1.2 billion for reserve savings, and to $930 million for gains from using larger generators —a total annual saving of between $1.74 billion and $2.55 billion.

Neither the survey authors nor Hughes purport to measure the costs of "under-coordination" with great accuracy. Nonetheless, together they can be taken as showing that, as of 1964, a movement toward optimal coordination could reduce the nation's electricity costs from $1 billion to $2 billion per year by 1980.

By 1972, a point midway between the FPC survey and the survey's target date for optimal coordination, how much coordination was achieved? Power companies in New England and those in New York have organized central dispatching for their respective areas. Many thousands of miles of high voltage transmission lines have been built.[25] And, since the Northeast power failure in 1965, the industry has organized itself into nine regional reliability councils which in turn are responsible to a national body representing both industry and government—the National Electric Reliability Council (NERC). The industry also reports the existence of twenty-two regional pools. But organizational titles such as "regional council" and "pool" can mislead, for they do not reveal the degree of joint planning and operation that underlies them.

It is not possible to determine conclusively the extent to which the industry is failing to achieve coordination benefits at the rate the survey's authors thought feasible. This would require a far more comprehensive study than can be done with publicly available information on company operations. The evidence that has been collected thus far from FPC documents and from the industry suggests that there should be considerably more coordination *at this time* than now exists.

Pooling

The words "pooling" and "coordinating" can be used to cover a variety of interrelationships among companies. But the crux of the relationship, from the point of view of the consumer, lies in taking three steps, the sum total of which can be defined as "pooling."

First, generating systems have to be connected by transmission wires. This is now the case in three separate physical areas—the East, Texas, and the remainder of the country. Within each of these areas most plants are physically interconnected. The three areas are connected with each other to a lesser extent.

Second, transmission reliability must be sought. Even with loose coordination, engineering studies of system reliability are desirable. Firms or member systems can compare their future production plans with each other and modify them to take transmission reliability into account.

Third, central control of electricity dispatching across companies is probably necessary to secure most savings in operating costs, reserve capacity, and generator economies of scale. This assertion is controversial, for surely, in principle, any two systems that are physically interconnected can share their reserves. But in practice if companies are not joined by an agreement to dispatch their electricity centrally—an agreement that commits each company to generate electricity in a way that minimizes total system costs—each company is uncertain whether the reserves of another are in fact available when needed. Hence a company, when planning additions to its own capacity and determining its own generating needs, will tend to discount reserves that are theoretically available for its use (for they are physically interconnected) but that are in the hands of another company.[26] Moreover, central dispatch represents a *commitment* to lower the total production costs of the separate power companies. Such a commitment, though it does not guarantee that the member companies will plan future capacity most efficiently, is more likely to lead them to plan future additions without overlap so as to approximate minimum regional costs. Conversely, a group of companies that planned their systems as a single unit would be drawn almost inevitably to dispatch centrally in order to realize additional savings in operating costs; hence the fact that they do not dispatch centrally suggests that they do not plan optimally.

Of course, a centrally dispatched pool may still fail to receive all the benefits of joint planning; a still greater degree of coordination may be necessary before firms will need to build no more capacity than a perfectly coordinated system would require. Conversely, a strong pool that interchanges power on an hourly or minute-by-minute basis and employs a central staff to originate (not merely to coordinate) construction plans may enjoy many of the benefits of reserve savings. The key question is the extent to which its members plan together—a question that in part turns upon the extent to which each member treats the reserves of other members as if they were its own.

Thus a degree of coordination equivalent to central dispatch is probably necessary to obtain full reserve savings. This degree of coordination is probably necessary to achieve economies of scale in the purchase of generators as well. Central dispatch is obviously necessary to achieve the savings arising from joint operating costs, but these savings are not as large as potential savings from sharing reserves. (The companies in the PJM system estimate that coordination reduces annual operating expenses by an amount equal to about 1.5 percent of total annual costs.)[27]

With these considerations in mind, a look at the degree of pooling that now exists suggests that the amount of electricity subject to pooling in 1970 was not substantially greater than in 1963. Table 4-1—which shows the roster of centrally dispatched pools and of looser arrangements—provides some indication of the limited extent to which integration has grown. From 1963 to 1970 for the nation as a whole, pools grew in size but not substantially in relation to total production in the regions of which they were part. As mentioned above, New England combined a number of independent companies into a single, centrally dispatched pool, and New York achieved the same level of coordination. But, in general, growth in coordination took the form of loose cooperation, not the formation of strong pools with central staffs that dispatched power and planned capacity additions.

A similar pattern emerges from an examination of pooling in each of the 16 study areas (see Table 4-2). Full pooling of total capacity existed in only 5 of the areas: New England, New York, PJM, TVA, and Michigan. In 10 other areas one or a pair of coordination groups to some extent planned jointly but did not centrally dispatch, and 2 of these same areas contained companies that had not joined a coordination group. (Only a single company operated exclusively in the Montana-Dakota area.) Most planning within the coordination groups consisted of reviewing plans initiated by one of the members rather than centrally designing plants to lower system costs. Coordination groups were not able to set strong area-wide standards for production and the acquisition of capacity. Overall, central dispatching units smaller than 10,000 megawatts controlled 61 percent of national capacity, and units smaller than 6,000 megawatts controlled 45 percent.[28]

Generating Equipment

Despite the very moderate growth of pooling, companies have become more likely than they were in 1964 to install large generating units. Planning future capacity is more coordinated now than then. Pools are larger, joint ownership of generating capacity is more common, and a bit more planning takes place on a regional basis.[29] Nonetheless, there is evidence that, in some parts of the country, companies are not taking advantage of possible economies of scale in generators.

Firms have submitted reports to the National Electric Reliability Council about the new generating capacity that they planned to install between 1971 and 1980. On the assumption that thermal power is most cheaply generated in units that range from 800 to 1,300 megawatts in size, it would appear that approximately 51 percent of the new thermal generating capacity that companies plan to install will consist of units smaller than efficient scale (less than 800 megawatts in size). Significantly, these figures take into account only large units that are to be used for base load; they do not consider the generally smaller units ordinarily used only to supply part of peak demand.[30]

Table 4-1. Electric Power Pooling by Region and System, 1963 and 1970

Region	1963 systems	Power dispatching status[a]	1963 capacity (percent of region)	1970 systems	Power dispatching status[a]	1970 capacity (percent of region)
Northeast (I)	Boston Edison Group	P	8.6	New England Power Pool (tentative)	(P)	16.5
	Upstate New York Interconnected	P	17.2			
	Southeastern New York Power Pool	P	19.9	{New York Power Pool][b]	(P)	34.0
	PJM Interconnection	P	41.4	PJM Interconnection	(P)	38.7
	Total		87.1	Total		89.2
East Central (II)	American Electric Power System	P[c]	20.1	American Electric Power System	(P)[c]	20.5
	Michigan Pool	P	20.1	Michigan Pool	(P)	20.6
				Cincinnati-Columbus-Dayton Pool	(P)	9.4
				Central Area Power Coordination Group	(C)	20.0
	Total		40.2	Total		70.5
Southeast (III)	Tennessee Valley Authority	P[c]	41.3	Tennessee Valley Authority	(P)[c]	27.3
	Carolinas-Virginia Group	C	24.2	Carolinas-Virginia Power Pool	(C)	30.8
	Southern Company	P[c]	17.2	Southern Company	(P)[c]	21.1
	Florida Group	C	12.9	Florida Group	(C)	19.0
	Total		95.6	Total		98.2
North Central (IV)	Illinois-Missouri Pool	P	23.0	Illinois-Missouri Pool	(P)	23.3
	Commonwealth Edison & Central Illinois	P[c]	29.9	Commonwealth Edison & Central Illinois	(P)[c]	33.5

Region	Entity			Entity		
	Interconnected utilities of					
	Eastern Wisconsin	P	15.0	Eastern Wisconsin	(P)	15.5
	Upper Mississippi Valley Pool	C	15.4	Upper Mississippi Valley Power Pool	(C)	17.4
	Total		83.4	Total		89.7
South Central (V)	Middle South Systems	C	14.8	Middle South Utilities	(C)	15.2
	Gulf States Utilities	P[a]	8.5			
	North Texas Interconnected	C	15.4	{Texas Interconnected}[b]	(C)	44.3
	South Texas Interconnected	C	20.3			
	Total		59.0	Total		59.5
West Central (VI)	Eastern Missouri Basin Power System	C	28.5	Eastern Missouri Basin Power System	(C)	23.7
	Rocky Mountain Pool	C	45.7	Rocky Mountain Power Pool	(C)	46.7
	Total		74.2	Total		70.4
Northwest (VII)	Pacific Northwest Pool	C	100.0	PacificNorthwest Pool	(C)	100.0
Southwest (VIII)	California Power Pool	C	66.0	{California Power Pool}[b]	(C)	79.8
	Southern California Pool	C	14.7			
	Total		80.7			

Sources: Pool membership—FPC, *National Power Survey* (1964), Pt. 1, and FPC, *The 1970 National Power Survey* (1971), Pt. 1, Chap. 17; capacity—FPC, *Electric Power Statistics*, 1964 and 1970 issues.

a. *P* designates a pool with central dispatching of power across several companies; *C* designates a looser system without central dispatching.

b. Braces designate a larger pool formed from systems that were separate in 1963.

c. All member companies under the same financial control.

Table 4-2. Power Capacity, 1970, and Planned Additions to Capacity, 1971–80, by Study Area

| | | | | Planned additions to capacity, 1971–80 | |
| | | | | | |
Study area	Power system	Status[a]	1970 capacity (thousands of megawatts)	Average size of plant (megawatts)	Reserve margin (percent of capacity in excess of peak load)
A	New England Power Pool	pool	13.6	631	21.8
B	New York Pool	pool	21.8	760	34.5
C	PJM	pool	29.7	729	24.9
D	American Electric Power	separate	11.0	1,075	29.0
	Allegheny Power	separate	4.2	634	27.9
	Ohio Edison	coordination group	10.0 { 3.5	830	18.5
	Cleveland Electric		3.2		
	Duquesne Light		2.2		
	Toledo Edison		1.1 }		
	Cincinnati-Columbus-Dayton	pool	4.8	704	15.8
	Kentucky Utilities	coordination group	5.5[b] { 1.3	545	19.0
	Indianapolis Power & Light		1.5		
	Public Service of Indiana		2.6 }		
	Ohio Valley Electric	separate	2.4	—[c]	—
	Louisville Gas & Electric	separate	1.6	394	32.8
	Northern Indiana Public Service	separate	1.4	532	28.1
	Southern Indiana Gas & Electric	separate	0.4	505	—
E	Virginia Electric & Power	coordination group	18.8 { 4.9	758	21.8
	Carolina Power & Light		3.9		
	Duke Power		6.7		
	South Carolina Electric & Gas		1.9		
	3 companies (800 MW each)		1.4 }		
F	Tennessee Valley Authority	government regional system	19.8	1,029	21.8
G	Southern Co.	coordination group	13.4 { 11.8	515	20.2
	5 companies (<1,000 MW each)		1.6 }		
	Florida Power & Light	coordination group	13.2 { 5.6	548	26.0
	Florida Power Corp.		2.3		
	Tampa Electric		2.0		
	4 companies (<1,000 MW each)		3.3 }		
H	Michigan Pool	pool	9.9	755	15.7
I	Wisconsin Electric Power	coordination group	5.0 { 2.6	435	19.0
	4 companies (<1,000 MW each)		2.4 }		

Table 4-2 (*continued*)

Study area	Power system	Status[a]	1970 capacity (thousands of mega-watts)	Planned additions to capacity, 1971–80 Average size of plant (mega-watts)	Reserve margin (percent of capa-city in ex-cess of peak load)
I	Union Electric	coordination group	8.1 ⎰ 4.7 ⎱	544	18.0
	Illinois Power		{ 2.3 }		
	Central Illinois Public Service		⎱ 1.1 ⎰		
	Commonwealth Edison	separate	12.2	741	12.7
	9 companies (<1,000 MW each)	separate	3.0	516	—
	6 companies (<700 MW each)	coordination group	2.6	426	—
	Northern States Power	coordination group	6.4 ⎰ 3.4 ⎱	511	—
	10 companies (<800 MW each)		{ 3.0 }		
	U.S. Dept. of Interior	government regional system	2.8	438	—
	4 companies (<900 MW each)	separate	1.5	616	—
J	Texas Utilities	coordination group	20.8 ⎰ 8.2 ⎱	575	—
	Central Southwest Corp.[d]		{ 2.4 }		
	Houston Light & Power		{ 6.3 }		
	City Public Service		{ 1.7 }		
	5 companies (<800 MW each)		⎱ 2.2 ⎰		
K	Middle South Services	coordination group	27.2 ⎰ 6.7 ⎱	617	—
	Central Southwest Corp.		{ 2.8 }		
	Gulf States Utilities		{ 3.9 }		
	Oklahoma Gas & Electric		{ 2.0 }		
	Southwestern Power		{ 1.5 }		
	Kansas City Power & Light		{ 1.6 }		
	Kansas Gas & Electric		{ 1.2 }		
	Southwest Public Service		{ 1.7 }		
	26 companies (<1,000 MW each)		⎱ 5.8 ⎰		
L	Montana-Dakota Utilities[e]	separate	0.3	—	—
M	5 companies (<600 MW each)	coordination group	0.9	303	—
N	Southern California Edison	coordination group	36.9 ⎰ 9.4 ⎱	594	26.2[f]
	Los Angeles Dept. of Water & Power		{ 4.5 }		
	Pacific Gas & Electric		{ 12.8 }		
	San Diego Gas & Electric		{ 1.4 }		
	California Dept. of Water Resources		{ 1.2 }		
	Arizona Public Service		{ 5.0 }		
	9 companies (<700 MW each)		⎱ 2.6 ⎰		

Table 4-2 (*continued*)

| | | | | Planned additions to capacity, 1971–80 | |
| | | | 1970 capacity (thousands of megawatts) | Average size of plant (megawatts) | Reserve margin (percent of capacity in excess of peak load) |
Study area	Power system	Status[a]			
O	Public Service Co. of Colorado ⎫		⎧ 2.4 ⎫		
	U.S. Bureau of Reclamation ⎬ coordination	5.0	⎨ 1.4 ⎬	345	30.5[f]
	5 companies (<500 MW each) ⎭ group		⎩ 1.2 ⎭		
P	Bonneville Power		⎧ 4.7 ⎫		
	Chelan County Public Utilities		1.1		
	Grant County Public Utilities		1.9		
	Pacific Power & Light		1.1		
	Seattle City Light ⎬ coordination	28.7	⎨ 1.5 ⎬	486	23.5[f]
	U.S. Corps of Engineers ⎭ group		8.2		
	Idaho Power		1.3		
	Utah Power & Light		1.0		
	British Columbia Hydro & Power		3.4		
	12 companies (<1,000 MW each)		⎩ 4.5 ⎭		

Source: Information submitted by regional councils to the National Electric Reliability Council for the years 1970 and 1971, as collected by the authors in February and March of 1972.

a. For purposes of this table, "pool" is defined as a system whose members plan jointly and dispatch power centrally; a "coordination group" plans jointly but does not dispatch centrally; and a system labeled "separate" neither plans nor dispatches with other power producers.

b. Figures rounded.

c. Dashes indicate data not available.

d. Central Southwest Corp. also controls two companies that are members of the Southwest Power Pool.

e. Other companies serving Study Area L are listed under Area I.

f. For the year 1975.

Of course, even a perfectly coordinated national system might install some base load units smaller than 800 megawatts to supply areas where coordinated demand would not be large enough to justify that much generating capacity. Yet, the 1964 survey estimated that a nationally coordinated power system would install only about 12 percent of its new thermal equipment in the form of units smaller than 800 megawatts. Even if the survey's authors seriously underestimated the need for smaller units, 51 percent of total capacity in small generators seems a very high percentage.

A comparison of smaller, unaffiliated companies, members of "coordination groups," pools with centralized planning and dispatching, and fully integrated holding companies suggests that the greater the degree of integration, the more likely that larger generators will be installed. Table 4-2 gives grounds for concluding that increased coordination increases the probability that a firm plans to install large baseload units. If, for example, 10,000 megawatts (or larger) units that centrally dispatch are compared with 10,000 megawatts (or larger) units that are more loosely coordinated, it is found that all but two of the former plan to install generators that on average are larger than 700 megawatts and that all but two of the latter plan to install generators that on average are smaller than 700 megawatts.[31] Of course, plans to install smaller units might simply reflect pessimism about the future performance of large units; their propensity to break down has been a matter of some speculation. But it seems improbable that pessimism should prevail more strongly among loosely pooled companies than among those using central dispatch or among holding companies. It is more likely that centralized planning for larger areas has led companies to install larger units. This conclusion is supported by independent efforts to measure the effect of increased coordination upon the size of generating units that firms plan to install.[32]

A rough numerical estimate of the importance of this tendency can be made by assuming that the larger coordination groups, by ordering larger generating units, could reduce their capacity costs by about 10 percent (assuming a 50 percent increase in size and a cost elasticity of 0.8).[33] Since these groups will account for about one-half the increase in electricity capacity, the saving, nationally, amounts to about 5 percent of the cost of new production facilities. The 1964 survey's estimate of this saving was about 2 percentage points higher—a reasonable discrepancy considering that the survey applied its calculation to replacement of old generators as well as to expansion to meet new demand. Essentially, the firms' plans to expand during the 1970s seem to replicate the survey's pattern for the uncoordinated nation.

Reserve Capacity

The most important saving that coordination can yield is the saving in the reserve needed to meet a given standard of reliability. The 1964 survey stated that if firms were coordinated at the 4-sector level, they would collectively require reserve generating capacity equal to 16.8 percent of peak 1980 demand. This would allow adequate maintenance overhauls, would provide some capacity in the case of an underestimate of demand, and would let the system meet the reliability standard of no more than a day of load lost every ten to fifteen years. Without coordination, significantly more reserve would be needed to do the same job.

This estimate is misleading. A system's reserve requirements depend upon a number of factors, including the size of generating units and their mix within a system, the number of units, and the duration of demand peaks (which can influence the time available for maintenance). Forced outage rates (affected by type of equipment, fuel used, and weather), errors in predicting future demand, and the configuration of transmission lines also play a part. Although these factors vary from region to region and system to system, the survey used drastically simplified assumptions and applied them uniformly to all regions of the country. More important, the survey's authors overestimated the reliability of new, large generating units and thereby underestimated the reserve level needed to meet the reliability goal, even with perfect coordination.[34]

Nonetheless, recent engineering studies that use more complex assumptions bear out the survey's basic conclusion: closer coordination than currently exists can yield significant savings in reserve capacity. Mabuce, Wilks, and Boxerman (1971), after taking into account unit size, the mix of sizes within a system, varying forced outage rates, and possible forecast error, concluded that, as a system grows larger, the percentage of reserve capacity needed to meet a given reliability standard is reduced significantly until the system reaches 40,000 to 50,000 megawatts in size. They calculated, for example, that doubling the size of a 15,000-megawatt system reduces the reserves needed to meet a standard of a day's outage in ten years from 31 to 21 percent, and pooling the facilities of three 10,000-megawatt companies would reduce the reserves needed from 35 to 21 percent.[35] Casazza and Hoffman (1969) estimated that doubling the size of a 15,000-megawatt system reduced reserve requirements from 26 to 21 percent of capacity.[36] Assuming that the costs of adding transmission lines needed to connect separate units were substantial, they suggested an optimal system size of 15,000 to 30,000 megawatts for the early 1970s.[37] This estimate probably erred on the low side by overstating the transmission penalty on the supposition that links would be built only to coordinate reserve use, whereas in fact many of the necessary transmission links between units have been built to improve the reliability of emergency interconnection.[38]

Together, the engineering studies and capacity forecasts of Table 4-2 provide the basis for a rough estimate of the extent to which full coordination at, for example, a system size of 20,000 to 40,000 megawatts, would reduce reserve costs. Such systems would lie closer to 16-area than to 4-sector coordination. If we assume that companies are now fully coordinated at a level of 10,000 megawatts (a considerable overstatement), increasing the size of fully coordinated units to between 30,000 and 40,000 megawatts should save reserves equal to 9 percent or more of capacity.[39] Since firms accounting for roughly two-thirds of the capacity added over the 1970s would be involved, the reserve reduction might approximate 6 percent of national capacity.[40] If all companies were to coordinate to the 4-sector level, then the pools would be at least 150,000 megawatts and probably would exceed 175,000 megawatts. Achieving this extent of coordination would almost certainly move the whole question of reserve requirements outside the framework employed in current engineering studies. Very likely the additional gains in going from 16-area to 4-sector coordination would be limited.

The Coordination Problem

Where do our calculations and the engineering studies cited and the original survey of 1964 come out? Is there a "problem," a serious lack of coordination, or not?

The survey's compilers may have overstated the benefits of coordination. Moreover, numerous transmission lines have been built since 1964, and many loosely coordinated organizations have been created—the possible nuclei of future, stronger central planning. Still, the commission erred in its 1964 estimate of the strength of existing coordination. At the same time, the price paid for failure to operate groups of companies as unified systems has shot up sharply. Construction costs increased from about $130,000 per megawatt in 1964 to about $300,000 per megawatt in 1972. Given an expected peak demand of 600,000 megawatts in 1980, every percentage point of capacity saved means a $216 million cut in the annual electricity bill. Thus saving 4 to 6 percent of capacity would save between $850 million to $1.3 billion per year.[41] Savings from the use of cheaper generators would also be substantial. Companies plan to install about 380,000 megawatts of new and replacement capacity before 1980; every percentage point saved from taking advantage of scale reduces the annual bill by $136 million. We calculate the potential savings from building units larger than the present ones at about 5 percent of newly installed capacity, or about $680 million per year. Assuming some additional savings from lower operating costs and increased ability to take advantage of demand diversity, a figure for total annual savings of $2 billion (or 3.5 percent of total 1980 operating costs) seems reasonable and conservative.[42] Further, this figure does not take the cost of environmental injury into account. The value of preserving natural environment that unneeded capacity would otherwise damage is obviously a matter of subjective opinion; but, equally obviously, the value is large, and it must be added to the savings in construction costs.

From all of these calculations, we conclude that coordination is seriously inadequate. In fact, the problem was still as troublesome in 1972 as it seemed to the Federal Power Commission in 1964.

On the face of it, the presence of inadequate coordination is puzzling. Since firms ordinarily try to reduce their costs in order to increase their profits and since the economies of scale and risk reduction in coordination imply opportunities to reduce costs, why haven't the firms coordinated to the 16-area or even the 4-sector level? There seems to be no straightforward answer. From interviews with executives both in unpooled companies and in companies which belong to pools come indications that bargaining over how to divide the potential gains from coordination among partially competitive, partially regulated companies has not worked well. Several obstacles that grew out of the regulatory process and affected the financing of new projects within the industry militated against combining small units into larger ones. These obstacles made it more profitable for individual regulated firms to forgo cost efficiency than to move together toward optimal coordination.

This is not to assert, in keeping with Averch and Johnson, that regulation by limiting profits (but allowing firms to earn more than the cost of capital) encouraged inefficient expansion of capital expenditures for rate base. Though such an analysis might explain why some firms preferred a less efficient but more capital-intensive production process, it does not readily apply to electricity production. For one thing, additions to the rate base favored by regulators, such as underground power lines and better safety facilities, have been opposed by electricity companies because of their expense. For another thing, the postulates of Averch and Johnson would suggest that in the early 1960s—when controls on rate of return were not very effective—the companies did not need to maintain excess rate base to maximize their earnings and therefore at that time should have favored coordination.[43] But according to the same postulates, in the later 1960s—when rising costs and comparatively sticky regulatory price control squeezed their profits—they should have opposed it.[44] In fact, contrary to the Averch-Johnson theory, the firms' efforts to coordinate were at least as great, if not greater, in the late 1960s as in the early 1960s.[45]

Our more conservative interpretation is that competition and regulation combined to dampen the firms' desires to achieve coordination economies. There may be something to the well-known claim that regulation lessens a firm's incentive to become efficient.[46] But, more important, electricity companies in an area compete at the margin for the right to serve industrial and commercial consumers; they also benefit to different extents from pooling, with the smaller companies benefiting the most. Pooling, with cost reductions passed on by setting wholesale prices for bulk power at marginal costs to all retail members of the pool, would have benefited the smaller or least coordinated companies more, since they were the farthest from achieving the full economies of scale by themselves. Larger producers that had already achieved substantial economies of coordination often found it better to forgo some remaining economies than to pool with small firms, for otherwise the large firms risked the loss of markets through increased competition, which can more than offset the cost reductions the large firm might realize from pooling.[47]

The impasse over sharing the gains occurred at the same time that management problems in pooling became more evident. Members of committees that operate centrally dispatched pools have complained of the difficulty of making decisions when there is no superior authority with the power to resolve disagreements or to set aside dubious compromises.[48] The PJM Pool, in response to these criticisms, simplified its committee structure, reducing the representation of some of the smaller firms; it also abandoned efforts to design and to operate through committee new jointly owned generating plants. Whether simplification will end administrative problems is not yet known. Of course, as committee structure is simplified, the difference between a pool of separate companies and a single holding company tends to disappear.

Management of a pool involves important economic matters. Pools have great difficulty in apportioning certain costs, such as those of strengthening the transmission system. Such strengthening helps all members, but in varying and indeterminate amounts. Even when companies themselves agree on apportionment, state regulatory authorities are at times reluctant to allow companies to contribute to the cost of building a transmission wire in another state unless it is perfectly clear that customers in its own state will benefit.

Pools also find it more difficult than single companies to plan and operate as a single, "most efficient" system. A pool's method for apportioning operating costs is unlikely to maximize incentive for its members to operate the whole system most efficiently.[49] Methods for determining how much reserve capacity each member is to provide suffer similar defects.[50] Moreover, if it proves most economical to build the majority of new plants in the service areas of only a few members, what happens to the rate base of the remaining companies? Efforts to overcome such problems by creating joint ventures raise problems of their own.[51] SEC or AEC approval may be necessary for joint ownership; and small companies may use these regulatory proceedings to try to force their way into a pool or joint venture over the objections of the original proponents.

A further set of impediments to strong pooling has arisen out of recent concern with the natural environment. Most firms hold state charters or franchises making them responsible for providing an adequate supply of electricity for a particular area. These firms, in daily contact with the area's residents, strongly feel that obligation, and they also realize that future building sites are becoming scarce. A rural firm may realize that if it joins a group that plans to use all sites on a statewide or regional basis, its building sites will be taken now to supply a densely populated urban area; it may be left without sites when it needs them to serve its own area. A single firm with responsibility for serving both areas, or even a strong pool with a state franchise giving it such responsibility, would use the site to supply the city on the grounds that the city's needs are greater. As long as a firm is charged with the primary duty of serving the rural area, however, it will resist efforts to use the site capacity to serve another area. Further, it may resist joining a pool if it foresees that such efforts will follow. There is no way under present law for the urban firm to compensate the rural firm or its customers for the loss of its building sites; in fact electricity producers often cannot easily acquire sites outside their own service areas.

More important, if firms coordinated their plans on a statewide or regional basis, then some power plants conceivably would be constructed in areas that did not need power but were relatively inexpensive sites for large power plants. The residents of areas subject to this risk may simply not want to have plants built to supply consumers in distant areas. Why should they suffer the marring of the land, they may ask, so that others can acquire power painlessly? If for a firm coordinated planning means building others' plants in its service region, it may be under considerable local pressure not to join the centrally dispatched pool or holding company that designs the plan. The problem has been to find pricing and costing rules to compensate the residents of areas designated as sites for power plants for their loss of environmental quality. The development of such rules has not been very successful up to the present time; recent decisions of the New York Public Service Commission requiring firms to develop recreational facilities along the routes of their new transmission lines seem to point in the right direction, but they are scarcely sufficient.[52] Without some such "compensation" system, the opposition to amalgamation from smaller companies in rural areas is likely to continue.[53]

The question might legitimately be asked as to why, in the absence of agreement on coordination, separate companies did not arrange a merger. The answer is that the same problems of dividing the gains occur in a merger as in coordination; only they appear at the time of exchange of shares. If anything, the prospect of merger brings out greater personal hostility in managers because of their fears of losing power and authority.[54] In addition, company officials perhaps believed that the regulatory attitude was hostile to merger. Any such belief may seem odd in light of the fact that no state commissions, nor the FPC, nor the Securities and Exchange Commission (SEC) have turned down any important merger attempt since World War II. And FPC officials have sometimes urged companies to merge, as Chairman Joseph C. Swidler did in a speech to representatives of New England utilities in 1962. Nonetheless, in 1968 the Department of Justice intervened before the SEC to oppose American Electric Power's proposed acquisition of an Ohio company, and more recently it opposed a merger involving Boston Edison. It has now gone so far as to announce that it favors pooling via joint ventures and opposes mergers as a means to achieve coordination.[55] Thus companies may fear possible antitrust suits, for commission approval probably does not automatically confer immunity, and most electricity mergers would violate the letter of the Justice Department's strict guidelines.[56] In any event, the department's intervention before the commission, with its promise of protracting proceedings for months or years, is probably sufficient to discourage many potential partners from merging. Further, the SEC, proceeding under the authority of the Public Utility Holding Company Act of 1935, was engaged for many years in breaking up holding companies and restructuring them. This activity was aimed only at shady financial practices and dubious corporate structures, and Section 30 of the Holding Company Act (15 USC 79 h, i, j) specifically encourages mergers under certain conditions. Yet SEC "trust busting" may have made the industry sensitive about all holding company acquisitions.

In sum, a variety of managerial, regulatory, and social factors may have weakened the incentives toward rationalization. Of these, perhaps the most serious consisted of the problems in running a pooling organization by committee, combined with the problems in sharing gains of location and scale among firms. In any case, the movement toward rationalization did not proceed very rapidly in the 1960s.[57]

FPC Planning

The coordination problem and its causes have been examined in some detail for two reasons. First, the discussion reveals that the commission— which in 1964 set coordination as a major planning goal—has not been effective. Second, to understand the complexity of the problem and its causes is to go far toward forgiving the commission for its ineffectiveness.

Let us examine this latter proposition more closely. Given a complex coordination problem stemming from a variety of causes, what has the commission done to further coordination? The commission's major effort consisted of the writing and publication of the 1964 survey. The survey called public attention to the problem, and its existence encouraged firms to coordinate their activities. The commission then sought to follow up the survey with a number of actions presumably designed to spur the industry on toward greater coordination.

Encouraging Coordination and Planning

Soon after the publication of the survey, the Northeast power failure of 1965 focused public attention upon the problem of transmission reliability. The commission, with considerable help from the industry, produced *Prevention of Power Failures,* an extensive report on the subject. The Federal Power Act (16 USC 824 [1970]) authorizes the commission to "divide the country into regional districts for the voluntary interconnection and coordination of facilities for the generation, transmission, and sale of electric energy." Referring to this mandate and to the findings of the report, the commission called upon the industry to establish national and regional coordinating bodies. The industry then set up the regional councils, which subsequently have dealt primarily with transmission reliability and not with the economic aspects of coordination. They have encouraged firms to install load-shedding devices, which stop the spread of power blackouts by allowing the isolation and "quarantine" of an affected area, and have reviewed plans submitted by members for consistency with overall regional transmission reliability. They have not conducted planning exercises to produce the most efficient system consistent with reliability standards.

The commission also requests extensive information from the industry, including an annual survey of existing capacity, future installation plans, future demand estimates, and estimates of reserve capabilities.[58] This information, though useful, does not show the magnitude of the coordination problem or spur efforts to overcome it. The commission could obtain a better picture of the problem were it to ask for and compare (1) estimates of the reserves firms believe they must build to meet a given reliability standard and (2) engineering studies showing the reserves necessary to meet the same standard on the basis of planning a region as if it were a single system. Instead, the commission requests figures showing the percentage reserves that firms plan to build—a request that may be counterproductive, for it reinforces the popular but naive view that the industry's objective should be to build a certain percentage of reserve capacity. In fact, however, the industry's objective should be to meet a certain reliability standard with as few reserves as possible. This confusion may in part account for a feeling in the industry in the 1960s that the commission was telling it to reduce reserves, when in fact the intended message was to coordinate so as to reduce the *need* for reserves. Some industry representatives claimed that as a result reserves fell from 31 percent of peak capacity in 1960–63 to 19 percent in 1966–70 (*Electrical World*, Sept. 15, 1969). In any event, reserve percentages fell drastically in the 1960s without the increase in coordination necessary to preserve reliability. This in itself *contributed to the reliability crisis* of the past few years.

The commission has the power under Section 202(b) of the Federal Power Act to *require* firms to interconnect. Upon complaint of a state commission or a public utility, it can force a firm "to establish physical connection of its transmission facilities with the facilities of other persons (selling) electric energy" if it "finds such action necessary or appropriate in the public interest." Yet the commission has not used this authority as a weapon to promote rationalization.[59]

Expanding the Commission's Jurisdiction

Throughout the 1960s, the commission was laying legal groundwork which, in principle, could allow it to take more vigorous action to promote industry rationalization. The commission's jurisdiction over thermal facilities is, as pointed out before, limited to generating and transmitting facilities involved in producing electricity for resale in interstate commerce. Prior to 1962, to determine which facilities engage in interstate commerce the commission tried to trace the actual flow of electricity from a generating station to a recipient. Such a task was incredibly complex, and the results were quite subjective. In the 1960s, the commission resorted to a definition that potentially gives it jurisdiction over nearly all generating and transmitting facilities, so that the calculation of separate interstate flows became less important. The FPC began to argue that any facility *connected* to a facility that sells electricity in interstate commerce is itself in interstate commerce. It supported this argument with a theory that the electricity of such companies is "commingled" with that of others so that some electricity from interstate companies inevitably flows across connected interstate lines. On this theory, the commission asserted jurisdiction over Florida Power & Light, a firm that was located wholly within the state of Florida, that had no connections at the state line with any out-of-state system, and that had no contracts to sell electricity outside the state. Yet, because Florida Power's lines were connected to other Florida systems that, in turn, were connected to out-of-state systems, the FPC argued that the firm's commingled electricity is sometimes sent out of state. Although the scientific basis for this theory is uncertain, the Supreme Court upheld the commission in its assertion of jurisdiction.[60]

The immediate practical effect of asserting jurisdictions over Florida Power & Light and other primarily intrastate companies was quite limited. Such companies have had to obtain commission approval before entering into mergers and certain securities transactions; they submit information that the commission requests; and the commission can supervise their interstate wholesale electricity rates if they commence such sales. Yet, potentially, the assertion of jurisdiction might become important, for it could increase the commission's ability to push for the creation of larger power pools through interconnection. In the abstract, the commission's jurisdiction is now broad enough to allow it to reach virtually every important generating and transmitting facility in the country.

Although the Federal Power Act authorizes the commission to license power facilities built on navigable waters, the commission has not used this power to force increased coordination. In fact, in the Northfield Mountain proceeding, in approving the building of a transmission line that was allegedly too small to meet the region's needs, the commission stated expressly that it could not use individual licensing cases to make regional planning policy. The courts affirmed this position on the ground that the "statute does not in terms require that a water power project be integrated into an overall regional power plan."[61] On the other hand, in this type of plant, as in the case of steam turbine facilities, the commission has expanded its jurisdiction. In 1965 the Supreme Court upheld the commission's view that power facilities built on non-navigable headwaters of navigable streams fall within its licensing authority.[62] Such broadened jurisdiction would obviously help the commission develop regional coordination under its licensing power should it choose to do so.

Wheeling

The commission has occasionally been asked to require a company to "wheel" electricity: meaning to carry supplies purchased from another generating plant over its line to a customer within its service area. Compulsory wheeling could increase planning efficiency. The customer would be able to investigate all interconnected generating sources in order to determine the configuration of generation and transmission that minimizes his power costs. Large systems enjoying significant economies of size would have a greater opportunity to attract away customers from smaller, less efficient systems. Moreover, the owner of transmission lines would have no incentive to build high-cost generating facilities to serve his customers, for ownership of the lines would no longer make those customers his captives. The major limitation to compulsory wheeling as a force for more competition or for rationalization is the relatively small number of distribution companies that are free to shop around for electricity. Since 80 percent of the industry is vertically integrated, few buyers could seek alternative suppliers even if suppliers were compelled to wheel power.

In any event, the commission has refused to require wheeling. In the 1960s it read the Federal Power Act narrowly. Section 202(b), which gives it authority to compel interconnection, was construed to apply only to the joining of wires, not to the carrying of power across them.[63] The commission did not mention other possible sources of legal authority to compel wheeling, such as Section 205(b) (no public utility shall "subject any person to any undue . . . disadvantage") or Section 207 (the commission can require utilities to provide "proper, adequate, or sufficient [interstate] service").[64] It might, for example, have read into this general language the antitrust principle forbidding a firm that legitimately controls a "bottleneck" from using that control to prevent competition—a principle that courts have recently held applicable to a utility's control of transmission wires.

Environmental Actions

Since late 1969 the commission has taken a number of actions designed to help protect the natural environment. An Office of the Advisor on Environmental Quality has been created, and a Task Force on Environmental Questions was established. Specific environmental regulations now govern the construction of hydroelectric facilities, and FPC systematically collects data on fuels. Usually actions of this sort come in the form of orders that request information, that require compliance with certain antipollution standards, and that encourage, through liberalized accounting rules, the acquisition of land and expenditures on research and development.

These orders, if successful, should lead companies to do less environmental harm; they will not necessarily lead companies to plan jointly that system of new construction that optimally satisfies the conflicting demands for economy, reliability, and environmental protection. Put somewhat differently, the growing sensitivity to environmental harm—like growing concern with transmission reliability—has increased the importance of planning regional capacity on a single-system basis. The commission's particular environmental actions, however, have not specifically increased the pressure on industry to coordinate planning. They have done so only indirectly, insofar as general concern for the environment in itself pushed the industry toward rationalization.

Requests for Legislation

The commission, with reason, believes that the Federal Power Act was not designed to give it extensive power to compel rationalization of the industry. This view is not necessarily persuasive, but neither is it groundless. The legislative history of the act reveals very little that is relevant to this question. The elaborate statement in Section 202(a) concerning the commission's authority to encourage voluntary interconnection may be read as indicating an intent not to grant extensive authority to compel interconnection through other, broadly phrased, provisions of the act.

In light of this problem, in 1969 the commission asked Congress for legislation broadening its statutory authority. Lee C. White, the FPC chairman when the bill was proposed, testified in favor of a bill that would have given the commission explicit power to compel wheeling, to compel interconnection, and to require further rationalization.[65] Under the proposed legislation, one utility, for example, might have shared the generating capacity of another, even over the latter's objection, when such sharing would have produced cost savings. Moreover, by allowing the commission to speed the implementation of construction plans, the bill would have given the commission the power to induce companies to coordinate their planning. But John Nassikas, who was FPC chairman when hearings on the proposal were held, opposed this bill when he testified before Congress early in 1970. He argued that encouragement of voluntary coordination was sufficient to achieve rationalization.[66] Congress postponed action, and the prospects for passing a bill such as White had favored looked exceedingly dim in 1974.

The Perpetual Emergency

The practical obstacles to commission planning arise from the fact that the individual firms control most of the information needed to formulate a successful plan. How could the FPC compel the industry to coordinate? It might, of course, simply order a group of firms to produce a "future expansion plan" that takes proper account of economy, transmission reliability, and environmental injury. But the plan produced would be unlikely to fit anyone's idea of what is optimal. It would reflect bargaining among the firms—representing an accommodation of their conflicting interests, of the various interests of the local areas they serve, and of the possibly conflicting regulatory mandates set by a variety of agencies. In fact all of the forces now at work to prevent optimized regional planning and operation would also work to prevent the creation of an optimizing plan.

Whether, instead, the FPC's staff could successfully design detailed construction plans on its own is doubtful. Design of a detailed plan requires a firm grasp of a myriad of facts about each system, proper models that relate system size, shape, and composition to reserve needs and reliability requirements, a feeling for the importance placed upon environmental factors by the various groups affected, and the necessary experience with the system to make sensible judgments.[67] Unless it conscripts planners from the companies themselves, the staff will not have the ability to produce detailed plans for the nation's several hundred production plants and transmission networks.

Of course, it may be possible for the staff to design general, global planning models, on the basis of information submitted by the individual companies.[68] But such models provide only general targets, not specific optimal construction plans.[69] And, the application of any such models to a reluctant industry would be difficult. Firms must be given the opportunity to object to proposed models, particularly if the FPC or a state agency were to use them as a basis for a specific order to build or not to build. Objections can lead to lengthy administrative and judicial proceedings. The importance of avoiding such litigation would lead to compromise; and a final plan would embody the irrationalities of compromise, staff mistakes, and the results of bargaining among firms trying to reach a common "industry position."

In any event, the commission in the later 1960s lacked the will to pursue rationalization. It exhibited, instead, what might be called an "emergency mentality." It passed up many opportunities in the 1960s even within a conservative reading of mandate. The agency did not ask questions designed to expose the extent to which lack of coordination increases the need for reserves. It did not encourage state commissions and public utilities to lodge complaints that might give grounds for ordering further physical linkups of transmission lines. It did not ask power companies to undertake studies of how to minimize costs through coordinated development and operation of capacity. It did not offer models for restructuring the electric power industry (despite its considerable success in developing a model for pipeline networks in the Gulf of Mexico and in convincing gas transporters to use that as a guide for new construction). Yet the commission was extremely busy during all this period. What absorbed its attention?

The record suggests that in the field of electric power the commission let its priorities be set by external pressures. The Northeast power blackout of November 1965 produced public pressure to "do something" about reliability. President Johnson specifically requested FPC Chairman White, his former legal counsel, to uncover the causes of the failure. The commission, with substantial aid from the industry, responded with a three-volume report, *Prevention of Power Failures*, containing many specific recommendations for change. The commission went further: in White's words, the agency "shoved and cajoled utilities to install and use this equipment (to eliminate power overloads)" despite a feeling within the agency that the FPC had practically no legislative authority to do so. Similarly, a few years later, the commission's sudden concern for the natural environment constituted a response to intense pressure exerted by ecology groups acting primarily through the courts. The negative side of this phenomenon became evident in light of the fact that there was no outside agitation for power pooling: the agency lost interest in its own 1964 survey. The commission's planning activity in the 1960s consisted of separate reactions to what it saw as immediate problems. It did not act in accordance with any organized plan; it did not act as if it realized that economy, reliability, and protection of the environment are inter-related goals that call for coordinated industry planning.

The Need for Change

Louis Jaffe has written that planning was meant to be a major function of the independent administrative agency. Quoting Dean Landis and others, he remarks that the administrative process in such an agency typically evolves through two states: "first the identification of the admin-istrative process with the protection of the economically weak . . . and then, because private industry has appeared to fail in its organizing func-tion, the assertion of government responsibility to plan for the well-being of industry."[70]

This chapter suggests that to expect the FPC to plan for the well-being of the power industry (or the industry's customers) is utopian. The FPC has not been able to create a rationalized power industry. The causes of this failure go beyond any lack of adequate statutory authority. They spring in large part from the practical difficulties involved in having regu-lators make complex managerial decisions or in finding incentives for private managers that would lead them to make decisions more to the regulator's liking. The problems also derive in part from the tendency of the agency to respond to problems as they arise—incrementally, the tendency to pull away from sustained long-term planning in favor of attacks on whatever arises. The need to rationalize the industry remains.

This conclusion does not mean that all efforts to plan through regula-tion should be abandoned. It does suggest that the search for the best approach should be widened. Instead of asking only how regulation could be made more effective, those who frame public policy should also ask whether there are workable alternatives to regulation.

For example, the government might move to see that mergers take place that lead to an electricity industry controlled by ten to fifteen large,

privately owned companies. The argument against such an industry structure is that it would destroy possible competition among producers. Those
who make that argument must face the fact that state regulatory rules
and vertical integration already severely limit competition. In dealing with
this problem, proponents of competition might advocate changing the rules
and divorcing ownership of distribution from ownership of generating
facilities. Indeed, Leonard Weiss points to the possibility of separately
owned generating units competing across a common carrier transmission
system for the business of separately owned local distributing companies.
He maintains that consumers in the ten largest cities could support ten
to fifteen generating plants of efficient size within two hundred miles of
each city. In his view, significant competition among these units for the
city's business would be feasible.[71] However, it is difficult to see how such
competition and full rationalization could coexist. Minute-by-minute
power exchanges between units is necessary to produce the lowest-cost
power flow for an entire area. By agreeing in advance to supply low-cost
power to competitors, a firm would weaken its own ability to sign up
customers. Any important change in the configuration of power flows—
and it is the essence of competition to create, or threaten to create, such
change—might necessitate the rebuilding of portions of the transmission
lines to maintain total system reliability. Unless the cost of this is reflected
in every company's bids, competition is likely to take place at the expense
of reliability.

There are nonetheless good grounds for opposing the creation of large
private companies. But these grounds are not primarily economic. Rather,
they rest on the fear that firms of such huge size might wield undue political and social influence. And, there are some who believe that such firms,
interested in maximizing returns to shareholders, would prove insensitive
to environmental problems.

Instead of large private firms the industry might be reshaped to consist
of large production companies controlled by the government itself. Such
an arrangement might redirect institutional loyalties, leading engineers
and managers to subordinate diverse company goals to the creation of a
single, efficient production system. To convert managers to this mission
while developing a central regional staff to initiate planning studies would
speed the creation of a more rational production system. In principle,
public ownership might also make easier the problem of controlling electricity prices and taking proper account of environmental injury. Company
officials would not be judged in terms of their ability to raise stock prices

by increasing shareholders' returns; rather, they would be judged in terms of their ability to follow directives designed to yield economically proper prices—directives that allowed a reasonable return to invested capital, that attempted to set prices on the basis of incremental costs, and that might require appropriate deference to environmental problems.[72] But it is an understatement to say that managers of public enterprises have many more and different objectives than maximizing consumer welfare. It remains a major question whether in the United States managers responsible to the government would, or could, administer an economically sound but complex system of electricity prices.

The stock objection to public ownership is that public bureaucracies are inefficient. But the case for this as a universal proposition has not yet been made. Like private firms, some governmental enterprises have been successful, and others have botched their task.[73] A public corporation could be structured in a variety of ways, some of which would minimize the risk of inefficiency (particularly from political interference), while paying salaries to the same men now working for the industry to perform about the same jobs.

But there are other difficulties with public ownership. The most frequently made proposals for public ownership would separate distributing companies from the production companies that now control them.[74] Public enterprises would presumably have access to capital from the federal treasury, on favored terms. Basically, one must weigh the potential losses from these aspects of a radical change against the potential benefits of rationalization.

Although this chapter did not explore in detail the potential losses and gains from alternatives to the present inefficient regulation, it points up the need to seek such alternatives—if the nation is to obtain the benefits of rationalized planning. In any event, it has become apparent that achieving substantial cost savings for the consumer through the planning of electric power systems lies beyond the grasp of the Federal Power Commission.

CHAPTER FIVE

The Lessons of Regulation

OUR OBJECTIVE, as stated at the outset, has been to evaluate the performance of the Federal Power Commission in the 1960s. In measuring commission performance, we did not depend on internal technical criteria such as the absence of a large backlog of cases. What matters is the actual difference that commission performance makes in those spheres the agency is intended to affect. Consequently we ignored a number of technical, informational, and hortatory activities in which the commission engages and, instead, focused upon the commission's three major tasks: (a) classic "utility regulation" through control of the prices and profits of gas pipeline companies, (b) "rent control" through regulation of gas producer prices, and (c) "industrial planning" through coordination for the more efficient production of electricity.

Three conclusions emerge from this study. First, commission activity benefited the consumer very little if at all. The administrative costs of operating the commission, including the costs to litigants, ranged between $31 million and $95 million per year and probably averaged approximately $35 million. Although this expenditure is small when compared with gas and electricity revenues, it did not buy much. Measures of the effectiveness of gas pipeline price regulation indicate that pipeline prices were not lower than they would have been without regulation. Gas producer price regulation, which accounted for the largest portion of the administrative expense attributable to commission operation, caused more harm than good. Ceiling prices at the wellhead were set too low, creating a reserve shortage and a production shortage. In all probability, the gas shortage hurt residential consumers more than lower prices helped them. Efforts to plan for increased efficiency in electricity production achieved a few minor successes but did not gain for the consumer the considerable benefits that increased coordination might have provided. The full array of these calculations is shown in Table 5-1. Perhaps the commission's secondary activities—gathering statistics, reviewing construction plans, providing a forum for complaints—justified the administrative expenses shown there. But certainly FPC regulation did not achieve direct gains to consumers.

Second, the study adds support to the growing suspicion that regulation by commission is at best a clumsy tool for achieving economic goals. In each instance, the FPC responded slowly and inefficiently to changing conditions. Once the commission set ceilings on pipeline profit, it maintained them for months or years, despite changing economic conditions; it reversed them only after hearing numerous conflicting expert views in lengthy adjudicatory proceedings; and the profit ceilings it set only very generally approximated the actual economic costs of capital. As a result, the commission had little effect on pipeline price levels. Similarly, the commission responded slowly to the Supreme Court ruling that gave the agency a mandate to regulate gas producer prices. When it did respond, price-setting procedures were extremely cumbersome and time-consuming, and the resulting price ceilings were far from the competitive price level. The commission's attempts to deal with the electricity planning problem also reveal slow response and rather half-hearted effort. For a number of reasons, FPC actions moved the companies only very slowly and very approximately toward the goal of increased coordination and efficiency.

Table 5-1. Estimated Cost-Benefit Gap Accompanying FPC Regulation during a Typical Year in the 1960s

Millions of dollars

| | Costs of regulation[a] | | Benefits from regulation for consumers | |
Activity	Estimate	Range	Direct	Indirect or long-term benefits
Gas pipeline profit regulation	6.0	5.5–6.5	1–10	Insignificant
Gas field price regulation	21.1	21.1–79.1	Negative	Negative
Electric power systems coordination	3.2	1.8–4.7	Insignificant	Insignificant

Source: Column 1 derived from Table 1-1, p. 14; column 2 estimated on basis of information discussed in Chaps. 2–4.

a. The costs to litigants as well as the FPC costs incurred in rate proceedings are excluded, but general administrative expenses, the cost of certification proceedings, and the cost of evaluating electric power systems are included.

Third, the study shows the serious risks that flow from an agency's single-minded pursuit of lower prices. An important strain of regulatory thought views low prices as good in themselves and brushes aside any inefficiencies they may cause on the ground that such inefficiencies are simply the price paid for an improved income distribution. Chapter 2 recounts a case in which pursuit of such redistribution makes sense— where regulation seeks to lower prices to an approximately competitive level. Chapter 3, however, examines a case in which such pursuit is dangerous—where regulation seeks prices that are lower than a competitive level. More important, Chapter 3 shows that the distinction among prices that are higher than, roughly equal to, and lower than, the competitive level is not simply an economist's theory. Rather, the differences in these levels have great practical importance in supply—even supply for those whom the public-minded regulator wishes to help with price reductions.

Theories of Regulatory Failure

At the most general level, this study sheds light on theories advanced to explain why agencies perform badly or fail to achieve sensible objectives. Typically, those theories blame such factors as bad management, faulty administrative structure, or capture by the regulated industry for regulatory failure.

We should declare at the outset a prejudice against, or an intuitive suspicion of, any theory that attempts to explain agency failure in terms of a single variable. An agency's effect on the markets it regulates is the product of a number of elements. What will appear to be success or failure depends in part upon the nature of the task the agency is asked to perform. It may be easier for an agency to order information about securities disseminated to potential buyers or to have a moon rocket built than to make a major improvement in the quality of children's television or to set prices that duplicate those of a competitive market. In addition, an agency's success depends in part upon its statutory mandate; the task may be so defined in its mandate that agency performance is bound to appear a failure when compared with all conceivable ways a problem might have been approached. For example, tax incentives and penalties might reduce pollution more efficiently than the setting of physical standards by administrative decree. But what if Congress explicitly limits an environmental protection agency to the setting of standards? Further, an agency's performance is undoubtedly affected by the political climate in which it works. That climate helps to determine (1) the probability that Congress will overrule decisions or curtail expenditures of the agency, (2) the agency's ability to obtain cooperation from other parts of the government, and (3) the particular political rewards, if any, that accrue to commissioners from deciding cases. Finally, an agency's structure—the way in which it organizes and manages its work—obviously has something to do with its effectiveness.

Given this variety of elements that affect agency output, it would be surprising if any one factor could be responsible for numerous instances of apparent agency failure. Our study of the Federal Power Commission indicates weaknesses in the most commonly accepted theories and points toward other causes of failure that are embedded more deeply in the regulatory process.

Capture by the Industry

An agency has been captured by the industry that it regulates when that industry consistently obtains favorable decisions. It may do so, for example, by appealing to the expectation of regulators that their future careers are likely to be within the industry. Or capture may be less direct; there may be undue industry influence from inundating an agency with more information than it can obtain elsewhere—information that is biased toward the companies on points at issue. A "capture" theory of whatever sort implies that the regulated companies have on balance benefited from agency regulation. At the least, they ought not to have been harmed by it.

Contrary to this theory, experience with the Federal Power Commission during the 1960s shows that the regulated companies were hurt far more than they were helped by commission activities. Though direct supervision of pipeline company profits might be described as minimal, FPC supervision of the field price of natural gas was decisive. In holding natural gas prices down, the commission prevented pipelines from satisfying consumer demands for gas. To be sure, the early years of gas field price regulation favored a small number of established East Coast pipelines. (Since these lines held options on large amounts of reserves, price control helped them to maintain their profits, and shortages left them unaffected for a period.) However, these "benefits" for certain pipelines were not of great importance or of long duration. Field price regulation injured the pipelines more than direct profit regulation helped them.

Neither did other regulated companies benefit. Natural gas producers were seriously damaged by commission regulation that kept the price of natural gas well below market-clearing levels. Electric power companies in the long run gained nothing from the commission's failure to secure greater coordination in the planning of electricity production. Such planning in reducing costs would have helped many firms as well as consumers. In sum, if we judge "capture" by looking to results, there is little reason to say that the pipelines, the gas producers, or the power companies "owned" the Federal Power Commission.

Inadequate Personnel

Poor agency performance is often blamed on the staff. More, or better, or different staff would improve the situation—so the critics often say of any agency. Yet, though our judgment is necessarily subjective and impressionistic, there is no evidence that the commission's members and staff during the 1960s were inferior to those of other independent agencies, to the personnel of other executive departments, or, for that matter, to the employees of many of the companies being regulated. In any event, a call for "better personnel" does not suggest where one is to find them or make the case that society could put them to better use working on the Federal Power Commission than elsewhere. The "agency problem" more realistically requires efforts to determine how a commission with a staff of mixed abilities can perform more effectively.

It has recently been argued that it would help to appoint a different kind of commissioner—that lawyers should be replaced by economists. Whether such a change would significantly improve agency behavior is doubtful. For one thing, the policy that even such an economically oriented agency as the FPC applies is heavily dependent upon knowledge of law, politics, and detailed facts about the regulated industries. Moreover, economic theory rarely points unambiguously to a single policy conclusion. (Field price regulation, for example, found plausible support in economic theory, and distinguished economists advocated its adoption by the commission.) The political pressures upon the President when he makes appointments would not change; nor would the pressures upon an economist member arising from the need to prevent service failures, the need to complete a daily workload, and the need to satisfy possible political constituencies. What the advocates of appointing economists as commissioners really want is "good" economists—economists who will make decisions to their liking. One could just as easily call for "better commissioners."

Inadequate Mandate

The commission's legislative mandate, though perhaps not ideal, is no more than partly responsible for the inadequacies of its performance. It is an exaggeration to argue, for example, that the commission's limitations in authority over gas pipelines caused the gas shortage. Certainly, the commission's inability to control intrastate sales led to diversion of gas to intrastate industrial buyers and aggravated the shortage of gas available for residential heating. But to change the commission's mandate to allow intrastate gas regulation would not end the shortage; it would merely allow the commission to transfer gas from some potential customers to others. And such rationing, whether achieved through a system of commission-imposed prices or through direct end-use controls, would simply make producer price regulation a still more complex task, embodying the possibility of still more serious economic misallocation. Field price regulation and the gas shortage are products of too much legislative authority, not too little.

Alternatively, and more persuasively, one might blame the gas shortage on the commission's legislative mandate as interpreted by the Supreme Court. The commission was reluctant to regulate gas producers until the court found that the agency was required to do so. Efforts to change this legislative mandate were blocked by a presidential veto. Nonetheless, the commission has made no effort to test its mandate. If the FPC were to make an administrative finding that producers lack "monopoly power" and then were to use this finding as the legal basis for refusing to control prices, given the existing gas shortage, probably the courts would validate reduced controls.

The commission's legal authority to plan more effective electricity production is limited. Yet these limitations on its authority are only partly responsible for its failure to plan more effectively. Its powers to regulate pipelines are broad and in no way responsible for any regulatory failure.

Faulty Organization

Many critics of agency performance have looked for the causes of failure in the agencies' internal structure or organization. James M. Landis, for example, suggested in 1960 that agency chairmen be given additional authority.[1] In 1971 the Ash Council—a presidential study group—recommended that the position of commissioner be abolished. Instead, urged the council, substitute in each regulatory agency a single administrator directly responsible to the President.[2] Moreover, the Ash Council advocated de-emphasizing the agencies' adjudicatory function: agency chiefs would be given only thirty days to review the decisions of hearing examiners; and cases would proceed directly to a new administrative court, composed of judges appointed by the President and confirmed by the Senate. These proposals were designed to improve agency efficiency. They sought to dispense with the need for collegial decision making.

To provide that an agency's chief serve at the pleasure of the President might increase executive support for agency action; it might also, in principle, increase the extent to which an agency felt accountable to the electorate. Moreover, any effort to diminish a commissioner's responsibility for reviewing case decisions would be intended to free his time for the formulation of more general policy. The "faulty organization" school of thought emphasizes these points. Basically, these critics see agency problems as *management* problems.

Experience with the Federal Power Commission provides little reason to hope that the Ash proposal or similar "management reforms" would improve agency performance significantly. To have given more power to a single agency chief, to have made him responsible to the President, and to have diminished his responsibility for reviewing cases would not have prevented the gas shortage. Indeed, increased reliance upon staff work and recommendation could have led to lower ceiling prices and hence aggravated the existing shortage (since the FPC staff recommended lower prices than those set). Nor is it clear how the Ash recommendation would improve the commission's rate-making performance. In fact, removing one layer of adjudicatory review by a commission moderately familiar with the regulated industry might increase, rather than diminish, the possibility of rate-making errors.

The Ash Council's recommendations offer somewhat more hope in the area of planning. Planning problems are more obviously problems of policy making than adjudication, and the Ash proposals seem designed to lead agencies to spend more time in making general policy and less in adjudicating. To place responsibility in the hands of one man makes less likely those disagreements, compromises, and postponements that hinder the development of broad *consistent* policy. Letting cases proceed directly from a hearing examiner to an administrative court would allow the agency chief more time for general policy making.

But even here one must doubt the effectiveness of such reorganization proposals. A number of serious institutional and political obstacles that so far have prevented companies from coordinating planning on their own would remain. The single commissioner would still face the difficulties implicit in the compromises that plans submitted by coordinated companies involve, and he would find it difficult to draw up specific plans himself. Of course one might speed the planning process by giving the administrator the power to force companies to follow his suggested plans without judicial review. Yet it is difficult to see how one can deprive a private company, or the consumers, or citizens whose lives are affected by such a company's actions of the right to appeal to a court. There will always be claims that an administrator has exceeded his statutory authority or acted unconstitutionally. At best, a specialized reviewing court might speed the review process. Marginal improvement is the most one could hope for from the Ash Council proposals.

Administrative Ease

Theories about industry capture, poor staff, faulty mandates, and unwieldy structure miss the mark. A fair amount of validity must be granted, however, to the proposition that agency failures arise in large part from efforts to "process" work quickly—to avoid a backlog of cases—while raising as little controversy as possible.

Many of the FPC's problems reach it in the form of disputes—between gas retail distributing companies and pipeline companies, for example, or between pipelines and producers. The parties to any proceeding have the power to delay commission action through appeals to the courts. Further, the commission is aware that consumers and their political representatives, prone to react strongly to an interruption of service, will respond with somewhat less vigor to a price increase and are unlikely even to notice a failure to receive a price reduction. These conditions, along with a desire to reduce workload, explain a number of features of the commission's behavior.

An agency seeking a "good record" knows that an important part of the "record" is kept by the courts and by Congress. The lower the number of appeals cases and of bills in Congress to remedy problems in the agency's area, the better the record of the independent commission. Thus, to avoid controversy an agency may put a premium on negotiating compromises that will dissuade appeal to the courts. In the middle 1960s, when it was "too late" to avoid controversy, the Federal Power Commission abandoned its efforts to adjudicate "proper" area field prices and turned to negotiation among producers and pipelines to set the ceiling prices in Louisiana. The FPC also has tended to "negotiate" a "proper" rate of return with the pipeline companies in individual cases. Negotiation is likely to produce profit rates that an economist would think too high, and there are in fact pressures upon the commission leading it to resolve uncertainties in favor of higher profits. If the commission sets pipeline profit rates low, the companies take the case to court or at least reappear before the commission with a new request for a price increase. In contrast, the commission can set profit rates high without arousing buyer case appeals unless large individual buyer price increases are in the offing.

The commission has geared its procedures to reduce caseload, minimize complexity, and shorten the time cases take to complete. For example, rules that determine *future prices* by looking to *historical costs* sacrifice potential accuracy for workable procedure. Both pipeline and producer gas prices were "inaccurate" in that sense. To adhere to such rules rigorously when pipeline costs are falling—as in the 1960s—leads to higher pipeline profits. To adhere to such rules for producers when costs are increasing discourages service. Furthermore, the commission's efforts to use *historical averages* and *regional averages* to simplify producer field price regulation made it less likely that regulation would achieve the goals of reducing prices and clearing the market at the same time.

The search for administrative ease nevertheless has its proponents, and those critics who decried the commission's backlog of cases a decade ago may have done the consumer a disservice. Landis, for example, in assessing the FPC as an example of regulatory failure in the early 1960s, pointed out that it had completed almost none of the cases on its docket.[3] Worried by the backlog, the commission devised the area rate proceedings, a simpler administrative device with the result that uniformly low rates were set and a shortage created. In fixing rates, as in planning an efficient electrical system, one hopes for a technically accurate result. Results that are produced by compromising among the different positions presented to the commission approach the technically proper solution only by chance.

The Adjudicatory Process

In a way the FPC has the worst of two worlds. Despite the presence of considerable negotiation, the most important elements of the commission's rate-making process are adjudicatory, and this in itself impairs effectiveness. Such matters as ceiling profit rates and important allocational rules are determined after interested parties, usually the staff and a regulated firm, present facts and arguments to a neutral deciding body. A number of characteristics of the adjudicatory process make it ill-suited to the job of rate setting—at least if the commission pursues the classical goal of competitive prices.

First, an adjudicatory procedure is time-consuming. To obtain approval for a rate change requires marshaling a complex set of facts and arguments, presenting them to the agency staff, possibly to a hearing examiner, and then to the commission. The time required creates a conservative bias in the result—rates tend to remain at existing levels. Insofar as changes occur, the lag works consistently in the pipelines' favor—unreported when costs fall, anticipated with rate requests when costs increase. Yet outside these petty advantages the firms have little freedom to experiment with rates, even perhaps to try out profit-maximizing price cuts. Insofar as regulation tends to freeze existing prices, it does not tend toward any competitive ideal.

Second, the adjudicatory process cannot easily cope with decisions that rest upon speculation. In an unregulated, competitive industry, for example, managers try to predict future cost-and-demand conditions when determining their probable future output and price. Yet, when commissions determine a firm's future prices, they cannot easily do the same. To assess probable future costs, commissioners waver between depending on the company manager, who knows more about probable future costs than they do, and discounting his predictions of a cost increase because he may attempt to ensure a monopoly profit. It is not surprising, then, that the FPC has tended to use historical costs to determine future revenue requirements or that the commission has developed cost allocation rules that sacrifice, to the virtues of certainty, the flexibility that a firm might need to cope with changing market conditions.

Third, adjudication works best when the decision maker chooses among only a limited range of outcomes. He can list outcomes and hear arguments for and against each. Many rate-making problems, however, are polycentric, offering a wide range of possible results each of which, if adopted, has implications as to the desirability of other policies. Rate design poses a serious problem of this nature; for a vast number of rate structures might each yield the same total revenue, yet each will affect different groups of consumers differently. Commissions tend to leave rate design in the hands of the regulated company, subject to possible challenge from injured buyers. The procedure tends to freeze rate structure, for change brings with it the threat of challenge. It also can lead firms to propose structures that disfavor those buyers thought to have the worst chance of successful protest before an agency. Of course, it is possible to force a polycentric problem into an adjudicatory mold; experts, for example, might be hired to design an ideal structure, which an agency could adopt after allowing firms and buyers a chance to raise objections. But such a procedure still provides little opportunity for experiment or change. And insofar as rates are best approached by experiment or require subjective judgment or guesses, efforts to force such problems into an adjudicatory framework are not likely to succeed.

Fourth, adjudication requires standards that, in the case of rate making, are hard to come by. The overall objective or standard—seek to duplicate the effects of competition—provides little guidance, for it is difficult to know in any actual noncompetitive case what prices would be set by a hypothetically competitive firm. To ease decision making and to reach consistent results, commissions tend to introduce substandards. But these, like as not, move rate making away from its basic economic objective— toward "splitting the difference" between protagonists or toward sharing the benefits from production in such a way that no party to a controversy can be said to be divested of deserved property rights. Insofar as the administrative goal is efficient resource allocation rather than dispute settlement, an adjudicative proceeding is likely to make mistakes.

This appraisal does *not* mean that adjudication should under all circumstances be abandoned. What it does show is that adjudication is a clumsy tool for hitting economic targets. We neither propose a theory of regulatory failure nor believe that our findings conclusively prove or disprove any such theory. Yet those findings are suggestive; they cannot easily be explained through single-variable theories, such as those of bad management or industry capture. Theories that take account of multiple causes, especially causes embedded in the nature of bureaucracy and the adjudicative process, have far greater explanatory power.

Steps toward Reform

The behavior of the Federal Power Commission indicates the immediate desirability of three specific changes in regulatory policy. First, efforts to regulate the prices charged by natural gas producers should be abandoned. De-regulation in all likelihood would end the gas shortage, while competition among producers probably would keep prices near market-clearing levels.[4] Competitive prices would be higher than recent ceiling prices, by several cents per Mcf.[5] The government should consider changes in tax policy, such as abolition of the depletion allowance, rather than rely upon regulatory policy to capture any inordinately high producer rents that might follow from the price increases.

Second, the commission should consider relaxing, rather than tightening, its supervision of pipeline prices and profits. Our findings suggest that the pipelines face a certain amount of competition in many of their regulated markets. Such competition limits the extent to which they can raise prices above costs. That fact, together with the near impossibility of regulating prices in such a way as to eliminate monopoly profit, makes it most unlikely that regulation provides benefits worth its administrative cost. The commission should consider abandoning the cost-of-service price setting method and instead investigate the extent to which various pipeline markets are competitive. Where competition exists—where there are more than two gas pipelines and there are close substitute sources of energy— it could de-regulate. Where effective competition does not exist, it could set prices based upon costs and prices in the more competitive markets. Such a "comparative" price-setting technique, though approximate, is likely to be as effective as present rate-setting methods and to require less extensive supervision. The commission should begin to explore the details of such an alternative.

Third, energy policy planners, who are now groping with the problems posed by the need for economy, reliability, and environmental protection, ought not to look to traditional regulation for solutions. The need for coordination in planning and operating electricity systems is great. Electric power should be provided through unified systems that each serve several states and include several companies. Yet, the Federal Power Commission's history suggests that it cannot be relied upon to bring about any major change in industry structure, and Chapter 4 suggests that the reasons lie in the nature of the regulatory process itself. Policymakers should begin to study the desirability of injecting the government more directly into the planning process. Such governmental involvement might take a variety of forms, ranging from the creation of special task forces with power to order the building of particular lines and plants to the creation of industry/government regional power authorities with direct planning and operating responsibilities. Our study does not indicate to what extent such systems are preferable to the status quo; it indicates only that the status quo, and similar forms of regulation, will not solve the coordination problem. Thus policymakers must begin the study of very different institutional alternatives.

These three changes do not constitute a detailed program. Our basic objective here has been to assess the effectiveness of past commission action. That assessment indicates that it is expecting too much to ask a commission to undertake profit regulation or complex planning. As A. E. Kahn notes in *The Economics of Regulation*, some critics of the regulatory agencies suggest that "the present institution embodies the worst of both possible worlds—monopoly without effective control, private enterprise without effective incentive or stimulus, governmental supervision without the possibility of effective initiative in the public interest."[6] The performance of the FPC adds support to this view.

Notes

CHAPTER ONE

1. On the responsibilities of the FPC, see 49 Stat. 847, 848, 851; 52 Stat. 822.

2. See, for example, *Federal Power Commission* v. *Southern California Edison Co.*, 376 U.S. 205 (1964), on the jurisdiction and standards of the commission in setting electricity prices; and see *Federal Power Commission* v. *Northern Natural Gas Co.*, 346 U.S. 922 (1954), as an example of the way in which costs and prices have been calculated with regard to natural gas pipeline firms.

3. *South Carolina Generating Company,* in 16 *Federal Power Commission Reports* (hereafter cited as FPC) 52, 58 (1956). The statement that "costs are known" is open to question, for estimates of costs vary widely, and generally a compromise figure is chosen in preference to a determination that one of the estimates is most nearly correct.

4. *In the Matter of Kansas Pipe Line & Gas Company and North Dakota Consumers Gas Company,* 2 FPC 29 (1939).

5. *Phillips Petroleum Company* v. *Wisconsin,* 347 U.S. 672 (1954).

6. See President's Advisory Council on Executive Organization, *A New Regulatory Framework: Report on Selected Independent Regulatory Agencies* (1971).

7. Federal Power Commission, *Statistics of Interstate Natural Gas Pipeline Companies, 1970* (1971).

8. See Paul W. MacAvoy, *Price Formation in Natural Gas Fields* (Yale University Press, 1962), Chap. 3, for an early discussion of pipeline economics; subsequent analysis can be found in *Pacific Gas Transmission Company et al.*, 42 FPC 1046 (1969).

9. The so-called Atlantic Seaboard Formula is given in *Atlantic Seaboard Corporation et al.,* in 94 (N.S.) *Public Utilities Reports* 245 (1952). The costs assigned to service *j* are:

$$C_j = VC_j + (K/2)[Q_j/(Q_i + Q_j)] + (K/2)[Q_{jt}/(Q_{it} + Q_{jt})],$$

where VC is total variable cost actually incurred in *j*, K is total capital cost, and Qs are volumes consumed by *j* and other *i* demanders throughout the year as well as peak-load period *t*.

10. Federal expenditures for natural gas pipeline regulation are shown as $3.526 million in fiscal year 1968 according to *The Budget of the United States Government —Appendix, Fiscal Year 1970*, p. 930.

11. Compiled from "regulatory expenses" and consultants' charges reported by each of the interstate pipeline companies on FPC Form 2, "Annual Report for Natural Gas Companies." Allowing for reporting omissions and errors in allocating costs, the range probably was from $2 million to $3 million.

12. *Permian Basin Area Rate Cases,* 390 U.S. 747 (1968).

13. See *ibid.* and *Permian Basin Area Rate Proceeding et al.,* 34 FPC 159 (1965), Docket AR 61-1. (Cited hereafter as *Permian Basin Proceeding.*)

14. This estimate is based on statistics given in the *1968 Annual Report of the Federal Power Commission,* pp. 55–56. Technically speaking, price-increase requests were classified by the commission as suspended for 5 months after receipt, during which time the party making a request was enjoined from charging the proposed higher price. After 5 months the party could automatically put the higher price into effect. However, any increase collected in this manner was subject to refund to the extent that it exceeded the final rate allowed by the commission at the conclusion of proceedings. With 7,000 rates in suspension, considerable uncertainty and delay ensued for the industry.

15. *Permian Basin Proceeding,* p. 197. In the same source, see also the testimony of S. F. Sherwin, Exhibit 42-J (SFS-1), Schedule 17, Dockets AR 64-1 and AR 64-2. The estimates offered here include the costs of certification and of rate schedule review and so should not be attributed to area proceedings alone.

16. Producer commitments to interstate pipelines are given in the FPC annual reports. See esp. Federal Power Commission, *1969 (Forty-Ninth) Annual Report.*

17. Robert W. Gerwig, "Natural Gas Production: A Study of Costs of Regulation," *Journal of Law and Economics,* Vol. 5 (October 1962), pp. 69–92, and Paul W. MacAvoy, "The Effectiveness of the Federal Power Commission," *Bell Journal of Economics and Management Science,* Vol. 1 (Autumn 1970), p. 281, suggest a range from $10 million to $58 million for opportunity costs incurred through regulatory delay. The working figure is 17 cents per Mcf per month of delay, allowing alternatively for a 1-month delay or a 6-month delay.

18. FPC, *Statistics of Interstate Natural Gas Pipeline Companies, 1970,* Table 5, p. xiii.

19. FPC, *Statistics of Privately Owned Electric Utilities in the United States: Class A and B Companies* (1971), p. xvii.

20. These rough estimates of the number of schedules reviewed and challenged accord with the annual reports of the commission from 1965 to 1970.

21. *The Budget of the United States Government—Appendix, Fiscal Year 1970,* p. 930.

22. See Paul W. MacAvoy, "The Effectiveness of the Federal Power Commission," *Bell Journal of Economics and Management Science,* Vol. 1 (August 1970), pp. 277–80.

23. *Ibid.*

24. This estimate follows from assessing "in process" costs at $50,000 per annum, in keeping with average costs of $150,000 for a case completed in three years. It does not account for the possibility of lower or higher costs in any one year. If all cases were "single-rate" cases, costs for defense might have been as low as $100,000; but if all were complex interclass rate reviews, then defense costs might have been $3 million.

25. Note that some generating companies may have sold electricity to small buyers at uneconomically low rates in order to avoid expensive litigation before the commission. The largest number of cases before the commission were initiated by small cooperative electricity-retailing companies seeking to prevent power wholesalers from "discriminating" against them by charging a higher price than that charged other and often larger buyers. See docket numbers E-7120, E-7183, E-7273, E-7308, E-7344, E-7421, and E-7426 in Table 10 of the *Fiscal Year 1968 Annual Report* of the Federal Power Commission. We suspect that in fact the higher prices to smaller cooperatives reflected diseconomies of scale not present when electricity was sold to the largest retail buyers. Thus, from the standpoint of the electricity-generating company, the trade-off would have been (a) reduced costs of litigation against (b) prices below costs of production and distribution of electricity to small users; and

where the first exceeded the second, private losses were minimized, but social costs were incurred.

26. See, for example, *Gainesville Utilities Department* v. *Florida Power Corporation*, 402 U.S. 515 (1971).

27. FPC, *Statistics of Privately Owned Electric Utilities in the United States, 1970.*

CHAPTER TWO

1. See George J. Stigler, "The Theory of Economic Regulation," *Bell Journal of Economics and Management Science,* Vol. 2 (Spring 1971), p. 3.

2. Consumers are hypothesized as choosing between "no price savings today" and a range of savings from P_1 to P_2 as shown in the illustrative figure. They are not conceived to be choosing between prices that prevail when a regulatory agency exists and prices that prevail in an unregulated market. What the figure represents is a straightforward comparison of two agency-influenced price ceilings. Each level of demand resulting from a level of regulated price P can be estimated, so that the effects of degrees of regulation can be plotted by comparing, under the demand curve or function, $Q = f(P)$ for different P. Each comparison is made on the assumption that other factors affecting Q are held constant or else that their effects on Q have been removed as a matter of course.

There have been a number of attempts to make comparisons of this type. See Robert M. Spann and Edward W. Erickson, "The Economics of Railroading: The Beginning of Cartelization and Regulation," *Bell Journal of Economics and Management Science,* Vol. 1 (August 1970), pp. 227–44; Paul W. MacAvoy, "The Effectiveness of the Federal Power Commission," in *ibid.,* pp. 271–303; Merton J. Peck, "Competitive Policy for Transportation?" in Paul W. MacAvoy (ed.), *The Crisis of the Regulatory Commissions: An Introduction to a Current Issue of Public Policy* (Norton, 1970).

Fred M. Westfield, "Methodology of Evaluating Economic Regulation," in American Economic Association, *Papers and Proceedings of the Eighty-Third Annual Meeting, 1970 (American Economic Review,* Vol. 61 [May 1971]), pp. 211–17, has voiced objections to making comparisons between actual regulated price and perfectly competitive price. His objections appear to be beside the point, however, since this is not what the studies in question actually do. Rather, they compare alternative regulated prices, or they compare actual prices that prevailed before the advent of regulation or after the demise of regulation with prices that prevailed while regulation was in effect.

3. See David M. Winch, "Consumer's Surplus and the Compensation Principle," *American Economic Review,* Vol. 55 (June 1965), pp. 395–423. Gains in Area B are realized only under certain conditions. First, prices have to be greater than the economic costs of the additional output. This condition will not necessarily exist: costs of service as defined by the FPC, we have noted, are not economic costs except by chance equality of accounting overhead allocations with the opportunity costs of this production. Second, Area B is a good measure of aggregate gains of consumers only if the distribution of the gains is judged to be acceptable.

4. In order for the economy to gain, the lower price must at least cover the cost of supplying the additional gas consumed in Area B. Yet "cost of service" as defined in public utility proceedings does not necessarily take this factor into consideration.

5. Federal Power Commission, *Fiscal Year 1968 Annual Report,* p. 60.

6. Derived from data in Stephen Breyer and Paul W. MacAvoy, "The Natural Gas Shortage and the Regulation of Natural Gas Producers," *Harvard Law Review,* Vol. 86 (April 1973), pp. 976–78 and n. 118.

7. The results from regulatory proceedings may last longer than one year. But it

is impractical to estimate how much longer—an applicant denied a rate increase may reapply in one year or in five years. The present value of five years' benefits is $\Sigma B_i/$ $(1 + r)^i$ for year i and discount rate r. For five years and $r = 20$ percent, the value equals approximately 2.4 times one year's gains. The point is, however, that the applicant decides when to reapply. The approach here is to treat the interval of gains as limited to one year. In the case of especially large "savings" achieved by denying a rate increase, the applicant is likely to come back to the commission with a slightly revised proposal the next year.

8. Federal Power Commission, "Uniform System of Accounts Prescribed for Natural Gas Companies (Class A and B, C, and D) Subject to the Provisions of the Natural Gas Act in Effect on September 1, 1968," FPCA-10 (1968; processed), p. 1.

9. *Bluefield Water Works & Improvement Company* v. *Public Service Commission of the State of West Virginia*, 262 U.S. 679 (1923) at 692.

10. From price $R = P_{gas} + \{d + r(1 + T) [\Sigma(k_t - d_t)]\}/v$, it can be determined that the percentage change in price per percentage change in r is $(r\partial R)/(R\partial r) = [r(1 + T) \Sigma(k - d)]/R$, the allowed profits before taxes as a percentage of revenues. If profits and taxes were 20 percent of revenues and $r \simeq 0.05$, then a 1 point increase in r to 0.06 would imply a 4 percent increase in R. Similarly, for $B = \Sigma(k_t - d_t)$, or rate base, $B\partial R/R\partial B$ is equal to $r(1 + T)B/R$. The percentage change in price with respect to any given percentage "inflation" of rate base is equal to pre-tax profits as a percentage of sales. If the rate base were 20 percent too high, prices would be too high as well. The total effect from two "mistakes" would be prices 8 percent too high.

11. All three studies appeared in the *Bell Journal of Economics and Management Science:* Burton G. Malkiel, "The Valuation of Public Utility Equities," Vol. 1 (Spring 1970), pp. 143–60; Robert H. Litzenberger and Cherukuri U. Rao, "Estimates of the Marginal Rate of Time Preference and Average Risk Aversion of Investors in Electric Utility Shares: 1960–66," Vol. 2 (Spring 1971), pp. 265–77; John G. McDonald, "Required Return on Public Utility Equities: A National and Regional Analysis, 1958–1969," Vol. 2 (Autumn 1971), pp. 503–14.

On tests for membership in the same risk class, see esp. McDonald, p. 508.

12. The entire range of arguments concerning rate of return can be found in 17 major FPC decisions reached in the 1960s. In 8 cases reference was made to "comparable equity returns," and in 6 of these FPC considered "earnings-price ratios" of other companies explicitly. Rising debt costs figured in 2 cases, and in 2 others the correct rate was said to be a "matter of judgment"; these 4 all had higher allowed rates than those using comparable-earnings tests. But higher rates were also allowed in 5 other cases in which mention was most prominently made of the past successful history of the company. The various arguments do not seem to explain the results reached.

13. The combined effect of (a) allowing rates of return to exceed costs of capital and (b) allowing profit taxes to be included in costs is to dilute any direct effect of rate-of-return control on prices. The excess-profit margin is $(s - \rho)/(1 - t)$ where s is the allowed rate of return, ρ the cost of capital, and t the corporation profits tax rate. With $t = 0.5$ and $(s - \rho)$ close to 5 percent, probably this excess return of 10 percent on capital has approached the maximum that could have been earned by unregulated enterprises in the gas pipeline industry. In other words, the results probably were the same as if the government merely took 50 percent of noncompetitive profits, after the noncompetitive price had been set, leaving the other 50 percent as allowed after-tax margin over the cost of capital.

14. "Peak demand" in this context means the amount the customer takes from the pipeline during the system's maximum delivery period within the previous twelve months.

15. *Federal Register,* Vol. 13 (October 30, 1948), pp. 6371–76.

16. *Re Northern Natural Gas Company,* in 9 (3d Series) *Public Utility Reports* 15, 24 (1955). *Reports* cited hereafter as PUR.

17. *Ibid.* at 21–22. Issue can be taken with labeling the distance factor as the "prime determinant." There is general agreement that costs vary with both volume and distance, but there is no general finding that distance is more important. See Paul W. MacAvoy, *Price Formation in Natural Gas Fields: A Study of Competition, Monopsony, and Regulation* (Yale University Press, 1962), Chap. 3, for a numerical example of cost variation with both volume and distance.

18. *Re Northern Natural Gas Company* at 29, 30.

19. *Tennessee Gas Transmission Company,* 27 FPC 202 (1962) at 209.

20. *Ibid.* at 212. In fact, in the decision on Tennessee's price differentials, the commission declined to apply load factor and volume factors that would have permitted higher prices to be charged in New England.

21. Since most of Tenneco's additional mileage was in loops on its main line, rather than in a more indirect main line, and that is not the kind of mileage for which the rule allowed, there should not have been a difference in commodity prices on an Mcf-mile basis.

22. See *Atlantic Seaboard Corporation et al.,* 11 FPC 486 (1952), and Commission Opinion 225, 11 FPC 43 (1952).

23. Given that demand charges were set by peak loads, the formula reduced costs allocated to peak-load service relative to off-peak service when compared with costs as they would have been allocated on a volume basis. If the gas purchased during the three days of greatest demand during the year were bought entirely by retail utility buyers, then charges for this group would be reduced.

24. *Atlantic Seaboard Corp.* v. *F.P.C.,* 404 F 2d 1268 (1968) at 1271. See also Alfred E. Kahn, *The Economics of Regulation: Principles and Institutions* (Wiley, 1970), Vol. I, p. 99.

25. *Atlantic Seaboard Corp.* v. *F.P.C.* at 1270.

26. Further tests have been made of the effects of the historical costing procedure. It was hypothesized that the use of historical costs to set prices might have let pipelines make excessive profits in the sense that, as demand increased over time, unit costs fell with fixed prices. The test was to determine whether unit costs fell and margins increased for companies involved in cases in years immediately following landmark decisions. For the eight companies engaged in case proceedings in 1961 and 1962, this did not occur; in general, operating or out-of-pocket costs per Mcf declined from 1961 to 1967, but average receipts on regulated sales also declined and at a somewhat faster rate. No matter how receipts net of out-of-pocket costs were divided for accounting purposes (between depreciation, interest costs, and profits), these receipts did not increase per unit of sales or per unit of capital. Similar tests were completed for a sample of pipelines without regard to the occurrence of cases. Choosing the largest ten and the second largest ten pipelines, we reached similar results. By the measure $(R - AC)/K,$ equal to receipts from regulated sales minus operating costs per unit of net capital stock, the net cash flow per unit of capital expenditure did not increase on balance over the decade. There were increases in the middle 1960s and decreases in the late 1960s. This is shown by statistics for net cash flow per dollar of capital stock for "major classes A and B pipelines" as designated by the Federal Power Commission: $0.149 (1962); $0.160 (1964); $0.148 (1966); $0.090 (1968); $0.066 (1970). The failure of this flow to increase over time demonstrates that profits did not rise. This suggests once again that markets rather than FPC price setting put a ceiling on profits.

See FPC, *Statistics of Interstate Natural Gas Pipeline Companies,* annual volumes.

27. The term "A-J-W models" refers to Harvey Averch and Leland L. Johnson, "Behavior of the Firm under Regulatory Constraint," *American Economic Review*, Vol. 52 (December 1962), pp. 1052–69, and Stanislaw H. Wellisz, "Regulation of Natural Gas Pipeline Companies: An Economic Analysis," *Journal of Political Economy*, Vol. 71 (February 1963), pp. 30–43.

28. Price discrimination can be, and usually is, far more complex than simply having a single price for each class of customers. For example, each group could be charged a fixed fee, or demand charge, to obtain service and then a commodity price P_1 per unit of service used. To incorporate this and other complexities into the model does not change any of the primary results, however, and so the simpler, less realistic model is used throughout.

29. This follows closely on William J. Baumol and Alvin K. Klevorick, "Input Choices and Rate-of-Return Regulation: An Overview of the Discussion," and Israel Pressman, "A Mathematical Formulation of the Peak-Load Pricing Problem," both in the *Bell Journal of Economics and Management Science*, Vol. 1 (Autumn 1970), pp. 162–90 and 304–26, respectively. Although we discuss pricing rather than input-factor ratios, for testing purposes, our propositions do not differ in essence from the ones in these two articles.

30. The first-order conditions for maximum profits R subject to the constraint $(q_1 + q_2) \leq K$ include the price difference $P_1 - P_2 = \partial C/\partial q_1 - \partial C/\partial q_2$, the difference in costs of transport at the margin. Under conditions in which the firms can discriminate on prices for different amounts consumed by the buyer, the change in revenues on intramarginal units of sales is $q_1 \partial P/\partial q_1 = \partial \alpha_1/\partial q_1$, the change in demand charges. As such, the two terms cancel out and thus do not enter the comparison between buyers.

31. A collusive arrangement for pricing is not stable unless capacity constraints force each firm involved to produce less than it would find optimal. In the long run, the colluding firm will expand output as long as price exceeds marginal cost, whereas a collusive agreement to maximize the profits of the industry requires that marginal costs fall short of price (and equal marginal revenues). Thus, eventually, a workable collusive agreement on price must also include a collusive agreement to limit the output of each firm.

32. That is, first-order conditions for maximizing R subject to $q_1 + q_2 \leq K$ include $P_1(1 + 1/e_1) - P_2(1 + 1/e_2) = \partial C/\partial q_1 - \partial C/\partial q_2$, where $\partial C/\partial q_1, \partial C/\partial q_2$ are marginal costs of transport for the two classes of service. The elasticity of demand is the percentage change in sales that would result from a 1 percent change in price in the opposite direction. For example, if the elasticity of demand is e_1, a ρ percent drop in P_1 will cause q_1 to increase by $e_1 \rho$ percent.

33. The relationship expressed in equation 2-3 can be formulated alternatively as $MR_1(q_1) - MC(q_1) = MR_2(q_2) - MC(q_2)$, where $MR_1(q_1)$ and $MR_2(q_2)$ are the marginal revenues of the two services at outputs q_1 and q_2. (The marginal revenue is the effect on total revenue if the firm attempts to sell one more unit of output. Since the firm will have to lower its price to achieve greater sales, the marginal revenue is less than the starting price.) Equation 2-4 requires that the difference between marginal revenue and marginal costs be the same for both services and that this difference equal the value of a unit of capacity.

If all capacity is used in producing the output that maximizes profits and if a capacity larger than K could produce even greater profits, then the first-order conditions also require that marginal revenues exceed marginal costs for each service. Otherwise, marginal revenues must equal marginal costs in both markets.

34. The reasoning behind equation 2-4 proceeds as follows. Maximizing revenues subject to the two constraints calls for maximizing $L = P_1 q_1 + P_2 q_2 - C(q_1, q_2, K) +$

$\lambda[M - P_1q_1 + \gamma C(q_1, q_2, K)] + \mu(K - q_1 - q_2)$. The Kuhn–Tucker conditions for a maximum include:

$$(1 - \lambda)P_1(1 + 1/e_1) - (1 - \lambda\gamma)\partial C/\partial q_1 = \mu \text{ or } q_1 = 0$$
$$P_2(1 + 1/e_2) - (1 - \lambda\gamma)\partial C/\partial q_2 = \mu \text{ or } q_2 = 0$$
$$q_1 + q_2 = K \text{ or } \mu = 0$$
$$P_1q_1 - \gamma C = M \text{ or } \lambda = 0.$$

Assuming that both pipeline services are profitable at some level of output and that both constraints are binding (no part of current capacity is superfluous, and the profits allowed by regulation fall below the maximum possible unregulated profits), then these conditions imply:

$$P_1 = \frac{1}{(1 - \lambda)} \frac{(1 + 1/e_2)}{(1 + 1/e_1)} P_2 + \frac{(1 - \gamma\lambda)}{(1 - \lambda)} \frac{1}{(1 + 1/e_1)} (\partial C/\partial q_1 - \partial C/\partial q_2).$$

Here $q_1 + q_2 = K$, and $P_1q_1 - \gamma C = M$. In the text, $\delta = 1/(1 - \lambda)$.

Note that in equation 2-4 the terms λ and γ represent "regulatory constraint" effects on prices and outputs. The values they take can be inferred from the second-order conditions for maximizing profits subject to constraint. If marginal costs for transportation of the regulated service are constant as output changes, then the relevant second-order conditions for a maximum require that λ be less than or equal to one. If marginal costs are falling as output increases, λ also has to be less than or equal to one. But if marginal costs rise as output increases, λ can exceed unity. These results are demonstrated in detail in Paul W. MacAvoy and Roger Noll, "Relative Prices on Regulated Transactions of the Natural Gas Pipelines," *Bell Journal of Economics and Management Science*, Vol. 4 (Spring 1973), pp. 217–18 (n. 13).

35. The point is that the coefficients of P_2 and $[MC(q_1) - MC(q_2)]$ must be positive. In the case of $\lambda \geq 1$, $\delta \leq 0$ and $(1 + 1/e) \leq 0$ at the same time, so that the coefficients of P_2 and $[MC(q_1) - MC(q_2)]$ are both still positive, since the negative terms are multiplied together. This is demonstrated in *ibid.*, pp. 218–19 (n. 14).

36. Merely setting limits on total profits M can be compared with regulation by setting a maximum rate of return on capital. This rate-of-return procedure has the effect of enhancing the relative differences between unregulated and regulated prices shown above, at least when the procedure results in returns greater than the economic costs of capital. Consider the profit function $R' = P_1q_1 + P_2q_2 - r_1x_1 - r_2x_2$, where x_1 represents capital resources and x_2 noncapital resources available to the regulated firm at prices r_1, r_2, respectively. The restraint on profits is that $P_1q_1 - s_1x_1 - r_2x_2 = M$, where s_1 is the allowed rate of return on capital such that $s_1 - r_1 = V \geq 0$. The first-order conditions for maximizing $R = P_1q_1 - P_2q_2 - r_1x_1 - r_2x_2 - \lambda(q_1 + q_2 - x_1) - \lambda(P_1q_1 - \gamma s_1x_1 - \gamma r_2x_2 - M)$ include $(1 - \lambda)P_1(1 + 1/e_1) - (1 - \gamma\lambda)(r_1\partial x_1/\partial q_1 + r_2\partial x_2/\partial q_1) - (1 - \gamma\lambda)(s - r_1)\partial x_1/\partial q_1 = 0$ and $P_2(1 + 1/e_2) - (1 - \gamma\lambda)(r_1\partial x_2/\partial q_2 + r_2\partial x_2/\partial q_2) - (1 - \gamma\lambda)(s - r_1)\partial x_1/\partial q_2 = 0$. If marginal costs $\partial C/\partial q_1$ are defined as $(r_1\partial K/\partial q_1 + r_2\partial L/\partial q_2)$, then

$$P_1 = \frac{1}{(1 - \lambda)} \frac{(1 + 1/e_2)}{(1 + 1/e_1)} P_2 + \frac{(1 - \gamma\lambda)}{(1 - \lambda)} \frac{1}{(1 + 1/e_1)} \left\{ \frac{\partial C}{\partial q_1} - \frac{\partial C}{\partial q_2} \right\}$$
$$+ \frac{(1 - \gamma\lambda)}{(1 - \lambda)} \cdot \frac{1}{(1 + 1/e_1)} \cdot (s - r_1) \cdot \left\{ \frac{\partial x_1}{\partial q_1} - \frac{\partial x_1}{\partial q_2} \right\}.$$

The last term added on the right-hand side of the equation is greater than zero if the marginal cost difference is greater than zero, so that the relative price difference is enhanced when rate-of-return limits are set on regulated sales. It is as if there were a premium on costs for the excess allowed return; thus, whatever the effects on relative regulated prices from the regulatory constraint, these effects are greater under *this* regimen.

37. So far, in deriving conditions for relative prices the assumption has been that demands and costs are known and that regulation is continuous as well as certain. None of these conditions necessarily holds. Models with uncertainty should be constructed if they add greatly to the predictability of the certainty models. But, at this point, of the many promising uncertainty analyses, those based on monopoly market conditions with price as the decision variable differ little from the certainty-static models. (Compare the incisive review article by John J. McCall, "Probabilistic Microeconomics," *Bell Journal of Economics and Management Science*, Vol. 2 [Autumn 1971], pp. 403–33. McCall notes that "the strong sensitivity of results to stochastic assumptions is a clear warning that model building in probabilistic economics requires extreme caution and good sense" [p. 418].)

With models that assume stochastic variation in demand in all markets but greater variation where gas demand is highly elastic with respect to prices of other sources of energy, the finding is that prices under uncertainty would be lower than under certainty. (Compare Edwin S. Mills, "Uncertainty and Price Theory," *Quarterly Journal of Economics,* Vol. 73 [February 1959], pp. 116–30; Hayne E. Leland, "The Theory of the Firm Facing Uncertain Demand," Institute for Mathematics in the Social Sciences, Technical Report 24 [Stanford University, 1970; processed].) Here is a paradox. Since uncertain conditions occur most frequently in unregulated markets, almost by definition relative regulated prices shown by the models are higher than can be explained by the δ and e_1 terms in the coefficient for P_2. That is, uncertainty has the greatest effects in unregulated markets; yet these effects are manifest in regulated prices higher than justified by regulatory and demand conditions.

Of course, even continuous regulation could be uncertain, given that the profits allowed by case decision and administrative judgment have varied over time. The effect should appear in the estimated values of total profits M; because regulation could be either more or less severe, M would be subject to stochastic variation. The relative regulated prices would be uncertain in the same way as costs or demand were uncertain. The results would be the same: a pipeline company can be expected to act as if M were lower than actually was the case under FPC regulation. Given this state of affairs, rather than construct more complex analyses with uncertainty introduced explicitly, economists may as well evaluate the results from the certainty analysis in terms of whether some portion can be attributed to uncertainty.

38. The treatment here of average revenue as the commodity price, with zero demand price, is in line with the general practice of pipeline companies regarding demand price on industrial sales, according to a number of company executives who were interviewed.

39. In a few cases, there may have been a demand charge and a commodity charge on q_2. With $P_2^* = P_2 + w/q_2$ as the unit price, where w is the "demand" additive to the marginal or commodity charge, the equation stays essentially the same—that is, $P_1 = aP_2^* + b[mct(q_1) - mct(q_2)] + d$ with a, b as given above—but with the addition of a constant term d. The equation can be derived by substituting $P_2^* = P_2 + w/q_2$ in the appropriate objective functions for maximizing profits and then finding marginal pricing conditions as before in this chapter. If $\partial w/\partial q_2 \neq 0$, or charges in fact do vary with the amount of gas delivered, then an additional term appears. This additional term is the constant denoted d.

40. The eight companies are: Atlantic Seaboard, Colorado Interstate Corporation, Michigan Wisconsin Pipe Line, Natural Gas Pipeline Company of America, Tennessee Gas Transmission Corporation (a division of Tenneco), Texas Eastern Transmission, Transcontinental, and Trunkline Gas. (Note that Colorado Interstate is not located near the others.)

Information about these companies was taken from the annual volumes of *Statis-*

tics of Interstate Natural Gas Pipeline Companies issued by FPC from 1952 through 1967.

41. See, for example, Pietro Balestra and Marc Nerlove, "Pooling Cross Section and Time Series Data in the Estimation of a Dynamic Model: The Demand for Natural Gas," *Econometrica,* Vol. 34 (July 1966), pp. 585–612; Paul W. MacAvoy, "The Regulation-Induced Shortage of Natural Gas," *Journal of Law and Economics,* Vol. 14 (April 1971), pp. 167–99.

42. See Pietro Balestra, *The Demand for Natural Gas in the United States* (Amsterdam: North-Holland Publishing Co., 1967); H. S. Houthakker and Lester D. Taylor, *Consumer Demand in the United States, 1929–1970* (Harvard University Press, 1966).

43. The observations on regulated sales conform to market transactions in the sense that each set of observations is taken from a separate metropolitan region or market. But information on the forty-nine purchases by industrial buyers applies to fewer markets, since a number of them took place in the same metropolitan market regions. Also, prices for alternative industrial fuels were not obtained in sufficient detail to be useful. Therefore observations on industrial sales are more limited than they should be to indicate market behavior.

44. Division of a regression coefficient by its standard error can be used to test the hypothesis that the coefficient value is zero; the occurrence of a ratio greater than 1.6 generally leads to rejection of this hypothesis. For these effects to be statistically significant, the values of the coefficients divided by the values of the standard errors of the coefficients (shown in parentheses below the coefficients) should exceed 1.6; also, the coefficient of determination R^2 as a measure of "explained variance" from using the regression on the dependent variable q_1 should be close to 0.9.

45. Compare William S. Vickrey, *Microstatics* (Harcourt, Brace and World, 1964), pp. 337–38.

46. Here $P_1 - P_2 = \Delta P = (a - 1)P_2 + b[mct(q_1) - mct(q_2)] + d$ with $a = 1, d = 0$ because the samples q_1, q_2 have the same price elasticity and are carried by the same pipelines.

47. Compare Walter Y. Oi, "A Disneyland Dilemma: Two-Part Tariffs For A Mickey Mouse Monopoly," *Quarterly Journal of Economics,* Vol. 85 (February 1971), pp. 77–96, on the tradeoff between changes in demand and commodity prices along these lines.

48. *Ibid.,* pp. 84–85. For the retail utility sales, the term in b for $(1 + 1/e_1)$ should be replaced by $1 + (1 - Ns_1)/e_1$, where s_1 is the market share of the marginal consumer at the end of the line and N is the number of consumers. With the marginal consumers consisting of large retail buyers in the northern population centers, $1 - Ns_1 < 0$, and it is profitable to increase commodity prices at the farther locations by less than the marginal costs of additional transport.

49. Because errors in data on unregulated sales are more likely and can better be relegated to the dependent variable, a regression with P_2 as the dependent variable was worked out as follows:

$$P_2 = 1.104P_1 - 0.556[mct(q_1) - mct(q_2)] + 2.794L_1 + 5.098L_2 + 15.042L_3$$
$$(0.008) \quad (0.111) \qquad\qquad (0.248) \quad (0.714) \quad (0.535)$$
$$+ 9.163L_4 + 9.384L_5 - 9.717L_6$$
$$(0.705) \quad (0.819) \quad (1.003)$$
$$R^2 = 0.551$$

(The numbers in parentheses are the standard errors.)

50. Few further tests are possible with the L_i coefficients. The different pipelines have had different price levels for retail utility sales, perhaps because of different

degrees of regulatory control applied by the FPC but more likely because of historical variation in the prices paid for field supplies of gas. Earlier pipelines contracted at lower prices for gas supplies than pipelines constructed later, and, with these earlier prices in effect, the final sales prices of the earlier pipelines have been lower.

51. The fitted equation had P_2 as the dependent variable, as follows:

$$P_2 = 0.921AR_1 - 0.681[MC(q_1) - MC(q_2)]$$
$$(0.008) \qquad (0.132)$$
$$+ 2.699L_1 + 12.934L_2 + 3.096L_3$$
$$(0.297) \qquad (0.645) \qquad (0.856)$$
$$+ 5.468L_4 + 1.929L_5 - 0.681L_6$$
$$(0.983) \qquad (1.162) \qquad (0.132)$$
$$R^2 = 0.366$$

(The numbers in parentheses are the standard errors.)

52. If our reading of FPC motives is correct, it is easy to see how indicators of the economic costs of capital, such as those used in Tables 2-3 and 2-4, would be avoided. Prevention of controversy would be the goal, not analytical incisiveness.

CHAPTER THREE

1. 347 U.S. 672 (1954).

2. 15 USC 717(b) (1970).

3. *Interstate Transportation and Sale of Natural Gas,* H. Rept. 709, 75 Cong. 1 sess. (1937), p. 3. See also "Legislative History of the Natural Gas Act," *Georgetown Law Journal,* Vol. 44 (June 1956), p. 695.

4. This argument is advanced by Edmund W. Kitch, "Regulation of the Field Market for Natural Gas by the Federal Power Commission," *Journal of Law and Economics,* Vol. 11 (October 1968), pp. 243–80.

5. *Ibid.,* p. 256; *New York Times,* February 18, 1956.

6. The five areas were: (1) Permian Basin (Texas and part of New Mexico); (2) Southern Louisiana (including the offshore area in the Gulf of Mexico); (3) Hugoton-Anadarke (part of Oklahoma and Kansas); (4) Texas Gulf Coast; (5) Other Southwest (Mississippi, Arkansas, parts of Alabama, Louisiana, Texas, and Oklahoma).

7. On the development of the certification procedure, see Natural Gas Act, 52 Stat. 821 (1938), and 15 USC 717 (1964); *Atlantic Refining Co.* v. *Public Service Commission of New York,* 360 U.S. 378 (1959); Federal Power Commission, *Statement of General Policy,* No. 61-1, 24 FPC 818–20 (1960).

8. See *Southern Louisiana Area Rate Proceeding* (*Southern Louisiana Area*), 46 FPC 86, Opinion 598. Cited hereafter as *Louisiana Proceeding.*

9. See, for example, Paul H. Douglas, "The Case for the Consumer of Natural Gas," *Georgetown Law Journal,* Vol. 44 (June 1956), esp. p. 589, where he goes so far as to claim: "Competition in the field is limited by the domination of supply and reserves by a very few companies."

10. *Phillips Petroleum Company* v. *Wisconsin* 347 U.S. 672 (1954) at 685.

11. *Southern Louisiana Area Rate Cases* (*Austral Oil Co.* v. *Federal Power Commission*), 428 F 2d 407 (1970) at 416.

12. Clark A. Hawkins, *The Field Price Regulation of Natural Gas* (Florida State University Press, 1969), p. 248.

13. 34 FPC 159 (1956) at 182, n. 17; *Skelly Oil Co.* v. *FPC*, 375 F. 2d 6 (10th Cir. 1967); 390 U.S. 747 (1968).

14. Testimony of Professor Adelman before the Federal Power Commission, *Champlin Oil and Refining Co.*, Docket G-9277, p. 458 L.C., quoted in Paul W. Mac-Avoy, *The Crisis of the Regulatory Commissions* (Norton, 1970), p. 156; James W. McKie, "Market Structure and Uncertainty in Oil and Gas Exploration," *Quarterly Journal of Economics*, Vol. 74 (1960), p. 543.

15. As an example of this argument, see the testimony of Alfred E. Kahn in the Champlin Oil and Refining Company case, FPC Docket G-9277, p. 489.

16. Concentration was higher in the 1950–54 period in the mid-continent region, given that the four largest producers provided more than two-thirds of new reserves. But the four largest pipelines in this region purchased more than 90 percent of new reserves over this same period. The balance lay with the pipelines because high concentration on the supply side quickly disappeared, with the four largest producers providing only 28 percent in the 1956–58 period in the same region. See Paul W. Mac-Avoy, *Price Formation in Natural Gas Fields: A Study of Competition, Monopsony, and Regulation* (Yale University Press, 1962), Chaps. 5–7.

17. See *ibid.*, Chap. 8.

18. On this point, most of the economic theories of the regulated firm agree. The Averch-Johnson theory of the profit-maximizing firm subject to a constraint on rate of return implies no enhancement of the price paid for a noncapital input factor. See Harvey Averch and Leland L. Johnson, "Behavior of the Firm under Regulatory Constraint," *American Economic Review*, Vol. 52 (December 1962), pp. 1052–69; William J. Baumol and Alvin K. Klevorick, "Input Choices and Rate-of-Return Regulation: An Overview of the Discussion," *Bell Journal of Economics and Management Science*, Vol. 1 (Autumn 1970), pp. 162–90.

19. See MacAvoy, *Price Formation in Natural Gas Fields*, esp. Chap. 5.

20. This pattern occurred in the first complete area rate decision, *Permian Basin Area Rate Proceeding*, 34 FPC 159 (1965) at 160.

21. Assume that to discover and to produce a certain volume of gas and oil from a marginal well costs $100,000. Assume further that of this cost $70,000 is joint, $20,000 represents the separate cost of extracting oil, and $10,000 the separate cost of extracting gas. The producer will develop this well, selling both oil and gas, provided he can sell at least $20,000 worth of oil, at least $10,000 worth of gas, and an additional $70,000 worth of one or the other or both. He does not care whether the $70,000 comes entirely from gas sales, entirely from oil sales, or from some combination of the two. That will depend upon the relative strength of the demands of gas buyers and oil buyers for his products—a factor which will reflect supply and demand in each industry. Compare Alfred E. Kahn, *The Economics of Regulation: Principles and Institutions* (Wiley, 1970), Vol. I, pp. 79–83.

22. Correspondingly, a regulator would allow the hypothetical well owner mentioned in the preceding note to recover $100,000 by setting whatever combination of gas and oil prices was necessary to obtain this revenue. Similarly, the regulator would allow the owner of an intramarginal well (with, say, joint costs of $40,000, separate gas costs of $5,000, and separate oil costs of $10,000) to set whatever prices would obtain $55,000. Notice that in the intramarginal case if total production is sold for $55,000, the producer will lose $45,000 in rent, and gas and oil consumers together will pay $45,000 less than the free market price.

23. To be fair to the commission, joint production was not preponderant in the industry. After the mid-1950s, the number of joint wells diminished to the point where gas output from them accounted for less than 25 percent of total gas produc-

tion. And it has been strongly argued that exploration is "directional"—that gas and oil can be searched for separately, and usually one is not found as a result of a search for the other. Insofar as producers acted on this belief, exploration expenditures might have been more easily allocated to one or the other product. Nonetheless, joint expenditures were still sufficiently important to warp the pricing system.

24. Mr. Justice Jackson reached a similar conclusion in *Federal Power Commission* v. *Hope Natural Gas Co.*, 320 U.S. 591 (1944) at 645.

25. James M. Landis, *Report on Regulatory Agencies to the President-Elect* (1960), p. 54.

26. Some supporters of regulation argued that the supply of new gas is also fixed (or relatively inelastic). In their view a new gas price set below the level attainable in a free market would not cause much harm. Although the "low" price would cause a gas shortage, only a few potential customers would suffer, while all actual customers would benefit from lower prices. This view is enticing; yet all the problems that developed with the simpler arguments for tier pricing in fact apply to this rationale a fortiori.

27. Compare Paul G. Bradley, *The Economics of Crude Petroleum Production* (Amsterdam: North-Holland Publishing Co., 1967; New York: Humanities Press, 1968).

28. *Louisiana Proceeding,* Opinion 598.

29. U.S. Federal Power Commission, Bureau of Natural Gas, *Natural Gas Supply and Demand, 1971–1990,* Staff Report 2 (1972), Table 16, p. 123. The critical element in this estimate and forecast is the judgment of the industry's Future Requirements Committee as regards demand.

30. "Columbia Gas Will Limit New Commitments to Sell Natural Gas," *Wall Street Journal,* April 10, 1970, p. 36.

31. Testimony of M. D. Borger before the Federal Power Commission, *Louisiana Proceeding,* Docket AR 69-1, pp. 5–6, 8, 10 (in a preprint version of Borger's testimony).

32. Federal Power Commission, Bureau of Natural Gas, *The Gas Supplies of Interstate Natural Gas Pipeline Companies, 1968* (1970), p. 14; FPC, Bureau of Natural Gas, *Natural Gas Supply and Demand, 1971–1990* (1972), p. xi.

33. *Louisiana Proceeding,* Opinion 546-A. To the extent that the commission's policy reflected the view of its chairman at that time, it is interesting to note that the gas shortage prompted FPC Chairman John N. Nassikas to take a stance on a national issue outside his agency's jurisdiction. Because new gas reserves were in short supply, he urged that oil import quotas be maintained as an incentive for seeking gas. This position seemed to imply that oil prices should be kept uneconomically high to make up for gas prices kept too low by the FPC. In any case, quota maintenance was probably inexpedient within interrelated markets for energy sources, since higher prices for oil increase orders for gas as a substitute boiler fuel, adding to excess demand. See "Supplementary Views of the Chairman, Federal Power Commission: Impact on the Natural Gas and Electric Utility Industries," in Cabinet Task Force on Oil Import Control, *The Oil Import Question: A Report on the Relationship of Oil Imports to the National Security* (1970), pp. 369–89.

34. In principle, the distributors represented the residential buyers in bargaining with pipelines and thereby indirectly with producers for dedicated reserves. One must assume that the buyers did not understand their own preferences for reserves, or that the social cost of a production failure exceeds the sum of private costs to the affected buyers, before one can justify *economically* the commission's decision to set a particular reserve requirement *administratively.*

35. In theory at least, a longer waiting period for production imposes higher costs on the supplier, necessitating higher contract prices to the pipelines. This cost increase was not reflected in significantly higher prices on long-term contracts, however, during the period just before area rate regulation. See MacAvoy, *Price Formation in Natural Gas Fields,* pp. 262–65.

36. Federal Power Commission, Bureau of Natural Gas, *National Gas Supply and Demand* (1969), p. 18. A twenty-year reserve "backing" is equivalent to twelve years' "deliverability"—that is, twelve years' production at all field capacities from which the committed reserves come.

37. Calculated from data given in American Gas Association, *Reserves of Crude Oil, Natural Gas Liquids, and Natural Gas in the United States and Canada as of December 31, 1968* (1969), p. 126. Cited hereafter as *Reserves of Crude Oil and Natural Gas.*

38. The 1947 depletion rate is taken to be representative of depletion of old interstate pipeline reserves in 1964–68; for large-scale development of the interstate lines began approximately in 1947, and the initial reserves were probably being depleted at this rate.

39. The market analyzed here is delimited by the territory in which the pipelines taking gas for resale along the East Coast made their purchases. The area roughly comprises Texas Railroad Commission Districts 1–7 and 10; also Louisiana, Kansas, and Oklahoma.

40. The data used in the regressions and simulations were all obtained from publicly available sources. These consisted of the official publications of various federal agencies and the publications of professional associations related to the petroleum industry. A brief description of the data sources for each variable follows.

Reserves ΔR_{tj}: the figures used represent the additional reserves discovered in a given oil-producing district in a given year. The series is taken from American Gas Association, *Reserves of Crude Oil and Natural Gas,* pp. 120, 175–219. The data file contains the values for the 1954–68 period, expressed in billions of cubic feet.

Production ΔQ_{tj}: the figures in this series refer to the deliveries made by natural gas producers to interstate pipeline companies in 1967, in the first year of a basic contract. The figures were obtained from FPC Form 2 reports submitted by purchasing pipeline companies to the FPC, either in the succeeding year of the contract or two years thereafter.

The figures include additions to and modifications of the original contract. They exclude intrastate sales. The contracts have a nominal life of twenty years, although they remain in force until such time as the FPC issues a certificate permitting the discontinuation of supply from a given contract. The production is expressed in billions of cubic feet.

Prices P_{tj}: the price series relates to the production series described above. It is the average price at which the production in new contracts in a given year in a given district was sold to the interstate pipeline companies. The data are taken from the independent producer rate schedule filings in certificate applications.

Development drilling W_{tj}: figures for the period 1954–66 were obtained from the Review/Forecast issue of the *Oil & Gas Journal,* published annually the last week of January. The numbers refer to field wells completed by gas producers, including condensate producers.

Distance M_j: the variable expresses the pipeline distance between the center of a drilling region and the center of the area of consumption. Los Angeles is the consumption center for gas produced in Texas Railroad Commission (TRRC) Districts 7e, 8, 8a, and 9, the San Juan Basin (New Mexico Northwest), and the Permian

Basin (New Mexico Southeast). Cleveland is the consumption center for TRRC Districts 7b and 10, North Louisiana, Southern Louisiana, Southern Louisiana Offshore, Oklahoma, and Kansas.

Fuel price index fp_t: the price index for fuel, power, and lighting materials was obtained from the U.S. Bureau of Labor Statistics wholesale price and price index series. The average annual figures for the years 1955–68 were used.

Rate of interest i_t: the arguments for use of one or the other interest rate as the "economic indicator" are extensive and controversial and cannot be dealt with here. On institutional grounds, Moody's composite average of yields on public utility bonds was used; this rate indicated the costs of a major source of public utility funds, including pipeline company funds. The rate of equity capital could not have been independent of the composite bond yield, although it may not have been determined by the yield.

Capital stock K_t: the national stock of gas-burning furnaces shown as the annual shipments of gas furnaces under "heating equipment" in U.S. Department of Commerce, *Survey of Current Business,* as accumulated over the period 1954–68, and published biennially by the department in *Business Statistics.*

Oil price op_t: "Price at wells (Oklahoma)," as shown in *Survey of Current Business.*

41. The "hat" variables $\hat{W}_{tj}$, $\hat{P}_{tj}$ use values fitted from the first-stage regressions of the four endogenous variables on the purely exogenous variables, to reduce the effect of simultaneous determination of (a) both independent and dependent endogenous variations by (b) the exogenous variables. The simultaneity effect produces inconsistent estimates; two-stage least squares eliminated this inconsistency.

Compare with Phoebus J. Dhrymes, *Econometrics: Statistical Foundations and Applications* (Harper & Row, 1970), pp. 167–74.

42. The sets of variables $\Sigma a_i J_i$ and $\Sigma b_i J_i$ are district dummy variables taking the value one for observations from that district J and zero otherwise. This method of treatment of the geological differences between districts follows from Franklin M. Fisher, *Supply and Costs in the U.S. Petroleum Industry: Two Econometric Studies* (Johns Hopkins Press for Resources for the Future, 1964). The occurrence of similar gas deposits in a district from year to year results in a large coefficient for the dummy variable for that district; as such, these J variables approximate systematic geological conditions. The values of the coefficients, and their t-statistics, are as follows:

	a_j	t value	b_j	t value
J_1	104.15	2.98	86.07	0.18
J_2	−55.15	−1.64	−716.58	−1.51
J_3	147.83	4.23	1,002.06	2.13
J_4	64.60	1.85	−74.97	−0.15
J_5	−10.24	−0.23	−188.40	−0.40
J_6	123.49	3.54	−86.41	−0.17
J_7	214.22	6.15	5,937.45	12.53
J_8	225.04	6.45	−105.86	−0.19
J_9	305.87	8.72	782.70	1.21
J_{10}	212.48	6.06	−372.57	−0.59

where the values of a_j are in numbers of wells and the values of b_j are in billions of cubic feet of new reserves per annum.

43. The usual test for significance is a value of the ratio (estimated coefficient)/ (estimated standard deviation) greater than 1.6; here the ratio values are given in parentheses below the coefficients.

44. Three other constructs were fitted to the data, as well. One system used lagged values of the dependent variable $\Delta R_{t-1,\ j}$ and $W_{t-1,\ j}$ in place of the district dummy variables. The second was fitted in the logarithms of all variables, and the third was fitted in the logarithms of the demand variables only. Of the four systems, the one reported in the text simulates best the 1955–60 experience in reserves, production, and price.

45. This conclusion is based on the premise that supply conditions—as in the equations pertaining to wells and reserves—stayed the same in the 1960s as they had been in the 1950s. To the contrary, however, supply equations may have changed so that less new reserves would have been forthcoming at prices ranging from 20 cents to 28 cents. (If so, then prices would have been higher under market clearing —unless regulation itself had caused the supply functions to change.) An initial test for functional changes is to compare the actual reserves in 1961–68 with simulated reserves which are calculated on the basis of simulation values obtained at *actual* prices. These simulated reserves are 61.4 trillion cubic feet greater than the actual 36.6 trillion cubic feet shown in Table 3-3 (and 12.0 trillion less than the 110.0 for "market-clearing" prices). Thus it might be concluded that the supply functions changed over the 1960s. This could have occurred because of attrition of in-ground deposits (or other geological conditions), or it could have happened because of dampened supplier incentives under price controls. The first possibility implies that the conclusions of the following section on the shortage experience by consumers is overstated. But the second possibility implies that these conclusions are if anything understated.

46. "Statement of John N. Nassikas" in *Natural Gas Policy Issues,* Hearings before the Senate Committee on Interior and Insular Affairs, 92 Cong. 2 sess. (1972), Pt. 1, Tables 1 and 3, pp. 268, 270.

47. The period from 1962 to 1968 can be described as that in which gas sales were "reallocated" between classes of customers. Balestra calls 1950–56 an "innovating" period in which pipelines were built and service begun; 1957–62 was a "maturing" period in which more gas was sold to the same customers. See Pietro Balestra, *The Demand for Natural Gas in the United States: A Dynamic Approach for the Residential and Commercial Market* (Amsterdam: North-Holland Publishing Co., 1967), esp. sec. 4.3.4.

48. Reply Submittal of the FPC, Office of Economics, Initial Rates for Future Sales of Natural Gas for All Areas, Docket R-389A (October 1970), pp. 12, 19, of preprint supplied by FPC.

49. FPC, *Sales by Producers of Natural Gas to Interstate Pipeline Companies,* various issues.

50. For the kind of loss referred to here, economists use the term "consumers' surplus." Consumers' surplus is defined as the excess over the price charged which consumers are willing to pay for a given amount of a product rather than do without it. (See George Stigler, *The Theory of Price* [3d ed., Macmillan, 1966], p. 78.) When a market is at equilibrium, the market-clearing price equals what consumers are willing to pay for the last or marginal unit of output. Since consumers would normally be willing to pay more for intramarginal units of output, the equilibrium price affords them a savings or "surplus" on these intramarginal units. The savings of this kind which gas consumers who in fact experienced a shortage could have realized under unregulated conditions is a measure of the cost to them of FPC policy. The consumers' surplus created through the policy can be explained and diagrammed as follows:

At the level of production supplied under price ceilings Q_{FPC}, consumers, as represented by the pipelines, were willing to pay a price for gas not only above the FPC ceiling P_{FPC} but considerably above the market-clearing price P_{market}. Moreover, for each unit of additional production up to market-clearing levels Q_{market}, consumers were willing to pay more than the market-clearing price. Thus the area of the triangle ABF in the diagram below is equal to the difference between what consumers doing without gas were willing to pay for additional production ($Q_{market} - Q_{FPC}$) and what they would have actually had to pay for it under market-clearing conditions (equivalent to the rectangle $BFHG$). This surplus which consumers who actually did without gas would have obtained under hypothesized market-clearing conditions represents the losses to them from FPC price ceilings.

These losses to consumers doing without gas can be compared to the gains by consumers who obtained new gas production. These gains are represented by the area of the rectangle $CBED$. This area is the difference between the market-clearing and FPC price ($P_{market} - P_{FPC}$) multiplied by the quantity of new gas production they received (Q_{FPC}). If the area of triangle ABF were at least equal to the area of rectangle $CBED$, then the gains to those who received gas would offset the losses by those who had to do without.

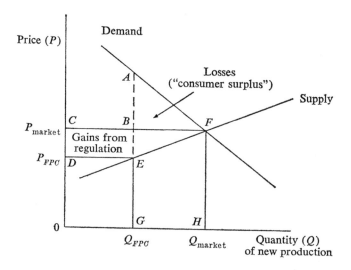

51. In other words, in the diagram given in the previous note, the length of line AB was, in fact, at least twice the length of line BE by the last years of the test period. Since the shortage of new production by 1967–68 exceeded the actual supply of new production, line BF was greater than line CB. Thus the area of the triangle ABF was at least equal to the area of the rectangle $CBED$.

52. Strictly speaking, the model shows consumer losses being at least equal to consumer gains only with regard to *additional* production during the test years. There may have been price changes on old production as well (because of the existence of "favored nations" clauses). Also, the supply curve may have shifted up and to the left for one of two reasons (see n. 45 in the present chapter). If the shift occurred because of depletion of deposits, so that supply pivoted on E in the diagram above and intersected the triangle ABF, the consumers' surplus was less than calculated here.

But if supply pivoted on E because of *regulation-induced* disincentives (fear of future price stringency, for example), then the area ABF has been correctly estimated.

53. See, for example, "Statement of Joseph C. Swidler, Chairman, New York State Public Service Commission," in *Natural Gas Policy Issues*, Pt. 1, p. 282.

54. *Southern Louisiana Area Rate Cases*, 428 F 2d 407 (1970) at 416, n. 9.

CHAPTER FOUR

1. Privately owned utilities account for about 75 percent of all electric energy sold in the United States. Nearly 92 percent of private sales to ultimate consumers are made by vertically integrated companies. Thus wholesale sales by private companies amount to about 6 percent of all sales according to Leonard W. Weiss, "An Evaluation of Antitrust in the Electric Power Industry" (paper prepared for a Brookings Institution conference, 1971), pp. 5, 6 (cited hereafter as "Antitrust in the Electric Power Industry").

2. *Report on Regulatory Agencies to the President-Elect*, prepared by the staff of the Senate Committee on the Judiciary, 86 Cong. 2 sess. (1960).

3. Federal Power Commission, *National Power Survey: A Report by the Federal Power Commission, 1964* (1964).

4. Federal Power Commission, *Prevention of Power Failures: Report to the President* (1967), Vols. I and II.

5. For a discussion of this strategy, see Alfred E. Kahn, *The Economics of Regulation: Principles and Institutions* (Wiley, 1971), Vol. II, pp. 77–86.

6. Weiss, "Antitrust in the Electric Power Industry," pp. 1, 5–6.

7. William K. Jones, *Cases and Materials on Regulated Industries* (Foundation Press, 1967), p. 14; *Federal Power Commission News*, Vol. 5 (February 25, 1972), p. 1.

8. FPC, *National Power Survey, 1964*, p. 14; FPC, *The 1970 National Power Survey* (1971), Pt. 1, Table 18.10.

9. Jones, *Cases and Materials on Regulated Industries*, pp. 26–35.

10. 16 USC 791–823.

11. 15 USC 79.

One of the charges against the holding companies was that rivalries among them prevented the formation of geographically contiguous systems of efficient size. See Twentieth Century Fund, Power Committee, *Electric Power and Government Policy: A Survey of the Relations Between the Government and the Electric Power Industry* (1948), pp. 343–50; Richard S. Wirtz, "Electric-Utility Interconnections: Power to the People," *Stanford Law Review*, Vol. 21 (June 1969), pp. 1714–33.

12. In *Public Utilities Commission of Rhode Island* v. *Attleboro Steam and Electric Company*, 273 U.S. 83 (1927), it had been held that selling electricity across state lines constituted interstate commerce.

13. See *Public Utility Holding Companies*, Hearings before the House Committee on Interstate and Foreign Commerce, 74 Cong. 1 sess. (1935), Pt. 3, pp. 2165–66.

14. The simulation models for determining these decisions are reviewed by Dennis Anderson, "Models for Determining Least-Cost Investments in Electricity Supply," *Bell Journal of Economics and Management Science*, Vol. 3 (Spring 1972), pp. 276–83.

15. The 1964 *National Power Survey* (p. 189) provides an example: Suppose the aggregate generating unit outages on a given power system are not to exceed reserves more than one day in ten years. For a hypothetical group of five identical power systems—every system consisting of twenty equal-size generating units and every unit

subject to an outage rate of 1 percent—the reserve requirement for each of the systems, based on separate operation, would be equivalent to three generating units, or 15 percent of total capacity. Thus for all five systems the aggregate reserve requirement would amount to fifteen generating units. On the other hand, if the five systems were to coordinate their use of reserve capacity, forming a pool of a hundred identical units, the aggregate reserve requirement would be reduced to only six units, or 6 percent of total capacity. The overall savings in capacity requirements would be the equivalent of nine generating units. See C. J. Baldwin, "Probability Calculation of Generation Reserves," *Westinghouse Engineer,* Vol. 29 (March 1969), pp. 34–40. The advice of T. J. Nagel of American Electric Power Co. has been helpful on this point and on many others.

16. Marc Nerlove, "Returns to Scale in Electricity Supply," in Carl Christ and others, *Measurement in Economics* (Stanford University Press, 1963); Phoebus J. Dhrymes and Mordecai Kurz, "Technology and Scale in Electricity Generation," *Econometrica,* Vol. 32 (July 1964), pp. 287–315; Malcolm Galatin, *Economies of Scale and Technological Change in Thermal Power Generation* (Amsterdam: North-Holland Publishing Co., 1968).

17. See William R. Hughes, "Scale Frontiers in Electric Power," in William M. Capron (ed.), *Technological Change in Regulated Industries* (Brookings Institution, 1971), p. 48, where this consensus view of elasticity is assessed.

18. According to Edison Electric Institute, *Report on Equipment Availability for the Eleven-Year Period, 1960–1970,* No. 71-26 (New York: EEI, 1971), pp. 5–7, forced outage rates for units larger than 600 megawatts were much higher in the 1960s than rates for smaller units. Smaller units, however, tend to be older units, so that the cause could be declining quality of workmanship over time. American Electric Power System officials report that newer equipment, regardless of size, has forced outage rates significantly higher than older equipment. They see no reason why size itself should affect the breakdown rate.

19. "PJM—America's Pioneer Power Pool," *Fact Card, 1970.*

20. *Electric Power Reliability,* Hearings before the Subcommittee on Communications and Power of the House Committee on Interstate and Foreign Commerce, 91 Cong. 1 sess. (1969), p. 362.

21. The survey of 1964 employed the figure of 12 percent. Various industry and state commissions in 1972 estimated the annual cost of capital investment to be 15 percent of the investment.

22. See FPC, *National Power Survey, 1964,* pp. 197, 286–87; Edison Electric Institute, "Supplementary Report on Load Diversity Based on 1962–68 Load Data" (New York: EEI, 1971; processed).

23. On safety margins and on the extent of actual 16-area coordination, see Phillip Sporn, "The U.S. National Power Survey—A Critique," CIGRE Paper 313 (Paris: Conference Internationale des Grands Réseaux Electriques, 1966; processed).

24. Hughes, "Scale Frontiers in Electric Power."

25. Approximately 22,000 miles of new high voltage line—345 kilovolt and over —were built between 1964 and 1970. See T. J. Nagel, "The National Grid—A Misconception," *Public Utilities Fortnightly,* Vol. 89 (January 6, 1972), p. 35, fig. 4.

26. Even when firms have contracts to buy and sell power, they cannot be certain those contracts will be adhered to or renewed. If Company X is free to sell its excess capacity elsewhere next year, Company Y will not design its system to minimize the cost of X-Y exchanges.

27. PJM's measurement of these savings consists of subtracting the actual cost of

supplying to an area (say, Area A) an increment of power out of a low-cost generator (say, located in Area B) from the cost of supplying power to that area out of a generator (in Area A) that would have been used if there were no coordination between areas. Since rates in the PJM region are set as though there were no coordination, Area A's company and Area B's company split this saving. In 1971, the savings amounted to about $31 million out of total sales of $2.2 billion (according to a letter to the authors from Wilmer Kleinbach, manager of PJM, March 27, 1971).

28. These findings are derived from submissions made by the regional councils to the National Electric Reliability Council for 1970 and 1971, as collected by the authors in February and March of 1972.

29. Projections at the beginning of the 1970s called for the joint building of 51 generating facilities with a capacity of about 37,000 megawatts between 1972 and 1976. This would constitute 15 to 20 percent of all new capacity planned for that period. *Electrical World,* Vol. 175 (March 15, 1971), pp. 55, 57–58.

30. The estimate includes only units larger than 200 megawatts, the assumption being that units below that size are intended strictly for peaking capacity. See Hughes, "Scale Frontiers in Electric Power."

31. In Table 4-2, the estimates of average size take into account only those planned units which will have a capacity of 200 megawatts or larger.

32. Weiss, "Antitrust in the Electric Power Industry," pp. 23–25, has compared the size of generating units built by members of twenty coordination groups (which *he* calls "pools") with the size of units built by firms outside the groups. He finds that members of nine such groups built larger generating units than did outside firms. His data also show that all members of centrally dispatched pools (which *we* call "pools"), except those in the new NYPOOL, built larger generating units than did outside firms. Moreover, holding companies tend to build larger units than do companies belonging to pools, so that perhaps not even strong pooling is sufficient to achieve the full benefits of coordination. The results from Weiss's regression analyses are unclear, however, with respect to the probable collinearity of certain variables.

33. Given that the scale differences are probably more than 60 percent, and with cost elasticity of 0.8, the cost differences are thus more than $(0.60) - (0.60) (0.80) = 0.12$.

34. Forced outage—stoppage of service necessitated by malfunctions and maintenance requirements—is figured as a percentage of total possible service hours. For units with a capacity of 800 to 1,100 megawatts, the FPC predicted forced outage rates of 11.8 percent during the first two years of service and 5.9 percent thereafter (*National Power Survey,* Pt. 2, p. 406). Actual forced outage for units 600 to 2,000 megawatts in size averaged 13.5 percent between 1960 and 1970 (Edison Electric Institute, *Report on Equipment Availability for 1960–1970* [EEI, 1971], p. 24). There has not yet been enough experience with the largest units, however, to predict future forced outage rates with confidence.

35. E. M. Mabuce, R. L. Wilks, and S. B. Boxerman, "Generation Reserve Requirements—Sensitivity to Variations in System Parameters" (unpublished paper received from E. M. Mabuce, Union Electric Co., St. Louis, 1972). In an accompanying letter the authors state that they used "numerical techniques rather than classical mathematics" and that "the several curves shown in our paper were derived empirically from results computed at many unique points."

36. From interviews with electricity managers, the authors of the present volume judge this to be a reasonable figure.

37. J. A. Casazza and C. H. Hoffman, "Relationship between Pool Size, Unit Size, and Transmission Requirements," CIGRE Paper 32-09, Haute Tension 22d,

1968 (Paris: Conference Internationale des Grands Réseaux Electriques, 1969; processed).

38. See similar studies by C. J. Baldwin, "Reserve Sharing Is Primary Benefit from Power Pooling," *Power Engineering*, Vol. 70 (April 1966), pp. 59–61; G. H. McDaniel and A. F. Gabrielle, "Load Diversity—Its Role in Power System Utilization," Institute of Electrical and Electronics Engineers, *IEEE Transactions, Power Apparatus and Systems*, Vol. 84 (July 1965), pp. 626–35.

39. We overstate the extent of existing coordination because any reserve saving figure derived directly from present engineering studies has to be discounted to reflect the fact that independent systems are now often physically interconnected; they now rely to *some* extent for planning purposes upon the availability of the reserves of others to meet emergencies. We assume that systems loosely coordinated with each other discount the worth of reserves held by others by, say, 50 percent—a figure that our interviews with electricity officials suggests is reasonable. This discount is reflected in our projection of a move by all company-sized systems from 10,000 megawatts (when most are less than that) to 30,000 or 40,000 megawatts.

40. One must use very crude methods to estimate reserve savings because engineering studies based upon the characteristics and future plans of individual systems throughout the nation—studies that would allow economists to determine the amount of potential saving more accurately—have not been completed. The Federal Power Commission and the National Electric Reliability Council publish statistics showing, region by region, future building plans and expected future reserve capacity. According to NERC, future plans are adequate to meet reliability standards. But these statistics cannot be used to determine the extent to which companies are overbuilding. The regions and the systems within them have different mixes of generating unit size; different fuels are used; weather conditions vary; the length of peak times varies; different regions use different assumptions about outage probability; and even the reliability standards that producers plan to meet vary from place to place. To determine the potential savings accurately, it would be necessary to examine engineering models or studies actually used for planning by individual systems. One would try to uncover the assumptions made about the value to a system of the reserves of others; then recalculate the system's needs under the assumption that the system treated all interconnected reserves as if they were its own; and finally compare results. Such studies, by using actual plans and by holding complicating factors and assumptions constant, would provide a better idea of the extent of possible reserve savings. The commission or NERC might undertake such studies, but so far they have not done so.

41. The rise in construction costs was estimated from announcements in *Nuclear Week* and other trade newspapers. The estimate is conservative in that it allows nothing for savings on the interconnection and pooling of *old* capacity. We judge that the location and sizing of old plants has been so far from optimal for central dispatch that—starting now—no cost savings on them would be achieved.

As for capacity, a 6,000-megawatt saving means $1.8 billion saved in construction costs. Assuming conservatively a 12 percent annual carrying charge, the annual saving comes to $216 million.

For reserves, we have calculated that coordination would save 6 percent in capacity, but possibly the reserves needed to serve capacity already installed cannot be reduced so easily.

42. PJM reports to us in private correspondence that coordination has produced operating cost savings of 1.5 percent, or about $31 million per year. Assuming in-

dustry operating costs of $40 billion per year by 1980, such a saving would amount to $600 million per year.

43. The Averch-Johnson analysis depends upon (1) a firm having monopoly power, the exercise of which is inhibited by regulation, and (2) a regulator that allows the firm to earn a rate of return that exceeds its costs of capital. In such circumstances a firm will increase its profits by borrowing at rate y to increase its capital investment, earning return x by raising its prices and returning the surplus $x - y$ to its shareholders. See Harvey Averch and Leland L. Johnson, "Behavior of the Firm Under Regulatory Constraint," *American Economic Review,* Vol. 52 (December 1962), pp. 1052–69. The argument that this effect has discouraged industry rationalization is made in William G. Shepherd and Thomas G. Gies, *Utility Regulation: New Directions in Theory and Policy* (Random House, 1966), pp. 12, 51–53.

It should be noted that the testable hypothesis from Averch-Johnson is the matter of increasing departures of capital-labor ratios from the least-cost ratio, as the rate of return allowed is reduced toward the cost of capital. See William J. Baumol and Alvin K. Klevorick, "Input Choices and Rate-of-Return Regulation: An Overview of the Discussion," *Bell Journal of Economics and Management Science,* Vol. 1 (Autumn 1970), pp. 162–90. The occurrence of increased capital costs from under-coordination does not imply increased capital-labor or capital-fuel ratios over those that would occur without electricity regulation. There is also no evidence that changes in the extent of coordination were caused by changes in rates of return—as would be posited by Averch-Johnson.

44. Cf. Thomas G. Moore, "The Effectiveness of Regulation of Electric Utility Prices," *Southern Economic Journal,* Vol. 36 (April 1970), pp. 365–75.

45. Cf. Baumol and Klevorick, "Input Choices and Rate-of-Return Regulation."

46. Moreover, in recent years, many producers have been unable to earn more annually than about twice their interest obligations to bondholders (68 percent had a debt cover of under 2.3; 34 percent under 2.0). See Federal Power Commission, *Statistics of Privately Owned Electric Utilities* (1970). Under mortgage indenture agreements, common in the industry, a firm cannot increase its indebtedness unless it will earn at least twice its interest obligation on existing and new debts combined. Thus many firms have had difficulty financing necessary new investment. Under such circumstances, they have no reason to seek to build unneeded plants.

47. See Bruce C. Netschert, Abraham Gerber, and Irwin M. Stelzer, "Competition in the Energy Markets," in *Competitive Aspects of the Energy Industry,* Hearings before the Subcommittee on Antitrust and Monopoly of the Senate Committee on the Judiciary, 91 Cong. 2 sess. (1970), p. 201.

48. The committee problem and disagreements over cost apportionment led to the breakup of two long-established groups: CARVA in Virginia and the Carolinas and ILLMO in Illinois and Missouri. Neither of these groups centrally dispatched electricity, but they were frequently cited as examples of close planning coordination. For example, see Hughes, "Scale Frontiers in Electric Power," p. 60.

49. A centrally dispatched pool will operate suboptimally unless the interests of each company and the pool as a whole are identical, which sometimes they are not. PJM, for example, encourages companies to dispatch electricity from the unit with the lowest incremental costs in the system by allowing the company owning that unit and the company that would otherwise have dispatched electricity from a unit with higher incremental costs to split the "saving." But the latter company may be reluctant to accept the offer when a lesser load means fewer sales to help cover its unit's *fixed* costs. Since it receives only half the "saving," its decision may differ from

that of a single company owning both units. Conversely, the company owning the low-cost unit may not wish to accept the offer if, for example, it has a fixed low-cost fuel supply which it would prefer to use where it can keep all resulting revenue—namely, in its own service area.

50. Most centrally dispatched pools allow each member company to provide reserves roughly in proportion to its capacity—an arrangement that may or may not produce optimal planning. State commissions, each anxious to protect the interests of the home state, may require a level of reserve capacity within the state that is excessive with regard to the system as a whole.

51. According to *Electrical World* (March 15, 1971), p. 57, U.S. electric companies plan to build 51 jointly owned plants by 1976.

52. See, for example, State of New York, Public Service Commission, Opinion and Order Granting Certificate of Environmental Compatibility and Public Need with Conditions (Opinion 72-2, January 25, 1972).

53. Direct opposition of environmental groups has delayed the construction of some transmission lines. This factor, however, has not been as important a cause of delay as is sometimes suggested. The Edison Electric Institute reported in 1970 that a survey of its members showed that late delivery of equipment, shortage of construction labor, and strikes were far more important causes (*Electric Power Reliability*, p. 484). The National Electric Reliability Council and the Edison Electric Institute suggest that in 1972 about a half-dozen planned transmission line installations were delayed by opposition from ecology groups. NERC, *Review of Overall Adequacy and Reliability of the North American Bulk Power Systems* (1971), Chap. 5; correspondence with J. Kearney, Edison Electric Institute, March 20, 1972.

54. See "Corporate Affiliation: The Promise and the Pitfalls," *Electrical World*, March 25, 1968, p. 22 (interview with Sherman Knapp, president of Northeast Utilities).

55. *Competitive Aspects of the Energy Industry*, Hearings before the Subcommittee on Antitrust and Monopoly of the Senate Committee on the Judiciary, 91 Cong. 2 sess. (1970), pp. 137–41.

56. See *California* v. *Federal Power Commission*, 369 U.S. 482 (1962); 41 *Federal Power Commission Reports* 846 (1969); 43 FPC 37 (1970); *Code of Federal Regulations*, No. 18 (1972), Pts. 1–149, sec. 2.11.

57. Edison Electric Institute figures show that about 40 mergers took place each year between 1961 and 1971, and nearly all of these involved firms with a total capacity of less than 1,000 megawatts each. This number is small in light of the several hundred private firms in the industry.

58. See Docket No. R-362, Order No. 383-1, FPC 37 (1970); Docket No. R-362, Order No. 383, 41 FPC (1969); 18 CFR (1972), secs. 211, 410.

59. We have examined the fifty-seven individual commission orders related to hydroelectric licensing issued between January 1969 and June 1970. Many of these orders dealt with minor matters; but the majority ended proceedings of two or three years' length. None of them contained conditions designed to force increased coordination.

60. 34 FPC 544 (1967); *FPC* v. *Florida Power & Light Co.*, 404 U.S. 453 (1972).

61. In re Western Massachusetts Electric Company, *Public Utilities Reports*, Vol. 76, 3d series (1968), p. 251; *Municipal Electric Association of Massachusetts* v. *FPC*, 414 F 2d 1206 (D.C. Cir. 1969), at 1208.

62. *Federal Power Commission* v. *Union Electric Co.*, 381 U.S. 90 (1965).

63. *Paris* v. *Kentucky Utility Co.*, 41 FPC 45 (1969) at 49. Cf. *Elbow Lake & Otter Tail Power Co.*, 46 FPC 675 (1971) at 679.

64. 16 USC 824(d), 824(f) (1970).

65. See the statement by former FPC Chairman Lee C. White in Martin Greenberger (ed.), *Computers, Communications, and the Public Interest* (Johns Hopkins Press, 1971), pp. 240–41.

66. *Electric Power Reliability*, pp. 590–912. See also *Federal Power Commission Oversight*, Hearings before the Subcommittee on Energy, Natural Resources, and the Environment of the Senate Committee on Commerce, 91 Cong. 2 sess. (1970), pp. 16–17, 39–43.

67. To obtain a rough idea of the importance of subjective judgment on even such a technical matter as the reserves necessary to meet a given standard of reliability, see G. S. Vassell and N. Tibberts, *Analysis of Generating-Capacity Reserve Requirements for Interconnected Power Systems*, IIE Paper 21 TP 92 (1971).

68. For a comprehensive survey of planning models, see Anderson, "Models for Determining Least-Cost Investments in Electricity Supply." Such models have been used by central planning authorities in a number of countries.

69. The models described by Anderson do not take into account the reliability level of existing transmission systems, environmental considerations, or the host of individual factors that affect the proper percentage reserve requirement for a particular system. In fact, Anderson describes models that go no further than to take a fixed percentage figure and assume that it represents a proper reserve.

70. Louis L. Jaffe, "The Effective Limits of the Administrative Process: A Reevaluation," *Harvard Law Review*, Vol. 67 (May 1954), p. 1107.

71. Weiss, "Antitrust in the Electric Power Industry," pp. 3–5.

72. See James R. Nelson, *Marginal Cost Pricing in Practice* (Prentice-Hall, 1964); Richard Pryke, *Public Enterprise in Practice* (St. Martins, 1972).

73. The Tennessee Valley Authority is generally acknowledged to be successful except in lowering environmental costs. On the other hand, experience with government-financed Rural Electrification Administration cooperatives is not a happy one from an economic point of view. Such firms enjoy government subsidized interest rates, which have helped to maintain small generating and distributing facilities of less than optimal size.

74. So far without success, proponents of such a system have introduced into Congress bills that would create a National Power Grid Corporation with directors appointed by the President. See H.R. 9970, 92 Cong. 1 sess. (1971). Their basic aim is the creation of regional corporations which would each own, plan, and operate generating and transmission facilities in a multistate area.

CHAPTER FIVE

1. *Report on Regulatory Agencies to the President-Elect* (1960), p. 85.

2. President's Advisory Council on Executive Organization, *A New Regulatory Framework: Report on Selected Independent Regulatory Agencies* (1971), pp. 5–6. The proposals in this report are examined in detail in Roger G. Noll, *Reforming Regulation* (Brookings Institution, 1971).

3. *Report on Regulatory Agencies to the President-Elect*, p. 55.

4. Price controls had a crucial effect on entry and on production in the 1960s. The controls suppressed entry, accelerated exit, and reduced production by reducing exploration and discovery by those companies that continued to operate. Thus it is impossible to gauge what supply concentration would be in a de-regulated market. We do know that concentration in new production was low in 1968 and 1969—sales from new production by the largest four producers ranging from 37 percent to

53 percent in the Permian, Mid Continent, and Gulf Coast market regions. In those same years, purchases by the four largest pipelines constituted respectively 50 percent (Gulf Coast), 76 percent (Mid Continent), and 90 percent (Permian) of demand. Given higher buyer concentration, conceivably under conditions of deregulation a preponderence of market power would remain with the pipelines on the buying side. In any case, there is no *new* evidence, beyond that in Chap. 3, showing producer market power.

For the most recent shares data and review of findings, see P. W. MacAvoy and R. S. Pindyck, "Competitive Market Conditions and Performance in the Natural Gas Industry" (testimony before the Subcommittee on Integrated Oil Operations of the Senate Interior and Insular Affairs Committee, December 13, 1973), Tables 1–18.

5. For a detailed econometric forecast of market-clearing prices under de-regulation, see P. W. MacAvoy and R. S. Pindyck, "Alternative Regulatory Policies for Dealing with the Natural Gas Shortage," *Bell Journal of Economics and Management Science,* Vol. 4 (Autumn 1973), pp. 454–98.

6. Alfred E. Kahn, *The Economics of Regulation: Principles and Institutions* (Wiley, 1971), Vol. II, p. 328.

Index

Adelman, M. A., 61
Adjudicatory process, 130–32
Administrative costs: of FPC, 8–11, 14, 122; of regulated companies, 13–14, 44
Administrative problems, of FPC, 129–32
"A-J-W models," 38
Alabama-Tennessee Natural Gas, 31
Algonquin Gas Transmission, 32, 74
American Electric Power Company, 91, 111
Area rate proceedings (natural gas), 8–10, 69–72, 86, 130. *See also* Montana-Dakota; Permian Basin; Southern Louisiana
Arkansas-Louisiana Gas, 74
Ash Council (*1970*), 2, 14, 127–29
Atlantic Seaboard Formula, 6, 36–37, 55, 135
Atomic Energy Commission (AEC), 110
Averch, Harvey, 108. *See also* "A-J-W models"

Benefits, from price regulation: cost/benefit gap, 123; measurement of, 18–22
Bluefield Water Works case (*1923*), 25
Bonds, of pipeline companies, 31
Boston Edison, 111
Boxerman, S. B., 106

Capacity of pipeline companies, effect of regulation on, 42
Capital, for energy development: cost problem, 9, 11, 29–33, 36–37, 68; rates of return on, 6–7, 22–33, 55, 63, 130
Capital equipment, and interstate sales of electricity, 12
"Capture" of regulatory agencies, 125–26
Casazza, J. A., 106

Central dispatching of electric power. *See* Coordination in electric power industry
Certification procedures (natural gas), 5, 9–10, 59
Chemicals industry, 46–47, 49
Cities Service Gas, 32, 74
Columbia Gas System, 37, 73
Commissioners, FPC, 126–29
"Commodity charges" (prices), 33–37, 39, 43, 50–51, 53
Competition: effect on prices, 18, 29, 37, 39, 47–48; in electric power industry, 109, 120; FPC role, 3; in gas production market, 60–63, 87–88, 133; in pipeline industry, 62, 133
Competitive prices, and the adjudicatory process, 131–32
Computers, use of, 91–92
Congestion, FPC concern with, 3
Congress, U.S., 57–58, 116–17, 125, 127, 129
Consolidated Gas Supply, 32
Consolidated Natural Gas, 73
Consumer interests: and the FPC, 1–3, 7, 18–19, 22, 33, 121–23; and the gas shortage, 75, 86; and price controls, 16–21, 60; transferral of rents to, 65, 69. *See also* Industrial consumers; Residential consumers
Contracts: re natural gas production, 61–62, 75–76; re natural gas transmission and sale, 5–6, 9, 33, 37, 43
Coordination in electric power industry, 91, 94–107, 133–34
Cost/benefit gap in FPC regulatory efforts, 123
"Cost-of-service" approach, 1, 4, 6, 11, 16, 23–28; proposed abandonment of, 133
Costs: in electric power industry, 11–13, 90–96, 98, 105–07, 109; in gas production, 7–10, 28, 64, 66–71, 130–31; in pipeline industry, 5–6, 23–24,

28–39, 43–44, 79, 130–31, 139; of regulation, 7–14, 21, 44, 86, 122; social, 3, 93, 96

"Cournot" elements, in price analyses, 48

Court system, and the FPC, 5, 24–25, 59–60, 66, 71–72, 88, 129. *See also* Supreme Court

Data collection, by FPC, 43

"Demand charges" (prices), 33–37, 39, 43, 50–51

Demand-diversity cost savings, in electric power, 92, 95–96, 107

Demand for gas: elasticity of, 44–52, 81; excess, 75–78, 86–87

Depletion allowance, 133

Depreciation, in cost analyses, 23–25, 33, 44

Distance factor, as pipeline cost, 33–34, 139

Dividends: in cost analyses, 30; and the FPC, 6, 19

East Tennessee Natural Gas case (*1965*), 31

Economic efficiency, of FPC, 2–4, 15

Economic models, of regulation effects, 38–54

Economic rents, in natural gas production: control of, 4, 122; transfer of, 69; windfall, 62, 64–66

Economies of scale: in electric power industry, 11, 92, 97–99, 108–09; in gas pipelines, 5, 18

Eisenhower, Dwight D., 58

Elasticity of demand for natural gas, 44–52, 81

Electric power: building-site problem, 110; costs of production, 11–13, 90–96, 98, 105, 107, 109; costs of transmission, 93–94, 106, 109; FPC role, 1–2, 4, 11–14, 67, 89; industry indebtedness, 155; local distribution of, 90; need for industry coordination, 94–119, 133–34; outage rates, 152–53; planning production of, 4, 89–90, 98–99, 105, 112–19, 121–23, 126–29, 133; production (generating) of, 49, 90–91, 93, 95–96, 99–107; profits in, 108; public ownership question, 120–21; transmission system, 89–91, 93, 97, 105–06, 112–13, 115; trend toward interconnection, 90–94

El Paso Natural Gas, 26, 31–32, 36, 74

Environmental considerations, in electric power planning, 89, 93, 108, 110–11, 116–17, 119–21

Equity, in energy development. *See* Capital, for energy development

Federal Power Acts: *1935*, 1; *1970*, 112–16

Federal Power Commission (FPC), 1–15; and the adjudicatory process, 130–32; administrative problems, 129–32; costs of regulation by, 7–14, 21, 44, 86, 122; legislative mandate, 127; lessons of power regulation, 122–34; organization of, 127–29; personnel, 126; planning production of electricity, 89–90, 112–19, 121, 126–27, 133; public v. private goals, 54–55; regulating natural gas pipelines, 5–6, 8–9, 16–55, 60, 122, 125, 127, 133; regulating natural gas producers, 1–10, 56–88, 125–27, 130; steps toward reform, 132–34. *See also* Court system; Data collection; Economic efficiency

Field surveys, by FPC staff, 12

Fixed costs, of gas pipeline companies, 33–38

Florida Gas Transmission Company, 27–31

Florida Power & Light, 114

Form 2 Reports, 43

Fossil-fuel plants, 93

FPC. *See* Federal Power Commission

Franchising, in electric power industry, 90

Gas. *See* Natural gas

Generating (capacity) costs, in electric power industry, 11–13, 90–96, 105, 107

Hoffman, C. H., 106

Hope Natural Gas Company case (*1942*), 24, 26

Housing, rent control laws in, 65

Hughes, William R., 96

Hydroelectric plants, 93, 116

Illinois, 73

Income, redistribution of: effect of regulation on, 19; FPC role in, 3–4, 124; in gas production industry, 65; by taxation, 21

Income taxes, in cost analyses, 23–24

Industrial consumers, of natural gas, 5–6, 20–21, 37–41, 46–48, 51–52, 69, 84–86, 127

Industry capture of regulatory agencies, 125–26

Inflation, 7

Interest rates, and pipeline regulation, 32
Internal Revenue Service, 21, 24
Intrastate sales of natural gas, 69, 86, 127

Jaffe, Louis, 119
Johnson, Leland L., 108
Johnson, Lyndon B., 118
Justice, Department of, 111–12

Kahn, A. E., 134
Kansas-Nebraska Natural Gas, 31
Kennedy, John F., 68

Landis, Dean, 119
Landis, James M., 127, 130; Landis Commission, 68, 89
Litzenberger, Robert H., 30
Location, role in pipeline price setting, 33–34, 139
Louisiana, 56, 69, 74, 86, 130

Mabuce, E. M., 106
McDonald, John G., 30
McKie, James W., 61
Maintenance, in electric power industry, 105–06
Malkiel, Burton G., 30
Management costs, in electric power industry, 94, 109
Management, of FPC, 128
Marginal costs: in electric power generation, 91; in production of natural gas, 70–71; in transport of natural gas, 43–44, 48
Market power (in gas production), 59–64, 66
Maryland, 12, 91
"Mcf-mile" method, of price setting, 34–36, 55
Mergers, and electric power industry, 111, 119
Michigan, 36–37, 99
Michigan-Wisconsin Pipe Line, 31, 34, 36
Midwestern Gas Transmission case (*1964*), 31
Minnesota, 36
Monopoly power, control of, 4, 59–60, 65, 72, 88
Monopoly pricing: FPC effect on, 17, 26, 28; in pipeline industry, 51–52
Monopsony prices for natural gas, 62
Montana-Dakota area, 99

Nassikas, John, 117, 146

National Electric Reliability Council (NERC), 97, 99
Natural gas: elasticity of demand for, 44–52, 81; excess demand for, 75–78, 86–87; exploration and development costs, 64, 66–67, 70–71; FPC regulation of production, 1–10, 28, 56–88, 125–27, 130–33; FPC regulation of transport, 1–2, 16–55, 125, 127; industrial consumers of, 5–6, 20–21, 37–41, 46–48, 51–52, 69, 84–86, 127; reserves of, 61, 75–85; residential consumers of, 5, 14, 21, 38–39, 46, 50, 75, 83–86, 122; shortage of, 56, 64, 69–87, 122, 127–28, 130, 133, 146; supply-and-demand analysis, 78–83. *See also* Pipeline companies
Natural Gas Act (*1938*), 1, 23, 25, 38, 57, 60, 74
Natural Gas Pipeline Company of America, 24–26, 32, 74
Natural resources, conservation of, 1
Negotiation, of rates on gas, 71–72, 129–30
"Net consumers' gains," measures of, 18–19
New England, 91, 96, 98–99
New Jersey, 73, 91
New Mexico, 36, 58, 61. *See also* Permian Basin
New York: blackout (*1965*), 2; electric consortium, 92, 96, 99; Public Service Commission, 111; regional market, 35–37, 73
North Carolina, 12
Northeast power failure (*1965*), 1, 112, 118
Northern Natural Gas, 26, 31, 34, 36–37, 74
Northfield Mountain (Mass.) proceeding, 114
Nuclear plants, 93

Oil. *See* Petroleum
Oklahoma, 56, 69, 86
Oligopoly pricing, 17, 60
Operating costs: in electric power industry, 91, 98, 107, 109; in pipeline companies, 22–24, 33, 44
Opportunity costs, for pipeline investors, 30–31
Organization of FPC, 127–29
Outage rates, 152–53

Pacific Gas Transmission, 32
Panhandle Eastern Pipe Line, 31–32, 36, 43

Peak demand, in electric power, 92, 106. *See also* Demand-diversity cost savings

Pennsylvania, 73, 91

Permian Basin (Texas–New Mexico), 8, 10, 58–59, 61, 63, 70–71, 85

Personnel of FPC, adequacy of, 126

Petroleum (oil): exploration and production, 9, 56, 60–61, 63, 66–67, 79; refining, 46, 48–49

Phillips Petroleum Company v. *Wisconsin*, 2, 7, 57–58, 68, 74, 88

Pipeline companies (natural gas), 2, 4–7, 56; costs incurred, 5–6, 23–24, 28–39, 43–44, 79, 130–31, 139; curtailment of deliveries, 74, 83–85; need for long-term commitments, 75–76; rates of return (profits), 16, 22–38, 41–42, 50, 52–55, 130, 133, 138, 140–42; regulation of, 5–6, 8–9, 16–55, 60, 122, 125, 127, 133; relations with gas producers, 62

PJM system, 91, 98–99, 109

Planning, by electric power industry, 98–99, 105

Planning (forecasting), by FPC, 2, 128–29; for electric power industry, 4, 89–90, 112–19, 121–23, 126–29, 133

Political goals, of FPC, 3

Political pressures, on regulatory agencies, 125–26

Pollution, 3, 73, 124

Pooling, in electric power industry, 97–101, 109–10, 119

Power. *See* Electric power; Natural gas

Prices, and the FPC, 1–15, 124–28, 130–32; in electric power industry, 91, 121; in production of natural gas, 56, 58–72, 78–83, 85–88, 123, 130, 132–33

Prices, discriminatory, 39, 50–52

Prices, in gas pipeline industry: effect of competition on, 18, 29, 37, 39, 47–48; FPC regulation of, 16–55, 122–23; without regulation, 40–41, 133; seasonal, 33, 36–37; zone, 34–36

Primary metals industry, 46–49

Production of electric energy. *See* Electric power

Production of natural gas: FPC regulation of, 1–10, 28, 56–88, 125–27, 130–33; profits in, 63; rationing in, 65, 69, 127

Profits, 1–2; in electric power industry, 108; in gas production industry, 63; in pipeline industry, 16, 22–38, 41–42, 50, 52–55, 130, 133, 138, 140–42

"Protectionism" and the FPC, 3

Public ownership of electric power, 120–21

Public Utility Holding Company Act (*1935*), 91, 111

Public utility regulation, 2, 16–22. *See also* Retail utilities

"Quality" of service, FPC concern with, 12–13

Rao, Cherukuri U., 30

Rate base: in electric power industry, 108, 110; in pipeline industry, 33

Rates. *See* Area rate proceedings (natural gas); Federal Power Commission

Rates of return on capital investment, 6–7, 22–33, 55, 63, 130

Rationing, in gas production industry, 65, 69, 127

Regional electric reliability councils, 89

Regulatory process: costs of, 7–14, 21, 44, 86, 122; in electric power industry, 89–90, 108–10; failure of, 122–34; in gas pipeline industry, 5–6, 8–9, 16–55, 60, 122, 125, 127, 133; in natural gas production, 1–10, 57–72, 81–83, 86–88, 125–27, 130. *See also* Federal Power Commission

Rents, economic, in gas production: control of, 4, 122; transfer of, 69; windfall, 62, 64–66

Reserves: in electric power industry, 113; of natural gas, 61, 75–85

Reserve savings, from coordination in electric power industry, 92, 95–98, 105–07, 154

Residential consumers of natural gas, 5, 14, 21, 38–39, 75; effect of gas shortage on, 83–86, 122; elasticity of demand by, 46, 50. *See also* Consumer interests

Retail utilities: elasticity of demand by, 52; regulated gas prices for, 21, 37–39, 41–42, 50–51

Seasonal pricing, 33, 36–37

Securities and Exchange Commission, 91, 110–11

"Service," in energy production and transmission: effect of price reductions on, 20; FPC control of, 1, 4, 12–13; contract rules re, 33, 37

Social costs, of energy production and transmission, 3, 93, 96. *See also* Pollution

Southern Louisiana, 58–59, 70–72

Southern Natural Gas, 32, 43
State regulation of electric power industry, 90–91, 109–10, 120
Storage costs, for natural gas, 44
Supply-and-demand analysis, in natural gas industry, 78–83
Supreme Court, U.S., 8, 65, 114–15, 123, 127; *Phillips* decision, 2, 7, 57–58, 60, 68, 74, 88
Surveillance activities, of FPC, 22
Swidler, Joseph C., 111

"Tangible" benefits from regulatory process, 17–18
"Tariff and service" contract rules, 33, 37
Tariffs (price schedules), filing of, 43
Taxes, income, in cost analyses, 23–24
Tax policy: changes needed, 133; and income transfers, 21
Telephone services, regulation of, 67
Tenneco, 35, 43
Tennessee Gas Transmission, 34, 36
Tennessee Valley Authority (TVA), 99

Texas, 10, 36, 56, 58, 61, 69, 74, 86, 97. *See also* Permian Basin
Texas Eastern Transmission, 35, 74
Tier pricing, for natural gas, 69
Transcontinental Gas Pipe Line, 35–36, 74
Transmission of electric energy. *See* Electric power
Transmission of natural gas. *See* Pipeline companies
Truman, Harry S., 58
Trunkline Gas Company, 36, 74

United Gas Pipe Line, 31–32, 74
Utilities. *See* Public utility regulation; Retail utilities

Water Power Act (*1920*), 90
Weiss, Leonard, 120
"Wheeling" of electricity, 115–17
White, Lee C., 116–18
Wilks, R. L., 106
"Windfall" rents, 62, 64–66

Zone prices, 34–36